James D. McCabe

Our Young Folks in Africa

James D. McCabe

Our Young Folks in Africa

ISBN/EAN: 9783743387379

Manufactured in Europe, USA, Canada, Australia, Japa

Cover: Foto ©Andreas Hilbeck / pixelio.de

Manufactured and distributed by brebook publishing software (www.brebook.com)

James D. McCabe

Our Young Folks in Africa

OUR

YOUNG FOLKS IN AFRICA.

THE ADVENTURES

OF

A PARTY OF YOUNG AMERICANS IN ALGERIA, AND IN SOUTH CENTRAL AFRICA.

BY

JAMES D. McCABE,

AUTHOR OF "OUR YOUNG FOLKS ABROAD," "PARIS BY SUNLIGHT AND GASLIGHT," ETC.

PHILADELPHIA:
J. B. LIPPINCOTT & CO.
1883.

PREFACE.

THE very kind reception given by the public and the press to "Our Young Folks Abroad" has encouraged the author and publishers of that work to offer a second volume, describing the adventures of another party of young Americans in a region as yet new to the readers of juvenile literature.

Four young Americans and a distinguished professor in a leading institution of learning in the United States meet for the first time on a steamer in which they are crossing the Atlantic, and finding their acquaintance a pleasant one, resolve to make a visit to Algeria. This is successfully accomplished; and the travellers are so much pleased with their experience of Northern Africa that they resolve to undertake an expedition "across the dark continent," from the Atlantic to the Indian Ocean. This resolve is speedily put into execution, and the "Young American Expedition to South Central Africa" successfully accomplishes the feat of marching from Benguela, on the Atlantic, to the river Zambezi, and thence to Durban, the capital of the British province of Natal, on the Indian Ocean, from which they return home by steamer.

The greater portion of the work is devoted to the journey through South Central Africa, a region comparatively unknown to Europe and America at the present day, and an earnest effort has been made to familiarize the young reader with countries, peoples, and customs which, in all probability, he will never have the opportunity of visiting.

The characters mentioned in "Our Young Folks in Africa" as belonging to the Young American Expedition are fictitious; but the natives, the negro chiefs, and kings who are introduced to the reader are real personages. The adventures which befell the travellers, the routes they travelled, the incidents of the journey, and the perils from which they escaped are based upon actual occurrences, and are drawn mainly from the experience of one of the most distinguished explorers of the regions described. They furnish a true picture of South Central Africa, and of the various nations which inhabit it.

It has been the aim of the author both to amuse and instruct, and it is believed that the work is sufficiently full of adventure to render its more solid portions acceptable to the general reader.

The illustrations can be relied upon as accurate, since they were made from sketches taken from life or nature.

J. D. McC.

GERMANTOWN, PA.,
    3d August, 1882.

CONTENTS.

CHAPTER I.
The Journey begun and the Party formed . . . 11

CHAPTER II.
A Visit to Algeria 22

CHAPTER III.
From Algiers to Constantina 42

CHAPTER IV.
The Country of the Kabyles 62

CHAPTER V.
The Young American Expedition to South Central Africa . . 95

CHAPTER VI.
Into the Heart of Africa 104

CHAPTER VII.
Adventures in the Black Man's Country . . . 127

CHAPTER VIII.
From the Bihé to the Zambezi . . . 150

CHAPTER IX.
Adventures in the Lui Country . . . 210

CHAPTER X.
On the Zambezi 239

CHAPTER XI.
To the Indian Ocean 283

ILLUSTRATIONS.

	PAGE
Frontispiece.	
The Old Harbor of Marseilles	11
In the Suburbs of Algiers	13
An Arab Tribe on the March	14
In the Atlas Mountains	15
Interior of a Kabyle Home	16
Algerian Method of Irrigation	17
The Plain of Metidja in Algeria	19
A Dandy of Algiers	20
Scene in Algeria	21
An Arab Encampment	22
An Arab Maiden of Algeria	23
Arabs of Algeria	25
Wandering Arab of Algeria	26
An Algerian Shop	27
Kabyle Armorers at Work	28
An Algerian Foot-Bath	29
Kabyle Woman and Child	30
A Mohammedan at Prayer	31
Arab Woman Churning	32
Algiers from the Sea	33
An Arab Cemetery near Algiers	34
Bazaar at Algiers	35
A Pleasure Resort near Algiers	36
A Public Writer at Algiers	37
A Dry-Goods Store at Algiers	38
An Algerian Beauty	39
Street in the Arab Quarter of Algiers	41
Dellys	43
Bougie, and Hill of Gouraya	44
Arab Woman and Child	45
Roman Relics at Philippeville	46
Lion-Shaped Rock, Harbor of Bona	47
An Arab Market in Algeria	48
Desert Horsemen	49
Constantina	51

	PAGE
Roman Bridge at Constantina	52
Bey's Palace, Constantina	53
The Roumi enjoy a Moorish Bath	55
"Balek!"	57
The Great Mosque, Constantina	58
A Marabout of Kybalia	59
Marabout rousing the Kabyles to Revolt	61
The Arab Guides	63
Country between Constantina to Setif	64
An Arab Douar	65
Mohammedan Cemetery	66
Bou-Kteun	67
The Amin of Bou-Kteun	68
The Gates of Iron	69
Kalaa	71
Scene in the Grand Kabylia	72
Kabyle Women	73
Fountain of Kalaa	74
Kabyles on the Watch	75
Ben-Ali-Cherif	77
Ben-Ali hunting with the Falcon	79
The Disciples of Tofail	81
A Kabyle Child	83
Kabyle Men	85
Kabyle Husbandman	86
Kabyle Oil-Works	87
House of Ben-Ali-Cherif at Chellata	88
A Koubba, or Marabout's Tomb	89
Group of Kabyle Women	90
The Djurjura Range	91
Defile of Thifilkoult	92
Fort National	93
An Algerian Village	95
A Genuine Negro Minstrel	96
Kabyle Pottery Works	97
A Kabyle Funeral	99

ILLUSTRATIONS.

	PAGE
Ruined Church near Benguela	101
Government House at Loanda	103
The Pilot's Boat at Loanda	104
San Paul de Loanda	105
The Mountains of Benguela	108
Benguela	111
Negro Village near Benguela	113
The Valley of the Dombe	115
Mundombe Women, Vendors of Coal	116
A South African River	117
Mundombe Women and Girls	119
Mundombe Men	119
A South African Forest	121
Articles manufactured by the Natives between the Coast and the Bihé	123
African Rat	124
Tree-Ferns of Africa	125
On the Cuverai	128
King Chimbarandongo	129
Encampment of the Expedition near Chimbarandongo's Village	130
The Negroes of the Party constructing Huts in the Encampments	131
Skeleton of a Hut	132
Specimen of the Huts used by the Expedition	133
Man and Woman of the Huambo	133
Tomb of a Native African Chief	134
Capôco's Sweetheart	135
Ant-Hills found between the Coast and the Bihé	136
Weapons and Implements of Native African Manufacture	137
Dumbo's Wives	139
Cassoma	140
The Urivi, or Trap for Small Game	141
Ganguella, Luimba, and Loena Women	142
African Women pounding Maize	143
Bridge over the River Cubango	144
Ant-Hills on the Banks of the River Cutato of the Ganguellas	145
Caquingue Blacksmiths' Tools	146
Caquingue Blacksmiths	147
Ant-Hills Thirteen Feet High, covered with Vegetation, on the Banks of the River Cutato	148
View of the Exterior of the Village of Belmonte in the Bihé	150
Silva Porto's House at Belmonte	151
Plan of the Village of Belmonte in the Bihé	153
Woman of the Bihé, digging	154
Biheno Carrier on the March	155
Palisades used for the Defence of African Villages	156
Articles manufactured by the Bihenos	157
Articles made by the Bihenos	159
A Bihé Head-Dress	160
Crossing the Cuqueima	166
Quimbande Man and Woman	167
Quimbande Girls	170
Quimbande Woman carrying her Load	171
The Sova Mavanda, masked, and dancing in the Camp	174
Ditassoa—Fish of the River Onda	175
Tree-Ferns on the Banks of the Onda	176
Cabango Woman's Head-Dress	177
King Chaquiunde	178
Lake Liguri	179
A Luchaze of the Banks of the River Cuito	180
Luchaze Tinder-Box, Flint, and Steel	181
A Luchaze Woman on the Road	182
Luchaze Woman of Cambuta	183
South African Buffalo	184
Luchaze Man of Cambuta	185
Articles manufactured by the Luchazes	186
Village of Cambuta, Luchaze	187
Luchaze Pipe	187
Luchaze Fowl-House	188
Luchaze Woman of Cutangjo	189
The Cuchibi	189
Luchaze of the Cutangjo	190
Moene-Cahenga, Sova of Cangamba	191
Luchaze Articles	192
Hatchet of the Ambuellas of Cangamba	192
Ambuella Pipe	193
The Quichobo	194
The Sova Cahu-heñ-eñ	195
Ambuella Woman	195
The King of Ambuella's Eldest Daughter	196
The King of Ambuella's Youngest Daughter	197
Cuchibi Canoe and Paddle	197
Drum used at Ambuella Feasts	198
Ambuella Chief	199

	PAGE		PAGE
Ambuella Hunter	199	Houston and the Lion	249
Royal Village of Cahu-heú-úe, on the Cuchibi	200	The Camp at Sioma	250
		The Cataract of Gonha	251
Ambuella Arrow-Heads	201	Carrying the Boats Overland at the Cataract of Gonha	253
Assegais of the Ambuellas	201		
Fording the Cuchibi	202	The African Elephant	255
Fish of the Cuchibi	203	The Canoes in the Rapids	257
Chipulo or Nhele	204	The Camp near Quissequc	260
The Malanca	205	The Last Boat over the Cuando	262
Ant-Hills of the Nhengo	206	Mr. and Mrs. Gaillard	267
A Luina Hunter	208	Encampment of the Gaillard Family in Lechuma	269
Luina Shield	209		
Luina Houses and Hoes	211	Interior of Mr. Gaillard's Camp in Lechuma	271
Luina Pipes for smoking Bangue	212		
Iron Implement used as a Handkerchief by the Luinas	213	The Burial of Eliazar	273
		Mozi-oa-Tunia	275
Luina Milk-Pot	213	Mozi-oa-Tunia. The West Falls	277
Luina War-Hatchets	215	Professor Moreton measuring the Falls	280
Luina Earthenware	216	Crossing the "Great Salt Pan"	284
Luina Man	217	The Odeo	285
King Lobossi	218	The English Quarter at Shoshong	287
Gambella	219	The Opumbulume	290
Matagja	221	Khama	291
Wooden Platters of the Luinas	223	Khama chasing the Ongiris	293
Wooden Spoon of the Luinas	224	Ant-Hills near the Limpopo	295
Luina Hatchet	226	A Night Visit from the Lions	297
Luina Woman	228	Store in Pretoria	298
Luina War-Club	229	Natives of the Transvaal	299
Luina Assegais	231	A Transvaal Farm	301
The Defence of the Burning Camp	234	Professor Moreton at Pretoria	302
A Zambezi Canoe	240	The Drakensberg	304
The Paddles	240	Near Pietermaritzburg	306
The Songue	241	Professor Moreton and the Negroes of the Expedition	309
Slot of the Songue	241		
Itufa House	247		

CHAPTER I.

THE JOURNEY BEGUN AND THE PARTY FORMED.

IN the saloon of the Belgian royal mail steamer "Nederland" one afternoon early in February, 1878, were gathered four young Americans, busily engaged in examining a map opened out on the table before them. From the

THE OLD HARBOR OF MARSEILLES.

earnestness with which they bent over it, and the eagerness with which they expressed their views upon the question they were discussing, a stranger would have supposed they were endeavoring to settle some matter of more than usual importance. And so it was to them, for they were attempting to decide upon their movements after the steamer should land them safely upon the shores of the Old World. They had sailed from the United States strangers to one another, but, being almost the only saloon passengers on the ship, had soon drifted into a pleasant intimacy, which became more pronounced and pleasant with each succeeding day of the voyage. As is often the case with persons thus thrown together, they soon began to compare notes as to their plans of travel abroad, and finally resolved to cling together and see the Old World in company. They were all as fine specimens of the young manhood of their native country as the most patriotic American could desire, and were all looking forward eagerly to the enjoyments which new lands and strange customs promised them. While they are thus engaged in looking over their map, we may present them to the reader.

The young man on the extreme right of the group was George Ashton, a native of Philadelphia. He was tall, broad-shouldered, and finely made,—a very athlete in appearance,—with hair, eyes, and complexion as dark as a Spaniard's. At Princeton, where he had recently taken his degree, he had been noted for his excellence in athletic sports of all kinds, and had been as remarkable for his powers of endurance as for his great physical strength. To sound bodily health he united a disposition of unusual amiability and generosity, and had been one of the most popular members of his class. Three months previous to his introduction to the reader he had come of age, and a few weeks later had had the misfortune to lose both of his parents, who died within a few days of each other. By their death he had come into possession of one of the largest fortunes in his native city. Greatly saddened by the double sorrow which had befallen him in the death of both his parents, he had resolved to leave America and pass a year or two abroad. In pursuance of this plan he had taken passage on the ship that was now bearing him across the Atlantic.

Next to Ashton stood Philip Lee, a young Virginian, his companion's junior by one year. Like the former he was tall and dark, but was more lightly built. He was strikingly handsome, and was in all respects a worthy representative of the distinguished family whose name he bore. Like Ashton, he was an orphan. His father had fallen in battle during the civil war, and his mother had died a few years after the return of peace. He had sailed from home for the purpose of spending the spring and summer in Europe, and intended returning to America in the fall to complete his course at college.

The third member of the group was Walter Hubbard, the son of a wealthy merchant of New York. He was but nineteen, but was well grown and manly looking for his age; and though he had enjoyed at college the reputation of being the wildest and most audacious member of his class, he was, withal, a warm-hearted, generous fellow. As it was his father's intention to take him into business with him, he had allowed the young man to sail for Europe in order that he might see something of the Old World before settling down to the work of his life at home.

The fourth and last member of the group was a stout, hardy-looking young man,—Robert Houston by name. He was the only son of one of the

IN THE SUBURBS OF ALGIERS.

most noted mine-owners of the Pacific coast, a man of immense wealth, and had grown up with scarcely a wish ungratified. Naturally disinclined to study, he had not availed himself of the opportunities at his command, and consequently was the inferior of his companions in education. Yet he greatly atoned for this deficiency by his sound, practical good sense, his straight-forward and honest nature, and his hearty generosity, qualities which had at once made him a favorite with his new friends.

As we have said, they were each and all fine, manly fellows, and fair representatives of the rising generation of the United States.

14   OUR YOUNG FOLKS IN AFRICA.

Their examination of the map before them interested them very much, and an eager and animated discussion was going on among them. It grew more animated every moment, and it was evident that they were far from coming to an agreement. At length the young Californian, with a good-natured laugh, withdrew from the group, and throwing himself in a lounging position upon one of the seats, began to whistle softly to himself.

AN ARAB TRIBE ON THE MARCH.

"Now, Houston," said Ashton, turning to him with an air of vexation, "that's too bad. Will you never be convinced?"

"I am entirely convinced of one thing, boys," replied Houston, "and that is, that we shall never reach an agreement in this way. We've been arguing this matter for the past six days, and we are no nearer a decision than when we began."

"But we must come to a decision," said Philip Lee. "It would be too bad to break up so pleasant a party. We shall be at Antwerp, the captain says, on the sixteenth, four days from this. Surely we ought to be able to agree upon some plan that will enable us to stick together."

"For my part," said Houston, "my mind is quite made up."

"Then let us have your plan, my boy," cried Hubbard. "It seems to me you have the levellest head in the party, and it may help us to know what you intend doing."

"Thank you," replied Houston, laughing; "I am not going to depend upon my 'level head,' however. I shall make use of another man's. In a few words, my plan is this,—to join Professor Moreton and travel with him."

IN THE ATLAS MOUNTAINS.

"Where does he intend to go?" asked Ashton.

"I don't know," was the reply; "but he said to me last night that he had mapped out a very interesting journey, and was only sorry that he would be obliged to make it alone. He wants company, and, from the manner in which he spoke, I think he wants me to go with him. I have quite made up my mind to do so. It does not matter much where I go, and I think the time spent with him will be not only pleasant but very profitable to me."

"That's not a bad idea," said Ashton, reflectively. "We have seen enough of the professor since we have been shipmates to be sure that he would be a pleasant and congenial companion. As he has a definite plan of travel marked out, however, we should all have to surrender our own schemes and accept his. Still, we should be free to separate from him at any time if we saw fit."

"So far so good," said Walter Hubbard, who had been listening thoughtfully. "But it seems to me we are overlooking one thing, and that the most

INTERIOR OF A KABYLE HOME.

important: Professor Moreton may be willing enough to take Houston for a companion, but the question is whether he would like to have our whole party at his heels."

"There's but one way to find out," said Houston, quickly, "and that is easily accomplished. Let's go at once and ask him."

"I like your Californian bluntness, Houston," said Ashton, laughing.

"That's the way we do things in 'Frisco,'" replied Houston. "None of your Eastern beating about the bush with us. If we want to ask a man a question we put it to him squarely, and expect a prompt answer."

"Well, Houston," said Philip Lee, "I like your plan, and I propose that we seek the professor at once, and put the question to him. It will end this perplexing discussion."

"I left him on the deck, smoking, when I came in here half an hour ago," said Hubbard; "and as he generally takes a long smoke after lunch, we shall

ALGERIAN METHOD OF IRRIGATION.

probably find him there now. What say you, fellows, shall we do as Houston suggests?"

There was a general affirmative answer; and the party at once left the saloon to seek the professor.

"The professor," as he had been called by the young men, was none other than Henry Moreton, until recently the distinguished professor of mathematics in one of the leading colleges of the United States. Though but forty years old, he had won an enviable reputation in his own country, and his name was not unknown in Europe. He was a short, thick-set man, with red hair and beard, and the keenest and cheeriest of blue eyes, yet with an expression which denoted rare determination and firmness of character. For ten years he had filled his position in his college with marked ability, and during that period he had never failed to spend his summer vacations abroad, so that he was already an experienced traveller. But now a sudden fit of weariness had seized him, and under its influence he had resigned his chair with the intention of spending several years in foreign travel.

He was lounging idly in his steamer chair on the afternoon in question, dreamily puffing away at a huge "meerschaum," and gazing off at the sea, when the four young men approached him. He roused himself from his revery as they came up, and gave them a pleasant greeting.

"Professor," began Houston, who made himself the spokesman of the party, "we have come to ask you two questions. You said to me last night that you would like to have company in your travels. I mentioned this to our friends just now, and we have come to the conclusion that we should like to be your travelling companions. The questions we wish to ask are, first, Where are you going? and second, Are you willing to take us for companions?"

The professor listened quietly while Houston was speaking, sending huge puffs of smoke from his pipe, and keeping his gaze fixed all the while on the waves. When the young man had finished he answered slowly,—

"I will reply to your second question first. I shall be very glad, indeed, to have your company if my plans suit you. It may be that after you have heard them you will not be so anxious to accompany me. I shall go direct from Antwerp to Paris, where I have some business matters to look after. I shall leave Paris on the morning of the 22d for Marseilles, and shall reach that place early the next morning. On the afternoon of the 23d I shall sail from Marseilles for Algiers, where I hope to arrive on the morning of the 25th. I shall remain in Algeria during the month of March, making excursions along the coast and into the portion of the Atlas Mountains inhabited by the Kabyles. I hope to return to France by the first week in April. After that my movements are uncertain. Now, young gentlemen, you know my plans as far as I know them myself, and if you see fit to accompany me, I shall be heartily glad to have you for comrades."

"I, for one, have already made up my mind to go with you, professor," said Houston.

"And I too," said Ashton.

"In fact, professor," said Philip Lee, "we are all of one mind. We shall enjoy both being with you and the novelty of seeing a portion of Africa. But, tell me, what are the advantages of such a trip?"

"Many," replied the professor. "In the first place, you will see a country and a civilization almost unknown to American travellers. We will see something of Arab life, something of Moorish civilization, and a great deal of the Kabyles, who are the descendants of the old Berber race, the original inhabitants of Northern Africa. They are a most interesting people, and though they have been successively conquered by the Phœnicians, the Romans, the Vandals, the Arabs, and the French, they have never yet been completely subdued, but to this day retain something of their ancient independence. They are a brave, hardy race of mountaineers, and are the most industrious as well as the most warlike of the Algerian tribes."

THE PLAIN OF METIDJA IN ALGERIA.

"Is the country a safe one to travel through?" asked Hubbard.

"Entirely so. The present season is also the best for Algerian travel. The month of March is the most delightful of the year in that country; the roads are in good order, and the mountaineers religiously respect the obligations of hospitality to strangers. Besides, the French authority is so firmly established that the country is apt to be at peace for a long time to come."

"Then we may consider it settled that we go with you?" said Hubbard, glancing at his companions, who replied by affirmative nods.

"Not exactly settled," replied the professor. "We have yet four days before we reach Antwerp, and a week after that before I leave Paris. I would like you to think of the matter. If you still hold to your determination to go with me, you can join me in Paris the day before my departure. I can only add that I shall be very glad to have your company, and that I think the journey will be both pleasant and profitable to you. It will add comparatively little to your expenses, and you will return to France in time to arrange for your future movements."

A DANDY OF ALGIERS.

During the remainder of the voyage the Algerian trip was constantly discussed by the young Americans, and always with growing enthusiasm. Not even their first sight of the English shore, or the splendid run of the steamer through the English Channel, or the sail up the Scheldt,—perhaps the most interesting journey in Europe to one who is enjoying it for the first time,— served to draw their minds from the anticipated pleasures of the African trip.

When they parted from the professor at Antwerp they told him they had definitely decided to accompany him, and agreed to meet him in Paris in time to start with him for Marseilles.

From Antwerp Professor Moreton proceeded direct to Paris, but the young men remained in that quaint old city a day, in order to visit its interesting sights. From Antwerp they proceeded to Brussels, where another day was spent in exploring that city. The third day was occupied by the journey from Brussels to Paris, where they arrived on the evening of the 19th. The next two days were devoted to a hasty view of Paris and to preparations for their African journey, in which Professor Moreton rendered them valuable assistance.

SCENE IN ALGERIA.

It forms no part of our purpose to relate the incidents of the brief visit of our young travellers to the most beautiful city of Europe. They greatly enjoyed it, and looked forward with lively pleasure to the prospect of seeing it at their leisure upon their return from Algeria.

The morning of February 22d found the entire party comfortably seated in a first-class carriage of the Paris, Lyons and Mediterranean Railway. The train left Paris at a little after eleven, and Marseilles was reached the next morning at half-past six. As their steamer did not sail until late in the afternoon, the day was given to exploring the city, and many and interesting were the sights and scenes the party witnessed in the principal seaport of France.

CHAPTER II.

A VISIT TO ALGERIA.

OUR travellers were on board the steamer "Algeria," of the line known as the *Compagnie des Messageries Maritimes de France*, by four o'clock on the afternoon of February 23d, and promptly at five the ship sailed. A fine view of Marseilles, with its old and new ports and the heights rising in the

AN ARAB ENCAMPMENT.

background, was obtained by the party from the deck as the steamer glided out of the harbor and turned her head to the open sea. The afternoon was delightful, and a soft breeze came off from the shore bringing with it a faint scent of flowers. As the steamer passed into the Gulf of Lyons the professor pointed out a little group of islands lying near the coast. The nearest one he told his companions was the Ile D'If. They could easily distinguish the old castle with which it is crowned. This, he told them, was once a state prison, and in it the great Count Mirabeau was imprisoned by his father. He added that the castle was also the site of one of the most thrilling scenes in Dumas's

AN ARAB MAIDEN OF ALGERIA.

novel of "Monte Christo," it being the place from which the hero of the book made his wonderful escape.

The sea was quiet; and when the dinner-bell rang, the party went below with keen appetites, and did full justice to an excellent meal. When they returned to the deck, the twilight was settling down over the sea and the land was rapidly receding from view. As they were fatigued by their long journey from Paris and their tramp through Marseilles during the day, they went to bed early, and slept well, lulled by the gentle motion of the Mediterranean.

As Sunday was bright and fair, the day was spent mainly on deck. It was very pleasant to lounge there, enjoying the balmy sea-breeze and watching the quaint Mediterranean crafts, which they passed in considerable numbers. The sky was cloudless and the sea a deep blue, which so nearly matched the color of the heavens that sea and sky seemed to blend. The voyage was all the more enjoyable because it was so different from that across the Atlantic. The latter voyage had been rough and stormy in the main, with "a gray sea and a gray sky" almost every day. Every one of the party, save the professor, who was an old sailor, had been more or less uncomfortable on the Atlantic; but now, as the steamer glided gently across this quiet sea, they experienced a feeling of comfort and contentment, and declared it the very perfection of ocean travelling.

"I say, professor," said Houston, as Mr. Moreton drew his steamer chair to the place where the young men were lounging on the deck in the afternoon, "if you have no objection suppose you tell us something about this strange country we are about to visit."

"Willingly," replied Professor Moreton. "But first let me light my pipe. I can talk better at sea with a pipeful of good tobacco to inspire me."

So, lighting his pipe, the professor gave them the following account of Algeria between the whiffs of blue smoke which he blew from his lips:

"Algeria was formerly one of the Barbary States, but is now the largest and most important of the French Colonies. It lies in Northern Africa between the Mediterranean on the north, the Desert of Sahara on the south, Tunis on the east, and Morocco on the west. It comprises an area of about one hundred and fifty thousand square miles, and is a little smaller than the State of California. It contains nearly three millions of inhabitants, the greater portion of whom belong to the native nomadic races; with the exception of the Jews all the natives are Mohammedans. The European inhabitants number about two hundred thousand, more than half of whom are French. The country is generally mountainous, being traversed by lofty ranges of the Atlas Mountains, which run nearly parallel to the coast, and rise in some places to a height of more than seven thousand feet. The mountains are divided into two chains, the Great Atlas bordering on the Sahara, which contains the highest mountains, and the Little or Maritime Atlas between it and the sea. The interval between the two ranges is occupied by a plateau which is about one hundred miles wide in its western part and fifty in the eastern. The country bordering on the coast is known as *The Tell*. It is generally hilly, though in some places a flat and fertile plain extends between the hills and the sea, and the hills are everywhere intersected by fruitful valleys. In ancient times the country was very productive, and is gradually becoming so again under the rule of the French. The principal cities are Algiers, the capital, Oran, Constantina, and Bona. The people are nearly equally divided into what are known as the settled population and the nomadic tribes. The two principal native races are the Arabs and the Berbers. The former, who inhabit chiefly the southern parts of the country, are mostly true nomads; they dwell in tents and wander from place to place. A large

ARABS OF ALGERIA.

number of them, however, are settled in *The Tell*, where they carry on agriculture, and have numerous villages. The Berbers are the original inhabitants of the country, and are now called Kabyles. They still form a considerable portion of the population, and are distributed mainly over the mountainous parts of the province of Constantina. Many, however, are to be found in *The Tell* and in the plains. They have largely intermarried with the Arabs, and this amalgamation is still going on. They are a brave, hardy, active, and industrious race, living in villages, and engaging in agriculture and the cultivation of fruit-trees. They also make their own agricultural implements, guns, gunpowder, leather, carpets, and other articles in common use. We shall see much of them in our journey, and you will be able to form your own opinions of them. Another and a smaller class are the Moors, who are descended partly from the Arabs and partly from the ancient Mauritanians. They live in the towns and villages near the coast, and earn a scanty livelihood as small tradesmen or mechanics. There are about thirty thousand Jews in the colony, and these form one of the most influential classes of the population, owing to their wealth and commercial activity. Until 1865 they were excluded from all public offices, but an act passed in that year by the French Chambers declared all native-born Jews and Mohammedans entitled to all the rights and privileges of French citizens on placing themselves completely under the civil and political laws of the French. The Jews have rapidly availed themselves of these privileges.

WANDERING ARAB OF ALGERIA.

"Algeria is partly under civil and partly under military rule. The latter system prevails principally in the southern portions among the nomadic tribes. Nearly one-fourth of the area of the country and nearly one-half of the inhabitants enjoy civil government.

"The history of Algeria is very interesting, but I shall have to sum it up briefly. In ancient times the country was inhabited by two nations, the Massyli and the Massæsyli, who were rivals for the supreme power of the whole country. During the struggle between Hannibal and the Romans, Syphax, the sovereign of the Massæsyli, espoused the cause of the Carthaginian leader, while Masinissa, the prince of the Massyli, became the ally of the Romans. Upon the overthrow of the Carthaginian power, Rome rewarded Masinissa by bestowing upon him the dominion of Syphax, with the title of King of Numidia. During the Roman civil war, Juba, king of Numidia, sided with Pompey. He was defeated by Cæsar, and his kingdom was converted into a Roman province. The Roman rule was highly beneficial to the country; agriculture and commerce flourished, roads were built, and cities and towns sprang up. Christianity early obtained a foothold in the province, and spread rapidly. The country was enjoying a high degree of prosperity when the Vandals invaded Northern Africa and drove the Romans from it, about the middle of the fifth century. They almost destroyed the civilization introduced by the Romans, but their reign was of short duration. In the year 533 they were expelled by Belisarius, the general of the Eastern emperor, Justinian, and the country was restored to Christianity, and continued a province of the Eastern Roman Empire until about the middle of the seventh century, when it was overrun by the Saracens, who established themselves firmly in it. Under their rule it was divided into a number of petty states under independent

AN ALGERIAN SHOP.

chiefs; civilization rapidly disappeared, and the people sank into barbarism. In the eleventh century a religious sect, known as the Morabites, conquered many of the petty chiefs, overran the country, and laid the foundation of the dynasty of the Almoravides, which remained in power for nearly a century, and at one time ruled over nearly all of Barbary and a large part of Spain. This dynasty was succeeded by the Almohades, who ruled the country until 1273, when it was again divided into a number of small states. In 1505, Ferdinand, king of Spain, sent an expedition against the country, under the Count of Navarre. Oran and a number of other towns were taken, and in 1509 the Spaniards captured the city of Algiers. They continued to hold the country until the death of Ferdinand; but their rule was very distasteful to the Algerincs. In 1516 one of the native princes, hearing of the death of Ferdinand, sent an embassy to the famous Turkish pirate, Aruch Barbarossa, requesting his aid in an effort to drive out the Spaniards. Barbarossa readily complied with the request; but no sooner had he established himself in the country than he murdered the prince and proclaimed himself king of Algeria. He introduced the system of piracy for which Algiers became so famous in after-years, and by force and treachery extended his rule over a large part of the country. He was finally defeated, captured, and beheaded by the Spaniards, and was

KABYLE ARMORERS AT WORK.

succeeded on the throne by his brother, Hayradin, who, finding himself unable to cope successfully with Spain, placed himself under the protection of Turkey. The Sultan readily granted him assistance, and appointed him viceroy, or pasha, of Algiers. With the aid of the Turks he drove out the Spaniards, and then proceeded to extend his system of piracy. He strongly fortified Algiers, and built a long mole for the protection of his ships, upon which work he is said to have forced thirty thousand Christian prisoners to labor for three years. He built and equipped a strong fleet, and the Algerian corsairs soon became the terror of the Mediterranean. Spain and Italy were especial sufferers from their ravages, and in 1541 the Emperor Charles V., at the request of the Pope, led a strong naval and military expedition against Algiers. The fleet was wrecked by a fearful storm, and the army was routed by the Algerines, the emperor and a handful of his force making their escape with difficulty.

AN ALGERIAN FOOT-BATH.

"Meanwhile the Pasha of Algeria had been extending the boundaries of his province. Before the close of the sixteenth century he had carried his authority as far westward as the frontier of Morocco. The piratical operations of the Algerines were carried on at the same time with equal vigor, and these involved them in frequent wars with France, England, Venice, and other powers. The Algerian fleet was several times defeated and almost destroyed, and the city of Algiers itself was twice bombarded by the French, and almost reduced to ashes. The Algerian corsairs, on the other hand, swarmed in the Mediterranean, and several times cruelly ravaged the coast of Southern France. Treaties were made with the Mediterranean powers of Europe, but were broken without scruple whenever the Dey found himself strong enough to do so. Thousands of Christian slaves constantly languished in captivity in Algiers, and throughout Europe societies were formed for the purpose of ransoming them.

"The authority of Turkey during this period existed only in name in Algiers. In 1600 the janizaries obtained permission from the Sultan to elect their Dey or governor from their own number. After this the power of the Dey steadily grew stronger, while that of the Turkish pasha decreased. In 1705,

Dey Ibrahim declared his independence of the Sultan, and expelled the Turkish pasha. Thus the country passed into the sole power of the Dey, who was, in

KABYLE WOMAN AND CHILD.

his turn, ruled by the janizaries. These were natives of Turkey, recruited in Constantinople and Smyrna. No native of Algeria, even though the son of a janizary by a native woman of the country, could be admitted to their ranks. The janizaries continued from this time to elect the Dey, and frequently mutinied against and murdered the chiefs of their own selection. Turkey was so hampered during this period by her constant wars with Russia that the Sultan was unable to make any effort to recover his authority in Algeria. The Dey sent occasional presents to Constantinople as a token of nominal allegiance to the Sultan; but the regular tribute ceased, and all actual authority on the part of the Sultan was forever ended in Algeria. During all this while the Algerian pirates continued to sweep the Mediterranean, and many of the European powers endeavored to purchase exemption from their outrages by the payment of an annual tribute, which, however, did not always protect their vessels from outrage. In 1795 our own country had to pursue a similar course, and a handsome subsidy was paid by the United States to the Dey to secure peace. During the wars of the French Revolution and of Napoleon the constant presence of large European fleets in the Mediterranean put a check to the piracies of the Algerines. They were promptly resumed, however, upon the return of peace. About the same

A MOHAMMEDAN AT PRAYER.

time the second war between the United States and England came to a close. The Dey, thinking that the United States were too much crippled by the contest to punish his insolence, suddenly renewed his depredations upon American ships. He also threatened to reduce Mr. Lear, the American consul at Algiers, to slavery, and compelled him to purchase his liberty and that of his family by the payment of a large ransom. Several American merchantmen were captured by the Algerines and their crews reduced to slavery. The excuse offered by the Dey for these outrages was that the presents of the American government were not satisfactory. The President of the United States thereupon determined to bring the matter to a final settlement, and in May, 1815, Commodore Decatur was despatched to the Mediterranean with a fleet of ten ships of war, three of which were frigates. He was ordered to compel the Dey to make amends for his past outrages, and to give a guarantee for his good conduct in the future. On the voyage out Decatur fell in with the largest frigate in the Algerian service, near Gibraltar, and captured her after a fight of half an hour. Two days later he captured another Algerian cruiser. The fleet then proceeded to Algiers, but upon his arrival there Decatur found the Dey in a very humble frame of mind;

the loss of his two best ships and the determined aspect of the Americans, who threatened a bombardment of the city, terrified him, and he abjectly sued for peace. He was required to come on board of Decatur's flagship, and there sign a humiliating treaty with the United States, by which he bound himself to indemnify all the Americans from whom he had extorted ransoms, to surrender all his prisoners unconditionally, to renounce all claim to tribute from the United States, and to refrain from molesting American vessels in future. This bold example was followed by England. In 1816 a fleet was sent to Algiers, under Lord Exmouth, who bombarded the city, reduced it to ashes, and compelled the Dey to surrender all his Christian prisoners.

ARAB WOMAN CHURNING.

"Piracy was not suppressed, however. Italian vessels were captured in the Mediterranean, and the Algerian cruisers even carried their depredations into the North Sea. A day of reckoning was at hand, however. In 1823 a quarrel arose between France and Algiers. The house of the French consul was plundered, the consul himself was struck in the face by the Dey, and several outrages were committed upon French vessels. A French squadron was sent to Algiers, which took the consul on board, and for three years maintained an ineffectual blockade of the port. At length, in 1830, Charles X. sent a powerful naval and military force against Algiers. The city was captured on the 4th of July, and twelve ships of war, fifteen hundred brass cannon, and over ten million dollars were surrendered to the French. The Dey and his Turks were compelled to leave the country. Louis Philippe decided to retain Algeria as a possession of France; the French army was strongly reinforced, and Bona, Oran, and Bougie were captured. The Arab and Kabyle tribes now rose against their new rulers, and thus began the long war between the French and the natives of the country, which was not ended until 1847, when Abd-el-Kader, the great leader of the struggle, surrendered to General Lamoricière. Since then several insurrections have been attempted by the Kabyles, but each has been crushed by the overwhelming power of the French. During the last ten years the country has been peaceful, and the French authorities have been enabled to grant civil government to a large portion of the colony. The country is also growing in wealth and prosperity.

"And now, young gentlemen," said the professor, "I have made rather a longer story than I intended; but it may serve you as an introduction to the country, and help you to understand better what you will see during our travels in Algeria."

The next morning the professor and his companions were on deck by six o'clock. Land was full in sight, and in the distance the Atlas Mountains could be seen looming up against the sky. The steamer sped swiftly along, and soon the city of Algiers was plainly in view, rising like an amphitheatre from the water up the northern slope of Mount Boujarin, and presenting a picturesque and beautiful appearance which was

ALGIERS FROM THE SEA.

greatly heightened by the dazzling whiteness of the houses, as they rose in terraces up the side of the hill. The professor called the attention of his companions to the contrast between the whiteness of the houses and the rich green background of the mountain, and told them that this was the origin of the Arab comparison of Algiers to a diamond set in an emerald frame.

As the steamer passed between the long jetties and entered the port, he pointed out the Islet of the Marine (or, as it was formerly called, *El Peñon*) crowned with a lofty lighthouse, and told them it was the last spot in Algiers held by the Spaniards, and the scene of many fierce encounters. This island, he added, which was called by the Arabs Al-Jezireh, or "the Island," gave its name to the city. The mole connecting it with the mainland, he told them, was that upon which Hayradin had employed thirty thousand Christian slaves for three years. He pointed out the Kasbah, or citadel, on the highest point of the city, and other objects of interest.

By half-past eight o'clock the steamer was securely moored to her dock alongside the custom-house, and an hour later our travellers were comfortably settled in their quarters in the "Hotel d'Orient." While they are making themselves comfortable, we invite the reader's attention to a brief description of the city in which they are to begin their African journey.

Algiers was the ancient Icosium of the Romans, and under them was a place of some importance, but was less prominent than its neighbor Julia Cæsarea, the modern Cherchel. Its history has been related in the account we

AN ARAB CEMETERY NEAR ALGIERS.

have already given of the country. Since 1830 it has been the capital of the French colony of Algeria. It contains a population of about sixty thousand, of which about fifteen thousand are French and six thousand Jews. It is built in the form of an amphitheatre on the northern slope of a steep hill rising abruptly from the coast. It ascends the hill in the form of an irregular triangle, at the apex of which is situated the Kasbah, or citadel, the ancient residence of the Deys, about five hundred feet above the level of the sea. The city is divided into two towns, the old and the new. The latter, which is entirely modern and European, is built upon the lower part of the slope and along the shore; while the old town, which occupies the higher parts of the hill, is altogether Oriental in its character. The new town is well laid out, consisting of handsome streets and squares, and containing the government

BAZAAR AT ALGIERS.

buildings, the barracks, the hotels, and many handsome private residences. The streets are regular and spacious, and are adorned with handsome arcades. In the old town, or Arab quarter, the streets are dirty, narrow, and winding.

The houses are square, substantial-looking buildings, presenting to the streets only bare walls pierced with a few slits protected by iron gratings in place of windows. Each house has a courtyard, or quadrangle, in the centre, into

A PLEASURE RESORT NEAR ALGIERS.

which all the rooms look, and which is entered from the street by a low narrow doorway. All the streets of the city now have French names.

Algiers is surrounded by walls, and is strongly fortified on the water side, but its land defences are weak and exposed. Beyond the city walls are two handsome suburbs, and the surrounding country is sprinkled with elegant villas. The city is the residence of the governor-general of Algiers, of the prefect of the Department of Algiers, and of the various officials employed in the administration of the colony. It is also the seat of an archbishop and of a Protestant consistory, and has a chamber and tribunal of commerce, a college, various schools, a bank, a public library, a museum, and several theatres. It is well supplied with water, and there are numerous public and private fountains and baths. Of late years the city has become a favorite winter resort for invalids.

Our travellers remained in Algiers until the 5th of March, and during that time thoroughly explored the interesting city. One of their first visits was made to the harbor and the batteries defending it. Hiring a boat, they visited the ancient harbor and the Island of the Marine, and the battery of El Djerfna, which occupies a rock almost in the centre of the port. Lying at ease in the boat, and gazing up at the dazzlingly beautiful picture presented by the city, the suburbs, and the masses of hills in the background, Ashton said almost as if speaking to himself,—

A PUBLIC WRITER AT ALGIERS.

"It is hard to imagine, professor, that this handsome city could ever have been a nest of pirates. It seems made for the abode of peace. I can hardly realize that it was the scene of so much crime and suffering."

"It looks peaceful enough now," replied the professor, "and no doubt seemed equally so in its worst days. Yet, as I have told you, it has a terrible history. Do you see that lofty height off there to the westward?" he added, pointing to a dark mountain rising beyond the city and some distance west of it; "that is Boudjareah, and on those lofty heights still dwell in huts two powerful Arab tribes which in former days furnished the most daring and blood-thirsty of all the Algerian pirates. That large fort rising on the southern side of the city marks the site of the Gate of Azoun, where the Christian captives who would not accept the Koran were hung by the loins from iron hooks until they died. Up there on that height, on the opposite side of the town, in front of Fort Neuf, which you see rising there, is the Bab-el-Oued, or Oued Gate. There the Arab rebels were beheaded by the yataghan, for the

Arab Deys were careful even in such matters to show more mercy to followers of the Koran than to Christians. Even this harbor we are now sailing over was marked by its deeds of blood, for here helpless women who had incurred the anger of their lords were drowned, tied up in a sack between a cat and a serpent. Yes, they were a cruel and blood-thirsty race, and the best thing that has ever happened to the country is the rule of the French."

A visit was also made by the professor and his companions to the Cathedral of St. Philippe. This they found to be a showy church, but one singularly lacking in tastefulness in its adornments. It stands next to the palace of the governor-general, and occupies the site of the old Mosque of Hassen. The most interesting portion of it is a small chapel to the visitor's right on entering, which contains the bones of the martyr St. Geronimo.

"Who was St. Geronimo, professor?" asked Houston. "I never heard of him before."

"Geronimo," replied Professor Moreton, "was the only Christian martyr of Algiers who has been canonized by the church. His history is related by a Spanish Benedictine monk named Haedo, who published a description of Algiers in 1612. He tells us that during an expedition of the Spanish garrison of Oran in 1540 a young Arab boy was captured, taken to Oran, and baptized under the name of Geronimo. When he was about eight years old, he was recaptured by his family, and lived with them as a Mohammedan until he reached the age of twenty-five. He then returned to Oran with the intention of living thenceforth as a Christian. In May, 1569, he joined a party of Spaniards who embarked in a small vessel for the purpose of making a raid upon neighboring Arabs. The vessel was captured by an Algerian cruiser, and Geronimo and his companions were carried to Algiers as prisoners. Every effort was made there to induce him to renounce Christianity, but all in vain. He was sentenced to a most cruel death, and the sentence was promptly executed. His hands and feet were bound with cords, and he was thrown alive into a mould in which a block of *béton* or concrete was about to

A DRY-GOODS STORE AT ALGIERS.

be made. When the concrete containing his body had hardened, the block was built into an angle of one of the forts of the town then in course of construction. The exact spot was carefully recorded by Haedo, who closed his description with the following words: 'We hope that God's grace may one day extricate Geronimo from this place, and reunite his body with those of many other holy martyrs of Christ, whose blood and happy deaths have consecrated this country.'"

"Is the story true, professor, or only legendary?" asked Ashton.

"The sequel shows it to be true," was the reply. "In 1853 it was found necessary by the French authorities to demolish the fort, and on the 27th of December, in the very spot described by Haedo, the skeleton of Geronimo was found imbedded in a block of concrete. The bones were carefully removed, and interred with great pomp in this chapel. Liquid plaster of Paris was run into the mould left by his body in the concrete, and a perfect model of it was obtained, showing not only his features but the cords which bound him, and even the texture of his clothing. This cast is preserved in the government museum here, and we shall see it when we visit that establishment."

AN ALGERIAN BEAUTY.

A very interesting visit was made to the Grand Mosque, the most ancient in Algeria, and also to several other mosques, among which was that of Sidi Abd-er-Rahman the Thalebi, which contains the tomb of that saint, and tombs of a number of the pashas and Deys. The travellers went several times to the Government Library and Museum, which collections are contained in the ancient palace of Mustapha Pasha. Here the professor spent a large part of his time, devoting himself to the study of certain matters connected with Algeria, and leaving the young men to wander through the city at will. In the museum they saw the plaster cast of St. Geronimo, to which we have referred. The museum also contains some interesting Roman remains and a number of valuable Christian antiquities. The Permanent Exhibition of Algerian products, which occupies five of the large vaults beneath the Boulevard de Republique, also interested them greatly, as it enabled them to obtain a thorough comprehension of the products, manufactures, and natural history of the colony from the specimens exhibited there. They also visited the Kasbah, or citadel, which, as we have stated, occupies the highest point of the city. The fortress was erected in 1516 by Barbarossa, and was, until the capture of the city by the French, the residence of the sovereigns of Algiers. It was defended by two hundred pieces of artillery, and was considered almost impregnable. It contained the palace, a mosque, and one or two other buildings. After the siege the French cut a road straight through the centre, converted the mosque into a barracks, and used the remainder of the fortress for military purposes. It was in the vaults of the citadel that the enormous treasure we have spoken of was found by the conquerors. The view from the citadel is very fine. Below are the city and harbor, with the picturesque suburbs and villas stretching away on either side of the walls. Far away to seaward stretches the Mediterranean, an unbroken line of blue, while beyond the city lies the fertile plain of the Metidja, with the dark wall of the Atlas Mountains rising grimly from its farthest verge.

Our travellers were greatly interested in the city itself. It was a pleasure to stroll under the handsome arcades of the modern town, and look into the shops and bazaars with which they are lined. They found the arcades a pleasant refuge from the sun during the warm days, and a convenient shelter from the rains in bad weather. All sorts of people passed them in the streets, and various and quaint were the costumes they beheld. At every turn they met the French officers and soldiers in their gay uniforms, the Moors and Arabs in their turbans and long-flowing robes, and the Kabyles in their picturesque dress. Hubbard declared it was like walking through the "Arabian Nights," and that every moment he expected to encounter some character of those wonderful romances. He stoutly averred that he would not be surprised if the good Khalif Haroun Alraschid should slap him on the shoulder at any moment, and ask him to accompany him on one of his rounds, or if Sindbad the Sailor should buttonhole him and commence to relate one of his marvellous adventures. The native *cafés* were also interesting, and the party spent many pleasant half-hours in them, sipping the delicious coffee from the daintiest and most delicate of cups; the professor also enjoying a good smoke from one of the huge Turkish pipes provided at such places.

But pleasant as was the visit to the capital, it soon drew to a close. The

STREET IN THE ARAB QUARTER OF ALGIERS.

professor had engaged passage for his party on one of the steamers of the Valery line, which was to sail from Algiers for Bona on the 5th of March. From that place our travellers were to make their way across the Kabyle country back to Algiers.

CHAPTER III.

FROM ALGIERS TO CONSTANTINA.

THE steamer on which Professor Moreton and the young Americans embarked for their voyage along the coast was much smaller than that in which they had crossed the Mediterranean, but was, on the whole, very comfortable. The vessel sailed promptly at noon, and, as the day was bright and fair, they had a fine view of the city and coast until darkness hid the land from view. The city presented a very picturesque appearance as the steamer receded from it, fading gradually into an indistinct mass of white set in a dark background. The vessel's course was directly across the Bay of Algiers towards the open sea, and in a little more than an hour Cape Matifou was rounded, and beyond it could be seen the summits of the Atlas Mountains, among which our travellers were to spend much of their time.

The day was pleasant, with a fair wind and smooth sea, and the views of the coast were very beautiful as the steamer sped swiftly along. At half-past four the vessel dropped her anchor in the port of Dellys, an insignificant town, about forty-four miles from Algiers. The harbor is very insecure, and in bad weather steamers are not able to enter it. A delay of three hours was made, to land a portion of the cargo, and our travellers had ample time to survey the town with their glasses.

"This place is memorable in the history of the French conquest of the country," said Professor Moreton, "as it was here that the French were first initiated into the peculiar method of Kabyle fighting. Here every house was converted into a fortress, and each had to be taken separately. The French had literally to storm their way through the town. The defenders consisted of the very flower of the Kablye chivalry, and even the women fought desperately."

The evening was passed pleasantly on deck, the saloon being too warm, and the party enjoyed a pleasant night's rest, from which they were aroused about six o'clock the next morning by the sound of the anchor going over the side. They were soon on deck, and found that the steamer was lying in the harbor of Bougie, the principal seaport of Eastern Kabylia. Numbers of boats were hovering around the vessel, and as the Americans came on deck they were hailed by a score of boatmen urging them to land and see the town.

Upon learning from the captain that the steamer would not sail until two o'clock in the afternoon, the party decided to go ashore after an early breakfast. That meal ended, they repaired to the deck again. The professor selected a boat, the owner of which could speak French fluently, and ordered it alongside. As they pulled away from the ship they could see that the town was built up the side of a steep hill, and was divided into two parts by a deep ravine, which the boatman told them was called Sidi Touati.

DELLYS.

"It was in that ravine," said the professor to his companions, "that a tragedy occurred which shows the Kabyle character in its worst and best lights. In 1836 the French commandant, M. de Mussis, was invited to a conference there by the sheikh of Amzian, and was treacherously shot by him. The sheikh endeavored to excuse his act by saying that it was done in revenge for the murder of a Kabyle marabout, or 'holy man,' who had been killed by the French sentinels. His countrymen, however, sternly denounced the murder, and reminded the sheikh that he had just taken coffee with his victim. He became known as the man who murdered with one hand and took gifts with the other; and so great was the indignation of the Kabyles at his violation of the laws of hospitality that he was compelled to resign his office. He died in utter obscurity."

"I think I shall like the Kabyles," said Houston. "What I saw of them in Algiers gave me a good opinion of them, and from what you say of them, professor, they must be good fellows at heart."

As he spoke the boat touched the stony beach which bounds the harbor.

Our travellers sprang ashore, and the professor told the boatman to await their return.

"O Roumi," exclaimed the man, laying his hand on his breast, and bowing low, "you will find me faithful. I will await your coming at this spot."

"What did the man mean by calling you Roumi?" asked Philip Lee. "Is that the Kabyle for 'professor?'"

"No," replied Professor Moreton. "It is the title given by the natives

BOUGIE, AND HILL OF GOURAYA.

to all Europeans in this country. It means simply 'Christian,' and its origin is no doubt due to the fact that the first Christians of this region were members of the Roman Catholic Church. The Kabyle regards all Christians as belonging to that faith. He recognizes no difference between Romanism and Protestantism. Every European is in his estimation a Romanist. Hence the term 'Roumi,' which is by no means intended as a mark of respect in all cases."

Bougie occupies the site of a very ancient Roman town, called Salda by Strabo. It has been ruled by the Romans, Berbers, Arabs, Spaniards, and Turks, and each race has left behind it interesting memorials of its occupancy. Our travellers made a visit to the remains of the Roman fortifications, which are still visible in many places. The arch at the landing place, and the walls and towers on the hillsides behind the city, all belonging to the Saracenic system of defence, also interested them greatly. They strolled for several hours through the town, seeing many quaint and interesting sights, and climbing its steep streets, many of which are simply stairways leading to higher elevations. Some lovely views of the harbor and coast were obtained from the highest points of the city. The travellers were at length thoroughly fatigued by their climb, and were glad to return to their boat. They were on board the steamer by one o'clock, and at two the vessel resumed her voyage.

Towards seven o'clock the captain pointed out the town of Djidjelly, a small, unimportant place, marked by huge barracks and a hospital. The professor told his companions that this town was the scene of the terrible defeat of the expedition sent against the Algerines by Louis XIV. of France in 1634. During the night the steamer rounded Cape Bougarone, and about four o'clock on Friday morning anchored in the harbor of Philippeville.

ARAB WOMAN AND CHILD.

The professor and his companions were soon aroused by the noise of discharging the cargo and the shouts of the sailors. Coming on deck between five and six o'clock, they learned that the steamer was to lie at anchor until seven that evening. This would give them ample opportunity to visit Philippeville, and after breakfast they went ashore, and devoted the day to seeing the city.

Philippeville is a modern town, and is built on the site of the ancient city of Rusicada. After the capture of Constantina the French authorities at

Algiers resolved to establish a more secure communication with the former place than already existed by way of Bona. In 1838, therefore, Marshal Valée occupied the site of the ancient Rusicada, and to make good the title of the government to it, purchased the ground from the Beni Melch tribe for one hundred and fifty-three francs. Upon this site a city was founded, and named in honor of Louis Philippe, king of the French. It has grown rapidly in the forty years that have elapsed since then, and is now a handsome, well-built town, French in all its characteristics as well as regards its inhab-

ROMAN RELICS AT PHILIPPEVILLE.

itants. Its streets are arcaded in imitation of the Rue de Rivoli at Paris, its houses are European in appearance; and it contains a gorgeous church.

Yet, though entirely modern, Philippeville contains many interesting relics of the old city of Rusicada. The professor and his companions visited a number of these remains, among which were the well-preserved Roman reservoirs on the hill above the town, which still supply it with water; the ruins of the theatre, and some groups of inscribed columns. On one of these they found a rude but amusing sketch, evidently cut there by some Roman school-boy, representing an *aquarius*, or water-carrier, bearing his twin buckets joined by a pole.

The party returned to the steamer late in the afternoon, and towards half-past seven the vessel put out to sea again. When they awoke the next morning the ship was at anchor in the handsome roadstead of Bona. In a little while the steamer stood in towards the town, and, entering the well-protected harbor, was made fast to her place at the dock. As they passed in the professor called the attention of his companions to the singular shapes of the rocks in the harbor, one of which bears a remarkable resemblance to the figure of a lion.

LION-SHAPED ROCK, HARBOR OF BONA.

It was so perfect in every part that Ashton declared it might well be taken for some huge lion that had been turned to stone by the ancient gods, and placed there to guard the entrance to the port.

As Bona was the most eastern point of our travellers' wanderings, and the end of their voyage by sea, they were soon ashore, and in a short time after landing had secured comfortable apartments in the Hotel d'Orient, to the proprietors of which they had letters from their landlord in Algiers.

Bona, called by the Arabs *Annaba*, or "the City of Jujube Trees," was founded by them after the destruction of the ancient Hippone, or Hippo, one mile to the southeast of the present town, which was in a great measure built of the ruins of the old city. The town is thoroughly Eastern in appearance, consisting of narrow streets bordered by Moorish houses. A few of these are devoted to the shops or stalls of the natives,—shoemakers, jewellers, and blacksmiths,—who sit cross-legged on the narrow ledges of their shops and transact business between the whiffs of their long pipes. These industries are about equally divided between the Jews and the Mozabites, a remnant of the old Berber race. The latter still cling to the true Arab dress, a small bournouse without a hood, broad breeches coming to the knee, and a turban twisted like a coil of ropes. Our travellers noticed that one street bore the name of St. Augustine, and were not a little surprised to find all the shops in it occupied by Jews, and those all of one particular family.

The day being Saturday, the streets were full of Jews, dressed in gayly-

colored robes, but all wearing black turbans. In other respects the dress of
the wearer was according to his means and taste, but the turban bore the same
hue upon the heads of rich and poor alike. This surprised the young Americans, and they appealed to Professor Moreton for an explanation.

"Under the rule of the Arabs and Turks," said the professor, "the Jews
were treated with great harshness and cruelty, and were permitted to dress
only in the most mournful colors. They were compelled to wear black turbans
as a mark of the contempt in which they were held by the followers of the

AN ARAB MARKET IN ALGERIA.

prophet. Now, although given by the law every right and privilege of French
citizens, they still, in small towns like this, wear the black turban as a souvenir
of their former sufferings."

On the next day, Sunday, the 6th of March, the professor and his companions made a visit to the site of Hippone, which they reached by a Roman
bridge, restored to its ancient strength and proportions by the French. As
they walked along the professor told them that Hippone was originally
founded by the Carthaginians, and was, at a later period, one of the royal
cities of the kings of Numidia. From this it derived its Roman name of

Hippo Regius. Later still it was created a colony of the empire, and with Carthage was one of the wealthiest centres of Roman commerce in Africa. It was taken and reduced to ashes by the Vandals in 431, but was rebuilt under Belisarius, only, however, to be finally destroyed by the Arabs in 687. There was but little to interest the visitors in the ruins save some foundations which are said to be those of the basilica in which St. Augustine preached for so many years.

"Whether these ruins be those of the church or not," said the professor, "we know that this site was the scene of the labors of the great Christian Father, and it is worth the trouble of coming here to stand on the spot his feet once trod."

"Who was St. Augustine?" asked Houston. "I've often heard his name, but I know nothing of his history. Tell us about him, professor."

"Augustine," began the professor, "was the greatest of the four great Fathers or teachers of the Latin or Roman Church. No other man has ever exercised such power over the Christian church, and no other mind ever made such an impression upon Christian thought. He was of good family, and was born at Tagaste, in Numidia, in 354. His father was a pagan at the time of

DESERT HORSEMEN.

Augustine's birth, but his mother, Monica, was a devout Christian, who, by her example and prayers, converted her husband to the true faith, and also brought her son up in Christian ways and doctrines. When but a youth Augustine fell ill, and being in danger of death, expressed a wish to be baptized; but when the danger was past he deferred his wish, and, notwithstanding his mother's admonitions and prayers, he grew up without any profession of Christian piety, or any devotion to Christian principles. He finally plunged into a life of dissipation and immorality, in which he continued until he was thirty years old. Yet all this while he was a close and diligent student of the classic writers, especially of the Latin poets. He studied at Madaura and Carthage, and was early known for his intellectual attainments. In his thirtieth year he went to Rome as a teacher of rhetoric, and soon after accepted a similar place at Milan. There, in his thirty-second year, moved by the preaching of St. Ambrose, he became a convert to Christianity, and the next year was baptized on Easter Sunday. He then went back to Rome for a short time, after which he returned to his native country and spent three years in retirement, originating the system of solitary monasticism which derives its name from him. At the end of his three years' retirement, he went to Hippo to see a Christian friend, and while there was compelled by the unanimous voice of the church to accept the position of presbyter. He burst into tears when the demand was made upon him, but submitted to the will of his brethren. He served with great zeal as presbyter, and subsequently became the bishop of Hippo. His residence here covered a period of thirty-five years, and here he composed his 'Confessions,' his 'City of God,' and his other great theological works. He bore the leading part in the great controversies of his time, and was the ablest supporter of the Roman Church. He died in 430 while the Vandals were besieging Hippo, and was spared the sorrow of witnessing the destruction of his home."

Early on Monday, March 10, our travellers left Bona by the diligence for Philippeville. The ride was along the plain and across low spurs of foothills, and led through an uninteresting country. Philippeville was reached about nightfall, and the party spent the night there at a very comfortable hotel. On Tuesday morning they took the railway for Constantina, which was reached in the course of a few hours. The greater part of the route lay through a succession of sunny hills and groves, and the professor and his companions were hardly prepared for the startling change in the scenery when Constantina came in view. On the flat top of a bare rock, encircled by a magnificent mountain chasm, and rising a thousand feet above the cascades of the river Rummel, which washed its base, rose the principal city of Kabylia, presenting a grand and imposing appearance. They had seen nothing like it, and were greatly impressed by it. Upon reaching the station they proceeded at once to the Hotel de Paris, situated in the French quarter of the town, where they succeeded in obtaining excellent accommodations.

Constantina occupies the site of the once splendid city of Cirta, one of the most powerful communities of ancient Numidia. The Romans regarded it as the strongest position in that country, and it was made by them the converging point of all their military roads in Numidia. It was allowed by the early emperors to fall into decay, but was restored by Constantine the Great, from whom it took its present name. The picturesque beauty of its situation is unsurpassed by that of any city in the world, for nature seems to have constructed it entirely with a view to defence and artistic beauty. The rock on which it stands is nearly quadrilateral in shape, with its faces corresponding to the cardinal points of the compass, and sloping from north to south. Its sides rise perpendicularly nearly one thousand feet from the river Rummel, which surrounds it on the north and east. On the west it is connected by a neck of rock with the main land. The deep ravine through which the Rummel flows varies in breadth from two hundred feet on the southeast side to nearly four hundred opposite the citadel, and is spanned on the northeast side by four natural arches of rock, about two hundred feet above the river. One of these

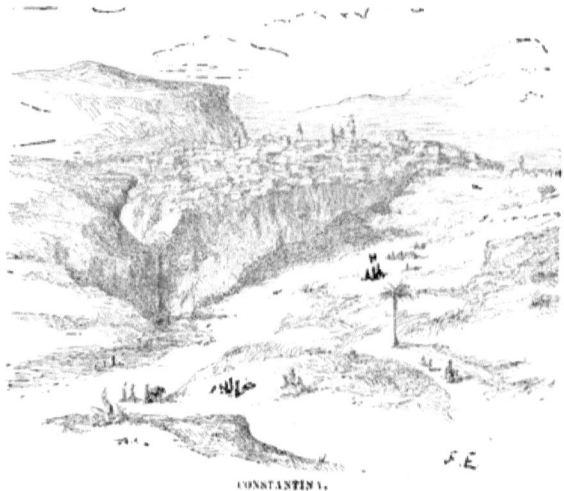

CONSTANTINA.

serves as a foundation for the bridge of El-Kantara. The city is partly French and partly Arab, each race occupying a distinct quarter. The population numbers forty thousand.

Professor Moreton and his companions remained at Constantina during the rest of the week. They found the city very different from Algiers. It was much more picturesque and interesting, and gave them a truer idea of Arab and Kabyle life than the capital. In passing the old Bab-el-Djedid, now called by the French "The Gate of the Breach," Professor Moreton called the attention of the young men to it.

"Constantina," said he, "was the most hotly defended of all the Kabylian strongholds in 1837. It was by this gate that Colonel Lamoricière entered the city at the head of his Zouaves. His success, however, was only the beginning of the hardest struggle. The city had to be taken house by house, and the gallant Lamoricière was severely wounded while directing the operations. The French gained steadily, however, and at last the Kabyles were crowded into the Kasbah, or citadel, on the summit of the rock. Driven to despair, they evacuated this strong position, and endeavored to lower their women by ropes into the ravine. Many of the ropes broke under the heavy strain, and the

ROMAN BRIDGE AT CONSTANTINA.

mangled bodies were piled up in heaps at the foot of the precipice. Numbers of the Kabyles, however, made their escape by climbing down the sides of the rock. The fall of the city greatly discouraged the natives, who had regarded it as impregnable, and the French authority was soon firmly established in the province."

The contrast between the French quarter of the city, with its rectangular streets and broad open squares, bordered with trees and adorned with fountains, and the tortuous lanes and Moorish architecture of the Arab quarter, was very interesting to the young Americans, and it seemed to them that in their

BEY'S PALACE, CONSTANTINA.

rambles through the town they were constantly passing from one world into another. They frequently walked out on the bridge of El-Kantara, an old

Roman structure restored by the French, and gazed down at the foaming river three hundred feet below; and on one of these walks the professor told them that an Arab poet had compared this river to a bracelet encircling an arm.

Through the courtesy of the governor of the province our travellers were admitted to the old palace of the Bey. This curious edifice was erected about sixty years ago by Ahmed Bey, the last of the native rulers of Constantina. Having determined to build himself the most gorgeous palace in Northern Africa, he stripped the ruins of Constantina, Bona, and Tunis of whatever was most beautiful in the way of Roman marbles and carvings, and built them into his new edifice. Thus, though the palace is in many respects the despair of architects, it preserves numerous rare and beautiful relics of Roman history, which would otherwise have gone to decay. The guide who accompanied the party through the palace called their attention to some curious frescos in the loggia or gallery,—crude, grotesque arabesques, seeming rather the production of a disordered fancy than of a mind and hand trained to art.

"They are the work of a French Roumi, as they call us here," said the guide, who was also French, in reply to a question by the professor. "Ahmed Bey, having completed his palace, was very anxious to adorn this gallery with frescos, which he had heard was the proper thing to do. Unfortunately he could find no artist among either his Arab, Moorish, or Jewish subjects capable of executing the task. At last he bethought himself of a French prisoner, who was confined in one of his dungeons. He caused the man to be brought before him, and astounded him by giving him the order to fresco the walls of this gallery. The poor fellow was a shoemaker, and had never touched a brush or pencil in his life. In vain he attempted to decline the honor, and protested that he could not paint. The Bey cut him short with the reply,—'You lie, you dog of a Roumi; all the Christians can paint. Go to your work. I will give you your liberty if you succeed; but will put you to death if you disobey me.' The poor shoemaker, thus made an artist in spite of himself, went to his task with a heavy heart and a trembling hand. The result you see before you in this odd mass of arabesques. At the appointed time the Bey came to inspect the work, and the poor Frenchman awaited his decision in an agony of fear, expecting each moment to hear the order for the bowstring or the yataghan. But Ahmed was delighted. He pronounced the work superb, and dismissed the 'artist' with his liberty and a handsome present. As he watched the man leave the palace, Ahmed observed with a chuckle to one of his attendants, 'That dog wanted to deceive me; but I was too wise for him. I knew that all the Christians could paint.'"

One evening during their stay in Constantina the professor and his companions strolled into a Moorish bath in the Arab quarter of the town, for the purpose of enjoying the luxury of "a good cleaning-up," as Hubbard expressed it. All had experienced the delights of the Turkish baths in New York and Philadelphia, and supposed that they would be even pleasanter here on their native soil. They were not long, however, in discovering the difference. Houston, in a letter to his father, written the next day, thus describes their experience. We give his account in preference to a description of our own:

"We were ushered," he wrote, "into a low, vaulted building, dimly lighted by oil lamps suspended from the ceiling. The light was made even dimmer by clouds of steam which floated among the arches. How the place did smell of soap! We were each shown into a closet, in which we removed our clothing

THE ROUMI ENJOY A MOORISH BATH.

and wrapped ourselves in large white sheets. Then we came out into the main hall, looking like a parcel of ghosts, and not a little nervous as to what was in store for us. We were then led to a marble bench and told to sit down. As soon as we had done so we found the heat had greatly increased. In a little while the perspiration was running in streams from every pore of our bodies, and our sheets were soon drenched with it. We were then taken into a room of milder temperature, where our sheets were removed, and we were each handed over to two stout, naked negroes. They were powerful fellows; and, as they could speak neither French nor English, we could not make them understand us, but had to submit ourselves to their mercy. Placing a white cloth on the floor for each of us, they laid us on our backs, and began rubbing the soles of our feet with pumice-stone. The professor, who can't bear his feet to be tickled, roared at this operation; but the negroes seemed to take this as encouragement, and rubbed his feet harder than ever. When they had finished with our feet they put their hands into small bags and rubbed us all over as hard as they could. I thought they would not leave a particle of skin on our bodies. We howled lustily, I tell you, but this seemed only to encourage the negroes to renewed exertions, and they smiled at us benevolently, and endeavored to show us by signs how much we were being benefited by the operation. All the while they climbed over our bodies, planting their knees on our legs, chests, and arms, until it seemed that they would fairly crush us by their weight. Not satisfied with scraping us in this way, they almost drowned us by drenching us with warm water thrown from silver vessels, which were in a marble basin under a cock fastened in the wall. The poor professor was a sight to behold. He looked like a boiled beet, and was spluttering and gasping for breath, and abusing the negroes with all his might. Suddenly the black fellows seized us, and placing each of our heads under a cock, let a large stream of water flow over our heads and down our bodies, while at the same time they kept drowning us with water from the basin. When we were about half dead they carried us to another side of the room and dried us with fine napkins, after which each respectfully kissed the hand of the person he had been torturing. We thought from this that our troubles were at an end, and were about to return to our closets when the black fellows stopped us, laid us down again on dry cloths, and began to rub our bodies with a kind of earth, which burned like quicklime. They did not suffer it to remain on us long, however, but drenched us again with warm water until we were clean. Then we were each seized without ceremony by a negro, who placed his two knees against the lower part of our backs, and, catching us behind by the shoulders, gave us a jerk that seemed to crack every bone in our bodies. We were rolled over, manipulated until our joints seemed dislocated, and pommelled in a way that seemed absolutely barbarous; and then, when the ordeal came to an end, we were released and smilingly shown into a room, where, enveloped in sheets again, we were permitted to lie down and rest for a little while before dressing. I was surprised to find how soon the sense of soreness left me. Coffee was brought to us, and to this the professor added a pipe. When we had rested, we dressed and went back to our hotel. I seemed to be walking on air, I felt so light and buoyant; and how I did sleep that night! Next morning I got up feeling cleaner than I had ever felt before, and without the least soreness or uncomfortable sensation."

It was rather a novelty to our travellers to sit in the cafés lining the principal square of the French quarter and listen to one of the military bands playing familiar operatic airs; but the band and the music seemed out of place in this old Berber stronghold; and the party liked better to roam through the Moorish quarter, the streets of which were only about five feet wide, and so crowded that locomotion was slow. Sometimes there would be a sudden cry of "Balek! Balek!" and the white-turbaned, long-robed natives

"BALEK!"

would crowd hastily against the walls of the houses, leaving a wide pathway for a horseman who would dash by, scattering the throng before him as he uttered his warning shout. Very pleasant it was to lounge on the stone benches of a coffee-house, sipping the fragrant beverage, and, in accordance with Eastern customs, eating it at the same time, and to watch the throngs leisurely passing along the street. Here sauntered by the swarthy Arabs in their white bournouses, the suspicious-eyed Jews, the haughty Turks, the dark-browed, fierce-looking Kabyles, heavily-turbaned Moors, with long flowing robes, and the gayly uniformed soldiers of the garrison. Each street in this quarter of the town has its specialty. One is devoted to the tailors, who sit cross-legged in their narrow stalls, and pursue their work in silence; another is given up to the blacksmiths, and echoes and re-echoes with the blows of the hammers upon the anvils; and another still contains the shoemakers, whose store of slippers seems inexhaustible, and sets you to wondering what can be the necessity for making so many slippers when nearly every native of Constantina goes barefooted. Other streets again are dark and silent, being lined with dingy walls pierced with grated openings for windows and low narrow arches for doorways. Veiled figures pass in and out of these archways, and once in a while you catch a gleam of a dark eye, which

THE GREAT MOSQUE, CONSTANTINA.

suggests that the women of Constantina may not be behind their Eastern sisters in beauty. Rising high above this intricate labyrinth of houses are the slender minarets of the mosques. The largest and most substantial is a square tower, shaped like a belfry, crowned by a dome and crescent, belonging to the Grand Mosque. From the highest gallery of the tower come floating down at intervals, all through the day and night, the deep-toned, bell-like voices of the muezzins exhorting the faithful: "Come to prayer! come to prayer! Prayer is better than sleep. There is no God but God; and Mohammed is the prophet of God!" Our travellers visited several of the mosques, the principal of which was the Grand Mosque, which the Arabs claim is the most beautiful in Algeria. The interior is adorned with columns of pink marble supporting rows of Moorish arches, and with tiles of painted faïence set in the walls. The pulpit, coarsely painted in red and blue, stands in the centre, and from this the Imaum recites the prayers. Upon the floor are spread carpets for the devotions of the rich, and mattings for those of the poor. The visitors were required to remove their shoes upon entering the mosques, and were provided with soft woollen slippers in their place.

A MARABOUT OF KYBALIA.

On Friday the professor and his companions went to see the performances of the fire-eating marabouts. These are held every Friday, and constitute the most curious spectacle to be witnessed in Constantina.

"These marabouts," said the professor, "belong to a sect founded about three hundred years ago by Mohammed-ben-Aïssa, from whom they take their name of Aïssaoui. The legend states that the founder was very poor, but that, instead of working to support his family, he devoted himself to meditation and prayer. This won him the favor of the prophet, who appeared to Aïssa's wife with baskets of provisions and to Aïssa with orders to found a sect. The whole object of these fanatics seems to be to show that nothing can hurt a true believer, but that everything can nourish him. Their fanaticism and jugglery give them great influence over the excitable Kabyles, and they have been the authors of almost every outbreak against the French. They take good care, however, to keep themselves out of danger when war actually breaks out."

By this time they had reached the place where the performances were to be held. Entering the hall, they found quite a large audience, principally of Arabs and Kabyles, with a sprinkling of French soldiers, assembled. These formed a ring; in the centre was an open space, in which a number of the marabouts were seated.

The performance began by the beating of drums and tambours, to which accompaniment the marabouts sang a wild, unearthly chant. This was continued for about a quarter of an hour, when one of them suddenly sprang into the middle of the ring with a hoarse yell, and began to dance frantically, swaying his body back and forth, and twisting it violently into various unnatural positions. All the while the most furious and unearthly cries burst from his lips. He was soon joined by another and another marabout, until half a dozen were howling and dancing in the ring. This portion of the ceremony greatly amused the young Americans, and Hubbard declared that the marabouts would prove even more popular in the United States than the negro minstrels.

"It's the best walk-around I ever saw," said Houston. "It must be rather tiresome, though."

He had scarcely spoken when two of the performers dropped to the floor from exhaustion. The mokaddam, or head of the order, then commanded the dancing to cease. In a few moments the drums and tambours struck up again, and two men sprang forward into the ring, and began to force their eyes from their sockets with large iron spikes. They drew them out to an almost incredible distance without seeming to feel the least pain. Another marabout now walked forward with his mouth full of red-hot coals of fire, which he had taken from a brazier in full view, and passed around the ring blowing out the sparks. A fourth drew a large bar of red-hot iron from the brazier and passed it repeatedly over his hands and face. It burned its way across the flesh, but the man seemed to feel no pain or inconvenience, and finally placed the bar in his mouth and held it there without support. Then another hideous-looking fellow came forward and began to chew the leaf of a cactus, paying no heed to the pricks of its dangerous and sharp spikes, after which he chewed up a quantity of broken glass and swallowed it. A sixth swallowed a living scorpion, a small snake, and a handful of iron nails. All through the performance, which lasted nearly two hours, the horrible yells of the marabouts and the beating of the drums continued with scarcely any intermission. The men appeared to be roused to the highest pitch of fanatical frenzy.

"Well, boys," asked the professor, as they passed out into the street again, "what do you think of the fire-eaters?"

"I am glad to have seen the performance once," replied Philip Lee; "but it disgusted me. I would not care to witness it a second time."

MARABOUT ROUSING THE KABYLES TO REVOLT.

"It's very curious, though," said Houston. "I'd like to know where the trick lies."

"They keep their secrets well," said the professor. "During the reign of Louis Philippe the French government sent the famous sleight-of-hand performer, Robert Houdin, to Algeria to show that these performances were not supernatural. He greatly surpassed the marabouts in his tricks and experiments, but could never learn the secret of theirs."

CHAPTER IV.

THE COUNTRY OF THE KABYLES.

THROUGH the assistance of one of the higher French officials at Constantina, whose acquaintance he had made, Professor Moreton succeeded in engaging a couple of Arab guides to conduct his party to Setif, and thence on to Bou-Kteun in Kabylia. For the use of the travellers five insignificant mules were all that could be procured, and these seemed scarcely strong enough for the journey. The guides, who spoke French very well, assured the professor, however, that the animals were fully equal to the task before them, having accomplished it often before. As the members of the party had left their baggage at Algiers, and had brought with them only the clothing necessary to the journey, they consoled themselves with the thought that the mules would be burdened with but little more than the weight of their riders.

Early on the morning of Monday, March 18, the guides were at the entrance to the hotel with the mules. Our travellers were soon in their saddles, and, with a hearty good-by to the landlord, set off for the city gate. As they passed out they were struck with the difference between their own appearance and that of the two guides. The latter were Arabs from the hills, and were fine specimens of their race. They were handsome fellows, tall and finely made, with dark complexions, rich, black beards, which set off their small, white teeth; and dark eyes, that were pleasant as a rule, but could flash with anger or grow cold with sternness. Their heads were small, and their arms and legs tapered to the wrists and ankles as delicately as the limbs of a blooded horse. They were dressed in red, with two bournouses, a white one underneath and a black one over it, the former fastened about their heads and flowing down over their bodies. Their lower limbs were encased in long boots of red Morocco leather, which came up to their knees, and to these were attached large iron spurs. They were magnificently mounted, the horse of the principal guide being a splendid gray with a large black tail, and that of the other a coal-black mare of the purest blood.

"Truly, professor," said Ashton, as they rode along through the open country, "we look like a band of captives who have yielded to the powers of these magnificent Ishmaelites."

The day was pleasant, but the country was uninteresting, and the travellers were not sorry when, late in the afternoon, they reached Setif, their halting place for the night. They found a tolerably comfortable hotel there, and, fatigued with their long ride, retired early.

Setif was in ancient times the principal city of this part of Mauritania. When the Saracens overran the country it made a memorable resistance to them, but was at length forced to yield. It is now occupied by a French garrison, and is a place of some importance, though it contains but little of interest to the visitor. It is situated on a large plateau a mile above the sea level, and is regarded as the healthiest spot in Algeria occupied by the French. It is fortified, and has four streets. Snow lies on the table land around it and in its streets for half the year, and during the remaining six months it is enveloped in clouds of dust. It is in the midst of a great grain-growing country, and is noted for its market, which is held every Saturday.

THE ARAB GUIDES.

Our travellers were off at an early hour on Tuesday morning, as they had a long ride before them. A few miles from Setif they came across an Arab douar, or assemblage of tents occupied by a portion of a wandering tribe. The professor asked one of the guides if this was a Kabyle tribe. The guide replied gravely that the occupants of the tents were Arabs, and added that the Kabyles never lived in tents, but always dwelt in villages built of stone. He then rode forward, and held a short conversation with an Arab, who came out of the camp to meet him. Returning, he told the professor that the douar was an encampment of marabouts, who owned the land from this point to the Kabylian frontier. He added that it was customary for travellers to stop, in journeying by such camps, and pay their respects to the sheikh. The professor promptly declared his readiness to conform to the custom, and the guide rode forward to announce the visit of the party, leaving his companion to conduct them to the camp.

The douar consisted of a circle of tents, about fifty in number, in the centre of which was an oval-shaped tent, the residence of the sheikh. The coverings of the tents were striped brown and yellow, and consisted of a coarse,

COUNTRY BETWEEN CONSTANTINA AND SETIF.

thick camel's-hair cloth, made by the women. This cloth has the property of swelling up in the rain, and so excludes the water. The sheikh's tent was constructed of much finer fabrics, with gayer colors, and at the apex rose a gilded ball with ostrich plumes, the symbol of authority. A number of fine horses were picketed near the doors of the tents, and the members of the tribe were gathered at their tent doors, and gravely saluted the visitors as they rode by.

Arrived at the centre of the camp, the party dismounted, and preceded by the chief guide, who was also to act as interpreter, advanced towards the tent of the sheikh, who stood waiting in his door to receive them. His greeting of them was courteous and kind, but stately and dignified. He invited them into the tent, which was richly hung with silk curtains, and ornamented with saddles, arms, and gilded boxes, but totally devoid of furniture. Seating himself cross-legged on a carpet spread on the ground, the sheikh invited his guests to do likewise; then, at a sign from him, an attendant brought in chiboukhs filled with mild tobacco, at which all present puffed away in silence for a while. The sheikh then asked the professor, through the interpreter, if the young men were his sons; and upon being told the true relations of the party to each other, said he had not thought the professor old enough to be the father of so many well-grown sons. He then asked if his visitors were English, and, upon being told that they were Americans, expressed his surprise that they

AN ARAB DOUAR.

should have made so long a journey to visit Algeria. He had heard that all Americans were very rich, and he hoped that Allah had blessed his visitors with an abundance of worldly goods. Some more conversation followed, and then, the pipes being finished, the interview came to an end. The sheikh accompanied his visitors to the door of his tent, and there bade them a grave farewell, and stood watching them as they remounted and turned out of the camp into the road again.

"I would not have missed this visit upon any consideration," said Ashton, as they rode along.

"Nor I," said the professor. "We have witnessed a perfect picture of pastoral life as it has existed since the days of Father Abraham."

At a little distance beyond the camp was a smaller one, a sort of suburb to the larger douar. Here a number of Arab women were engaged in washing and cooking. Farther on was a cemetery. The tombs were all of stone, for,

MOHAMMEDAN CEMETERY.

however satisfied the Arab may be to dwell in horse-hair tents during his pilgrimage on earth, he must have a covering of solid stone over his last home. Several of the tombs were surmounted by stone turbans, indicating that a true Mussulman slept below.

The rest of the day's journey was through a stony and chalky country, and over a difficult and tiresome road. Then, as night was beginning to fall, the party descended into a ravine, and crossing it, climbed up a steep hill, on which stood Bou-Kteun, the first Kabylian town on their route.

Before reaching the place Professor Moreton made inquiries of the chief guide respecting quarters for the night, and was told by the man that the entire party must proceed at once to the house of the amin or village sheikh, and ask hospitality of him. It is the custom among the Kabyles for travellers to do this, for the religion of these people commands them to receive strangers as the messengers of God.

The guide acted upon his words, and on entering the village led the party to the house of the amin. They were received with stately courtesy by the village chief, and also with a proud humility. The amin met the travellers at the door of his house, kissed their hands reverently, and conducted them to the principal room, where supper was soon served. During the meal he waited on his guests, and politely declined their request to share it with them. After supper coffee and pipes were served, and then the chief conducted his guests

BOU-KTEUN.

to their sleeping-room, and left them with a simple prayer that sweet sleep might bless them through the night.

Bou-Kteun, our travellers found the next morning, is a small mountain village, situate about half-way up the "Red Plateau," and commanding the pass known as the "Gates of Iron." It consists principally of wretched huts of stone; the sheikh's house being the only comfortable dwelling in the place. After the morning meal the sheikh took his guests to the summit of the tower attached to his house, from which they obtained a magnificent view. The mountains were all around them, stretching away in every direction, with scores of sharp, jagged peaks rising in dark-blue masses against the clear sky-line. On all sides could be seen the white Kabyle villages nestling among the mountain crags, and separated from each other by deep chasms. Fully twenty villages were in sight from the tower.

In reply to the questions of his guests, the sheikh told them that the Kabyle villages were united into federations. In times of war and danger, when a village is menaced by an enemy, signals are placed in the minarets of the mosque to appeal to the towns of the same party for aid. Thus the news of danger can be spread over a large space of country in a few hours.

The travellers left Bou-Kteun at an early hour, and the chief of the village rode with them for several miles, his duties as their host requiring him to see them safely on their road. During the conversation which enlivened the ride, the professor drew from the sheikh considerable information respecting the Kabyles. The Arabs, the sheikh declared, were lazy, and kept their wives like prisoners. The Kabyles were industrious workmen, and their women were perfectly free. They did not muffle themselves in veils, and mingled with the men in the daily pursuits of life. The Kabyles, he continued, did not confine themselves to their mountains, but could be found in all the towns and sea-ports busily engaged in trade. In their own country they built houses, were good carpenters, forged weapons, gun-barrels, and locks, swords, knives, pick-axes, wool cards, ploughshares, gun-stocks, shovels, wooden shoes, and frames for weaving. Their weavers and earthenware-makers were renowned throughout Northern Africa. They detested idleness, and had comparatively few beggars. When the amin had taken his leave, and turned back towards his village, the chief guide, who had agreed to continue with the party as far as Kalaa, quietly remarked to Professor Moreton that the Kabyle had forgotten to mention one branch of industry in which his countrymen excelled.

THE AMIN OF BOU-KTEUN.

"They are," said he, "the most shameless and skilful counterfeiters in the world, and make such clever imitations of five-franc pieces that the French Roumi themselves can hardly tell them from the genuine."

The road descended rapidly from Bou-Kteun to the bed of a river of the same name, which was followed until it fell into the Biban, a larger stream, the waters of which are strongly impregnated with magnesia. Then suddenly plunging down the side of the cliffs, by a series of frightfully steep zigzags,

THE GATES OF IRON.

the road reaches the Gates of Iron, situate at the end of a sharp turn, where a handful of determined men could hold a host in check. The first gate is a round archway cut by nature through the rocks. It is four yards wide, and proportionately high. About fifty feet farther on is another similar archway, and a short distance beyond there are two more, making four gates in all. The Americans were deeply impressed with the grandeur of the scenery and the strength of the pass. The professor asked the guide if it had ever been successfully attacked by an enemy of the Kabyles. The guide made no reply until they had passed through the first gate, and then quietly pointed to an inscription cut in the side of the cliff, high above the reach of the torrent, and which read as follows: "*L'Armée Française*, 1839."

After passing the Gates of Iron our travellers continued their way for some time through a deep mountain gorge, and early in the afternoon emerged once more into the open country. Passing the Beni-Mansour, the village of Thasaerth, famous for its guns and razors, Arzov, the streets of which were alive with the ringing of the blacksmiths' anvils, and some other towns, the party, late in the afternoon, entered the country of the Beni-Aidel, where the vegetation began to assume a fresher hue. In every direction they could see the white houses of the Kabyle villages embowered in trees and perched on the summits of the first range of mountains, beyond which the lofty peaks of the Atlas towered to the clouds. A few miles farther on the guide pointed out a large amphitheatre formed of rocky summits, at the back of which rose a detached mass or precipice of rock, crowned with a small city, whose white houses and slender minarets flashed and sparkled in the sunlight. This the guide told them was Kalaa.

"It is certainly the most remarkably situated place we have seen," said Philip Lee. "It seems to be hung in mid-air."

"Put a scene like that on the stage," said Ashton, "and people would say it was merely a freak of the artist's imagination."

"Well, all I have to say," said Houston, as he surveyed the lofty site, "is, that if I were a resident of this town I should keep a private balloon to go up and down."

Pushing on, the party were soon at the foot of the precipice on which Kalaa stood. Then began the ascent by zigzag paths up the steep side of the rock. The travellers continued to ride their mules until the first plateau was reached. Here the road became so narrow, and lay so directly along the face of the cliff, that the professor declared he preferred to trust to his own feet for safety. His example was followed by the entire party, and the rest of the ascent, which was long and fatiguing, was made on foot, the mules and the horses of the guides following slowly, and picking their way with caution. The city was reached at last, and the travellers paused for a while to rest before remounting their steeds; then, getting into the saddle once more, they rode through the city to the house of the principal amin or sheikh, to whom the professor had been given a letter of introduction by his host at Bou-Kteun.

They were received at the entrance to the house by the sheikh himself, a venerable old man, clad in a white bournouse. The reception was cordial and courteous. The sheikh read the letter of introduction carefully, and when he

KALAA.

had finished it pressed it to his lips and forehead, and, placing it in his belt, led his guests into the principal room of the house, where they were soon made to feel at home. The sheikh spoke nothing but the Kabyle language, but, as the chief guide was familiar with that tongue, the professor was enabled to carry on a conversation with the old man. In accordance with the custom of

SCENE IN THE GRAND KABYLIA.

the country, the party retired early. The next day was devoted to seeing the city and resting from the fatigue of the journey, and the travellers were enabled to see considerable of Kabyle life and customs.

Kalaa is an ancient city, and, unlike the majority of Eastern towns, is very clean. It contains a population of three thousand, all of whom are said to be rich, and is divided into four quarters, each of which has its sheikh. The inhabitants have a well-to-do air, and are busily engaged in manufactures. They make bournouses, which sell well all through Northern Africa, and have their factories or agencies in the principal parts of that region. The travellers were much impressed with the beauty of the women of Kalaa, whom

KABYLE WOMEN.

they met on the streets and at the bazaars without veils. They were almost white, were richly dressed, and were adorned with a profusion of valuable jewelry. For centuries the city has been a place of refuge, a sanctuary for person and property, throughout all the wild storms of war that have swept over the land. Its inaccessible position has protected it; and while the surrounding country has been scourged with fire and sword, Kalaa has remained unharmed upon its lofty rock.

The sheikh told the professor that the situation of the town had its disadvantages as well as its advantages. Water is scarce, and the inhabitants suffer frequently from this scarcity in the dry season. Several large basins have been cut in the rock in the town; but these, while containing a plentiful supply of water in winter, are totally dry in summer. Then the inhabitants have recourse to the little river Hamadouch, at the base of the rock. Water is brought from the stream in jars slung to the backs of donkeys, which toil

up and down the steep zigzags all through the warm season. Sometimes the
stream itself fails, and then the people of Kalaa would certainly perish from
thirst were it not for a hidden spring at the base of the rock. This spring,
the chief said, had been discovered several centuries before by a marabout of
great renown. Through the aid of the rich he had built a fountain over its
sources,—a small Moorish structure, with two pilasters of stone supporting a

FOUNTAIN OF KALAA.

pointed arch. This spring, continued the sheikh, was under the especial care
of the amins of the town, and the people were not permitted to use it until all
other sources had failed; then, if three of the amins gave their consent, the
machinery by which the flow of the water is regulated was put in order, and
the spring was thrown open to the public. But for the spring the sheikh did
not see how the people of the town could live during the droughts. Certainly
Allah had been good to them in allowing Yusef-ben-Khouia, the marabout, to
discover it.

The view from the city is very fine. The eye ranges over long stretches
of mountains, which break down into foot-hills, with wide valleys between

THE COUNTRY OF THE KABYLES. 75

them. On every plateau or level spot on the mountain-sides, or the lower summits, are seen the white villages of the Kabyles, surrounded by rich growths of trees and shrubbery. They are all in plain sight of one another,

KABYLES ON THE WATCH.

and the signals and beacon-fires are rapidly passed from one to the other. This is the Grand Kabylia, a country not yet wholly submissive to the French rule. It takes but a spark to kindle the fires of revolt, and send them leaping from crag to crag to summon the impulsive natives to arms. Yet the inhabitants are not only warlike; they are industrious as well. In the white towns and villages which stud the country are made the ammunition, guns, blacksmith work, bournouses, haiks, gossamer-like cloths, and jewelry which supply the markets of Morocco, Tunis, and the countries bordering the Great Desert. Dellys and Bougie are the seaports of Kabylia.

Professor Moreton and his companions left Kalaa early on the morning of Friday, March 22d. They descended the steep incline leading from the city to the ravine below on foot, and then, remounting their animals, set out again. Their ride on this day was to be but a short one, as they were to halt at the town of Akbou, a Kabyle stronghold of great importance. Professor Moreton had been furnished by a French official in Constantina with a letter of introduction to a family of considerable importance in Akbou, and had been strongly urged to remain there a day or two, in order to study the customs of the people from the most favorable point of view.

The day was cool, and our travellers found the clear mountain air refreshing and invigorating. The scenery was grand and inspiring, and even the mules seemed aroused to new efforts, and made better time than usual. The guides had been induced to continue with the party as far as Thizzi-Ouzzou, a short distance from Algiers, and the Americans were well pleased with the arrangement, as it spared them the necessity of engaging strange guides for the remainder of the journey.

Akbou was reached about one o'clock, and the party proceeded to the house of Ben-Ali-Cherif, the agha or noble, to whom their letter of introduction was addressed. Ben-Ali was a lineal descendant of one of the sisters of the Prophet Mohammed, and therefore of the proudest Oriental blood. He was a man of considerable wealth and of great influence among the Kabyles. He was past middle life, of noble and commanding presence, and his manner was marked by a coldness and stateliness in keeping with his proud lineage. He received the travellers courteously, and, after reading the letter of his friend at Constantina, begged that the professor and his companions would make his house their home during their stay at Akbou, and also expressed the hope that they would remain several days with him, in order that he might show them something of Kabyle customs. He spoke French fluently, and told the professor that he had been expecting this visit, his friend having written to him to prepare him for it. He added that he had arranged a hunting party for the next day, and expected a number of his friends to take part in it. He hoped his guests would do him the honor to join in the sport.

The agha then conducted his guests into the principal room of the house, where a light repast, consisting partly of French and partly of native dishes, was served. A handsome but rather effeminate-looking young man entered the room as the repast began, and taking his place at the table, was presented by the agha to his guests as his son. Professor Moreton attempted to draw him into conversation, but the youth answered only in monosyllables, with his eyes bent on the table. Noticing this, the agha smiled, and remarked quietly,—

"You must excuse him if he does not answer. It is not from lack of courtesy; but because he is not used to talk before his father."

"That's rather hard on the young fellow," whispered Houston to Philip

BEN-ALI-CHERIF.

Lee. "Only fancy me as mum as that in the presence of my governor. Why, the old gentleman would think I was losing my senses."

Later in the afternoon the agha directed his son to conduct the strangers through his pomegranate and orange orchards, which he assured them were worth seeing. He excused himself from accompanying them, as he was obliged to receive other guests who were beginning to arrive for the next day's hunt. Following their young guide, the professor and his companions left the house, and sought the orange groves. The fruit was thick upon the trees, and was just ripening. The young man, freed from the restraint of his father's presence, now found the use of his tongue, and proved as talkative as he had been silent at the table. He asked many questions concerning America, and said he would like to visit it; but it was too far and there was too much water to cross.

"But you would have nothing to fear," began Hubbard.

The youth interrupted him with a smile,—"I come of a race that despises fear," he said; "but if I should die, or be lost at sea, if anything should prevent my returning, it would break my father's heart. I am his only son."

When the party returned to the house, they found the court-yard full of strangers. Magnificent Barbary horses were grouped about the enclosure, handsomely caparisoned, and showing in every point their pure blood; and splendidly dressed and dignified sheikhs and Kabyles of the better class, each armed with a long inlaid gun, were chatting with one another and with their host. It was a bright and animated scene, and greatly interested the Americans. As they came up the agha made them acquainted with the most important of the new arrivals, and as some of these could speak French, an animated conversation soon sprang up between the Roumi and the true believers. One grave-browed sheikh, who had been watching Houston with considerable interest, said to him bluntly that American fathers must care very little for their sons, or they would never suffer them to go so far from home.

"But, perhaps," he added, "they have thought it best that you should see something of older and more civilized lands than your own. They must have great confidence in the Roumi with the red beard who is your guide; and he must be a very good and wise man to have the care of so many young men."

During the evening more guests arrived, until about thirty had collected under Ben-Ali's hospitable roof. In accordance with Kabylian customs, all spent the night at his house, and the court-yard was filled with attendants and a number of hangers-on who hoped to receive some of the fragments left from the bounteous feast with which the agha regaled his company during the evening. The professor expressed his surprise at the readiness with which the last-mentioned class were admitted, but was told by the sheikh to whom his remarks were addressed that it added to their host's greatness to have such a throng of dependents. It was very expensive, he admitted, but Ben-Ali was rich and could afford it.

The hunting party was astir by sunrise the next morning, and after a breakfast of coffee and light cakes the word was given to mount. The Americans were furnished by their host with horses, and each one was given a genuine Kabylian gun, which was more like a mediæval arquebuse than any other weapon. The stock was flat, and was surmounted by a hammer of flints, and the weapon was discharged by a wheel-shaped lock of curious construction.

"I'll carry the gun with pleasure, out of compliment to Ben-Ali," said Ashton to the professor; "but I hope I shall not be expected to fire it. I do not think I could do much execution with it."

BEN-ALI HUNTING WITH THE FALCON.

"And yet," said the professor, "it was with these weapons that the Kabyles made such heroic stands against the French, who had the advantage not only of the most improved modern arms, but also of artillery."

"Oh, as for that," exclaimed Hubbard, "the Kabyles and the guns are well suited to each other; but we 'Roumis' would find it hard work to do much execution with these old flint-locks."

At a signal from Ben-Ali the cavalcade swept out of the court-yard, and cantering through the town began the descent from Akbou to the plain of the river Sahel, where the hunt was to take place. A cautious pace was maintained while descending the steep road from the city, but this was succeeded by a brisk gallop when the plain was reached. Leaving the road, the party plunged into a low thicket bordering the river, into which a number of attendants had been sent to beat up the game.

"Look at Ben-Ali, professor," said Houston, his face aglow with admiration. "We thought him a fine-looking man last night; but now, in the saddle, he seems a very prince."

"He looks well, indeed," said Philip Lee; "but I think his mare the finer animal of the two. Did you ever see a more perfect beauty?"

The mare of the agha was indeed a beautiful animal. Slender and graceful in form, black as a raven's wing, and with her delicate veins clearly outlined beneath her glossy coat, she seemed fit only for the service of the "commander of the faithful" himself. She was caparisoned with a slender crimson bridle, and a saddle smaller in size and lighter in weight than those used by the Arabs, from which hung lighter stirrups. Her rider bestrode her as only a born rider could. He seemed to be conscious of the admiration of his Christian guests, and turning to them with a smile, patted the head of his beautiful steed and bowed low.

The horsemen rode along in silence until a shout from the thicket announced that a wild boar had been started. Immediately a series of yells broke from the company, and the whole cavalcade dashed forward as the boar burst through the undergrowth in his efforts to escape. The chase was long and exciting; but at length the boar, wearied with his run, turned and faced his pursuers. At the same moment several large African hounds sprang upon him and pinned him to the ground. A huntsman leaped down and gave the animal his death-blow with the yataghan, and the first part of the hunt was ended.

The cavalcade now halted for a short rest, after which the hunt was renewed. This time it took the form of a hawking party. One of the company explained to the professor that only the secular and religious nobles of the country—the djouads and marabouts—have the privilege of hunting with the falcon. At a sign from Ben-Ali an attendant approached with a fine bird, about as large as a pigeon, perched upon his shoulder. Our travellers noticed that the head of the bird was small, his beak short and strong, and his claws yellow and armed with sharp talons. Taking the bird from the shoulder of his servant, the agha perched it upon the leather glove of his right hand.

The company then rode along leisurely, and in a few moments a hare was started from the thicket. The agha at once removed the hood which had

THE DISCIPLES OF TOPAIL.

enveloped the falcon's head, and released it from the chain which held it to his hand. Instantly the bird soared swiftly into the air, rising in a straight line, and soaring so high that it seemed impossible for him to see anything upon the ground below. The agha explained to his Christian guests, however, that the bird never for a moment lost sight of its prey. Even as he spoke the falcon paused for a moment in the blue ether, and then, swooping down with almost the swiftness of lightning, disappeared in the thicket. It was explained to the professor and his companions, as the cavalcade rode forward in the direction of the bird's descent, that the falcon had found its prey, and that its method of despatching it was to swoop down upon it, double up its yellow claw like a fist, and strike the animal a sharp blow on the skull, which fractured it. When the horsemen reached the bird they found it bending over the body of the rabbit, picking its eyes out with its long sharp talons.

Thus the sport continued for some time, and noon found the huntsmen far from the city. Observing that his guests were somewhat tired, Ben-Ali proposed that they should repair to luncheon. The Americans were a little surprised by this proposition, as they could see no signs of provisions among the company, or any means of preparing food. As he spoke, the agha wheeled his horse, and galloped off towards a grove of trees in the distance, followed by the entire party. A ride of about ten minutes brought them to the grove, where they beheld a large tent erected, and two fires burning. A throng of servants and attendants were making preparations for an elaborate repast, and the odor of the savory viands was very appetizing. After a consultation with the most important of his native guests, the agha ordered the repast to be served under the trees of the grove, instead of in the tent, and selecting a suitable place, invited his guests to seat themselves. The meal began with a soup, which Houston declared was almost on fire with red pepper; and this was followed by pancakes and meats of different kinds, garnished with eggs or onions. These being finished, the principal dish of the meal was brought forward by two cooks, who were stripped to their waists, and who struggled under the weight of their burden. They bore a wooden dish, on which, covered with a napkin bordered with gold, was a sheep roasted whole, and still impaled with the spit. Having deposited the dish before the agha, the chief cook seized the spit with both hands, and, placing his naked heel against the hind quarters of the sheep, gave the spit a vigorous jerk, and drew it from the steaming body. Then the attendants served the mutton to the guests. The Americans did ample justice to it, and with one accord declared that they had never seen mutton properly cooked before.

"If I ever have an establishment of my own," said Ashton to his companions, "I shall certainly import a Kabyle for my cook, and shall have my mutton prepared and served after the manner of the true believers."

"Don't omit the drawing of the spit, and the blow of the cook's heel in the presence of your guests," said Houston, "or you will break the charm."

During the meal champagne was liberally served to the guests, to the surprise of the Americans, who were under the impression that the followers of

A KABYLE CHILD.

the prophet never drank wine of any kind. Ben-Ali must have seen their expression of astonishment, for he remarked quietly to the professor that champagne, being unknown to the prophet, was not included by him in the list of proscribed beverages, and that the faithful were therefore free to enjoy it. It was not "wine" in the sense of the Koran. At the close of the meal coffee was served in the most delicate of cups, and this was followed by light perfumed tobacco.

By the time the meal was half over, the Americans began to notice a steady and silent increase in the number of the persons present. Around each group of the agha's guests gathered a number of natives, who, lying or squatting upon the ground, were busily engaged in devouring the remnants of the feast, which were supplied to them by the servants of Ben-Ali. Their numbers continued to increase as the meal progressed, but the Roumi were unable to see from whence they came. They seemed to spring from the earth, so silently did they approach and take their places. The professor at length turned to the agha and asked who they were.

"They are Tofailians," replied Ben-Ali, calmly.

"What is a Tofailian?" asked Houston.

"Know, my son," replied the agha, gravely, "a Tofailian is a man who lives but to eat, and to eat at another man's expense. He scents a feast from afar, even as an eagle scents his prey. One of our poets has said of Tofail, from whom these parasites take their name: 'If he saw two buttered pancakes in a cloud, he would take his flight without hesitation.'"

"But why do you permit them to prey upon you thus?" asked the professor. "Surely, O Ben-Ali, to feed so many must cause a heavy drain upon your purse."

"It is an evil, certainly," replied the agha; "but one that we cannot cure. We cannot prevent their coming around us, and our religion forbids us to refuse them food. I will relate the experience of one of my friends, which will show you how adroit these people are in their efforts to obtain a good meal without paying for it. One of my friends, a man of rank and wealth, once gave an entertainment at his house, to which large numbers of our people were invited. A Tofailian, hearing of this, determined to share in the feast. He ran to the house, but could not enter, as the door was locked. He at once set to work to make inquiries concerning the family, and learned that one of the sons of the giver of the feast had recently departed on a pilgrimage to Mecca. The man was a genius in his way, and immediately conceived a plan for obtaining admission to the feast. Procuring a sheet of parchment, he folded it, sealed it with clay, and deposited it within the folds of his turban. Then rolling his garments in the dust, and procuring a long staff, he presented himself at the door of my friend's house, and sent him word that he had brought him a message from his son. The father at once hastened to the door, and greeted the seeming pilgrim warmly. 'You have seen my son?' he cried in delight. 'How was he? How has he borne the fatigue of the journey?' 'He was very well,' replied the Tofailian, feebly. 'How far had he gotten? Tell me all about him.' 'How can I answer you?' said the fellow. 'I am faint with hunger.' My friend at once led the man into the hall in which the feast was being served, and placing him at his right hand at the table, bade him satisfy his hunger. The fellow needed no second invitation, but fell to with a vigor which excited the admiration of every one at the table. My friend waited impatiently until the stranger had satisfied the cravings of his

KABYLE MEN.

hunger, and then asked, 'Did my son send me a letter?' 'Surely,' replied the Tofailian, who had now eaten quite heartily, and was prepared for the exposure that was to follow. 'Surely, I had forgotten.' Seizing a choice portion of a kid with one hand, and slowly untwisting the parchment from his turban, he handed the paper to the father. The fraud was apparent at a glance: the seal of clay was still moist, and not a line was written on the parchment. For a moment my friend was overwhelmed with astonishment; then a light broke upon him. 'Art thou a Tofailian?' he asked. 'Yea, in truth, verily,' replied the fellow, choking his food down as he spoke. 'Eat then,' cried my friend, 'and may Sheytan trouble thy digestion!' The

Tofailian was at once put out of the house, but he had succeeded in his efforts: he had dined."

A lounge of half an hour followed the luncheon, and then the party mounted to their saddles again, and set out on their return to Akbou. Soon after starting, at a sign from the agha twenty riders put spurs to their horses, and darting forward swiftly, soon disappeared in a cloud of dust. The remainder of the party also quickened their pace, but the flying horsemen were far ahead and completely hidden by the dust. Ten minutes elapsed, and then suddenly a wild yell rose from out the cloud of dust, and the twenty horsemen dashed like a whirlwind down upon the agha's party, their long bournouses flying in the wind and their guns flashing as they brandished them above their heads. Keeping their headlong pace until directly opposite the agha's party, they discharged their guns under the bodies of the horses opposite, and then wheeling suddenly were off again with almost incredible swiftness. Loading as they retired, they soon wheeled about and returned to the attack, firing, yelling, and shouting, retiring and advancing repeatedly, exhibiting the most magnificent horsemanship, and going through every detail of an attack upon a hostile force. These movements were kept up with spirit until the gates of Akbou were reached, and were watched with the keenest interest by the American Roumi. The city gates once reached, the cavalcade fell into line, and proceeded leisurely to the house of Ben-Ali, when, after taking leave of the agha and his American guests, nearly all the horsemen set out for their homes.

KABYLE HUSBANDMAN.

The next afternoon Professor Moreton and his companions left Akbou for Chellata. They were accompanied by Ben-Ali and several mounted attendants. The agha was desirous of showing his guests his birth-place; and during the ride he informed the professor that the house in which he was born was built by his ancestors several centuries before, and had remained in the possession of his family ever since.

It was night, and the moon was shining brightly when the party reached Chellata and dismounted before Ben-Ali's old home. Chellata looked very white and still in the clear rays of the moon, with the huge rock Tisibert rising above it like a dark phantom. Although it was early in the evening, scarcely a sound could be heard in the streets; a deep silence reigned over the entire

KABYLE OIL-WORKS.

town. Dismounting at the entrance to the agha's residence, the Americans followed their host through a beautiful Moorish court-yard surrounded by wide cloisters, and were shown into a handsome apartment, where a tempting meal awaited them.

During the evening they were visited by the venerable marabout sheikh who presided over the college maintained at Chellata by Ben-Ali-Cherif. There are many of these colleges scattered through Algeria; they are called *zaouias*, and are devoted to education and to the gratuitous entertainment of strangers. The principal studies, after the rudiments of the language have been mastered, are the law of the Kabyles and the Koran. The sheikh told the professor that Ben-Ali bore the entire expense of the institution at Chel-

HOUSE OF BEN-ALI-CHERIF AT CHELLATA.

lata, contributing to it every year a sum equal to about sixteen thousand American dollars.

The next day, Monday, the agha took his guests to visit the college, and after they had been served with coffee and pipes they were shown through the grounds by the sheikh, who had called upon them on the previous evening. The college was a strangely peaceful place, consisting of several buildings scattered among the tombs of the marabout ancestors of Ben-Ali-Cherif. Under a handsome dome reposed the most famous of these old-time saints, and over it the oak and tamarind trees waved their leafy branches. Through the little grove the professors of the college were leisurely strolling, conversing

A KOUBBA, OR MARABOUT'S TOMB.

in low tones, and here and there the visitors met students seated on the crumbling tombstones, poring over some work in Arabic.

As they strolled through the town, Ben-Ali informed his guests that it was market-day at Chellata. The narrow streets were filled with women busily engaged in buying and selling wares of various kinds. But few men or children were to be seen. The agha said the former were at work in the fields, and would not return until sunset, and the latter were in the mountains, looking after the flocks which were grazing there. The women, he added, not only performed the usual work of the household to which they belonged, but conducted almost all the various industries of the place, such as grinding at the mill, weaving cloth, and making vases of pottery. It was a very good arrangement, he thought, as it enabled the men to devote themselves entirely

GROUP OF KABYLE WOMEN.

to their fields, which were their chief sources of support, and it was only fair that the women and children should contribute their share to the earnings of the family.

"I have noticed," said the professor, "that your women enjoy much greater freedom than those of the Arabs, and mingle more freely with the men."

"Yes," said the agha, "we give them great liberty, especially the liberty to work. Still, we are very careful of them. The greatest delight of a Kabyle woman is to meet her neighbors at the town fountain and gossip with them. You will notice here, as in all our towns, that two fountains are provided, one for men and the other for women. Should a man be found at the women's fountain, we fine him a sum equal to twenty-five francs. We cannot stop the women from gossiping, but we try to preserve the men from the demoralizing influences of that habit."

The next morning our travellers bade adieu to Ben-Ali, warmly expressing their appreciation of his attentions to them. The agha seemed really sorry to let them go, and made them promise that if they ever came to Algeria again they would repeat their visit to him. They readily promised this, and with many good wishes for his health and prosperity, took leave of their noble host,

THE DJURJURA RANGE.

and set off from Chellata. The road led down the steep sides of the Djurjura Mountains, and by many white-walled and red-roofed Kabyle villages. It wound around the base of the precipice of Azrou-n'hour, on the summit of which rose the white tomb of a famous Kabyle saint. Opposite the cliff the mountain wall opened, and the road passed through a narrow defile in which the snow was still lying to the depth of more than a foot. This, the guide told the professor, was the Defile of Thifilkoult, and was one of the most famous mountain passes in Algeria. In former times the Kabyles guarded it with jealous care, and exacted a heavy toll from all travellers passing through it. The defile was cold and chilly, and scarcely a ray of sunlight entered it.

The guide said it was impassable in winter, as it was almost entirely filled up with snow.

DEFILE OF TRIFILKOULT.

Emerging from the defile, a glorious view burst upon the gaze of the party. Four thousand feet below them lay the great plains of Algeria, dotted thickly

THE COUNTRY OF THE KABYLES. 93

with white villages, and above them rose the snow-capped summits of the Atlas range, two thousand feet higher still. The road now led downward over chains of rocks of mingled flint and lime, past a well, called the Mosquitoes' Fountain, around which a group of Kabyle girls were chatting, and reached a lower level where flourishing fields of corn and orchards of olives were encountered. Then mounting another, but a lower ridge, the travellers late

FORT NATIONAL.

in the afternoon reached the immense fortress erected by the French after 1857 for the purpose of holding the mountain tribes in check. The fort was not built until fourteen expeditions had been sent by the French against the Kabyles. In 1857 Marshal Randon made a thorough conquest of this portion of the country, and determined to secure the hold he had gained by the construction of a military road from Algiers to a place called Souk-el-Arba (the Wednesday Market), where he intended to erect a powerful fortress. The site was admirably chosen. It was in the heart of the country of the Beni-Raten, one of the most powerful and warlike of the Kabylian tribes, and at a point where three great mountain ridges dropped into the plain of the Sebaou. The fort was at once begun, and called Fort Napoleon, in honor of the reigning emperor of the French, and the work was soon completed and armed. At the same time the military road was pushed forward with speed, and was at length completed. The Kabyles paid but little attention to the undertakings of the French while they were in progress, but when the works were completed they found that they gave their conquerors a hold upon the country which could never be shaken off. In 1871, the Kabyles, hearing of the reverses of the French in the war with Germany, endeavored to regain their independence. Fort National, as the great fortress of Marshal Randon had come to be called after the downfall of the empire, was beleaguered by large bodies of the mountain tribes. General Cérès was sent from Algiers with a strong force to its relief. He burnt the town of Thizzi-Ouzzou, in the valley below the fort, relieved the fortress, and inflicted a severe chastisement upon the Kabyles.

Professor Moreton and his party passed the night at Fort National, where they were hospitably entertained by the commandant.

The next morning, Wednesday, they continued their journey from Fort National to Thizzi-Ouzzou, in the valley below. They found the place springing up again from its ruins. New and substantial buildings were being erected, and the people seemed to be regaining their former prosperity.

Upon reaching Thizzi-Ouzzou, Professor Moreton paid and discharged the guides who had come with the party from Constantina. The young Americans were heartily sorry to part with the faithful fellows. They also looked up at the dark mountain wall over which they had clambered in their journey with regret. It had been a pleasant and deeply interesting tour to them, and one that would linger long in their memories. It was over now, and a few hours more would find them restored to the influences of European civilization. They reluctantly bade farewell to the guides, and watched them ride off in the direction of the mountains.

At noon they took their places in the old-fashioned diligence which was to convey them to Algiers. The journey was uneventful and uninteresting, and by five o'clock the travellers were once more in comfortable apartments in the Hotel d'Orient in the French quarter of Algiers.

The steamer for Marseilles had sailed from Algiers on the day previous to the return of the American travellers, and they were obliged to wait until the following Tuesday before they could leave Africa. At length, however, on Tuesday, April 2, they sailed for Marseilles in the steamer that had brought them from France a month previous.

CHAPTER V.

THE YOUNG AMERICAN EXPEDITION TO SOUTH CENTRAL AFRICA.

THE voyage from Algiers to Marseilles was pleasant, and as the weather was warm, our travellers spent most of their waking moments on deck. On the first night out, Ashton startled his companions by suddenly turning to them and exclaiming:

"Boys, do you know this Algerian trip has given me the African fever?"

AN ALGERIAN VILLAGE.

The professor, who came up at this moment, glanced at him in some alarm. "Are you afraid of being ill?" he asked.

"No, no, professor," replied Ashton, laughing; "that is not what I mean.

I am not ill, nor in any danger of becoming so. I mean that the little I have seen of Africa has inspired me with a longing to know more of that country, and that I intend to gratify my desire."

"It is too late to return now," said the professor. "In a fortnight the heat in Northern Africa will be unbearable. Egypt, Morocco, and Tunis, the only countries open to travellers of our race, will be practically closed against you."

"I have seen all of Northern Africa that I care for," said Ashton. "My wish, professor, is to follow in the footsteps of some of the great African explorers; to cross South Central Africa from ocean to ocean. All the time we were in Algeria I kept thinking of the Great Desert that lies south of it, and of the countries that lie beyond that. I have been reading a great deal about the journeys of Livingstone, Stanley, Cameron, and the other explorers of this dark region, and I left home with half a notion to give a couple of years to such a journey."

A GENUINE NEGRO MINSTREL.

"It would no doubt be a very interesting journey," said the professor, slowly; "but it would be one that would try every power of your mind and body. It would be difficult, dangerous, and enormously expensive. I myself have frequently thought I would like to attempt it, but I should never be able to raise the money necessary to the undertaking."

"Is the expense the only obstacle to your making the journey?" asked Ashton, quietly.

"Well, yes," replied the professor, hesitatingly. "If I had the money, I would willingly incur the danger and the fatigue."

"Will you go with me if I assume the expense?" continued Ashton.

"My dear boy," cried the professor, "you don't know what you are talking about."

"I have not spoken thoughtlessly," said Ashton. "I know, from what I

KABYLE POTTERY WORKS.

have read, the dangers with which both the natives and the climate would threaten me; I know that such a journey would cost a very large sum of money; and that the fatigue would be trying in the extreme. Yet, in spite of all this, I am resolved, if I can find companions, to make the attempt to cross Africa. As for the expense, you know my father left me a large fortune, which would enable me to assume the cost of the whole undertaking without feeling it."

"Granting all that, Ashton," said the professor, "don't you think it would be unwise to attempt such a journey merely for the pleasure of sight-seeing?"

"That is not my only motive," replied the young man. "I am ambitious, professor. I have no taste for a mercantile life, and but little liking for politics. In any profession I might enter at home I should have to work my way up slowly to a position of prominence, if, indeed, I should succeed in attaining one. Such a journey as I propose would make me famous in a year or two."

"You had better think of this matter seriously," said the professor.

"I have been doing that ever since we landed in Algeria," said Ashton; "and the more I think of it, the more firmly I am resolved to make the attempt. I ask you in entire good faith, Professor Moreton, will you go with me?"

"I will think of it," replied the professor. "I have some money to spare, and if I accompany you, I shall contribute my share to the expenses of the journey."

"When shall I know your decision?"

"On the day after we reach Paris, which will be next Saturday, the 6th of April."

So saying, the professor lit his pipe, and began to stroll up and down the deck.

The other members of the party had listened in silence to the conversation between the professor and Ashton. As the former walked away, Houston turned to his companion, and said, slowly,—

"Look here, Ashton, old fellow, it's very plain that you believe in the old adage, which says, 'While two make company, three make a crowd.'"

"Why so?" asked Ashton.

"Because," replied the young Californian, "while you are eager enough to have the professor for a companion in your grand African exploring expedition, you have taken good care not to ask any of us to join your party."

"I was about to lay the whole matter before you when the professor came up. Believe me, nothing would please me better than to keep our whole party together for the expedition I propose."

"That being the case," said Houston, "you can have my answer now. I'll go with you. My governor has fixed me very comfortably as regards money, and has given me leave to travel where I please for the next three years. All he asks is that I shall keep out of trouble and get back home safe. I am your man for the African expedition."

"And you, boys?" asked Ashton, turning to Lee and Hubbard.

"I must think of it," replied Philip Lee. "To join your party will compel me to change all my plans for returning to college. If I go, I shall not be a burden to you, Ashton, as I shall claim the right to contribute to the cost of the journey. I will talk to the professor about it. I am alone in the world, as you know, and have no one at home to consult as to my movements. I will let you know my determination by the time we reach Paris."

"I will join the party on one condition," said Hubbard. "I shall have to write home for my father's consent, and if he gives it, I will go with you. He knows the professor very well, and has great confidence in his judgment. If

A KABYLE FUNERAL.

the professor decides to go with you, I will get him to write to my father and urge him to consent. That point gained, nothing else stands in my way."

During the remainder of the voyage the proposed expedition was energetically discussed. Professor Moreton was astonished to find how much information Ashton had acquired concerning the countries he wished to visit. He had evidently been a close student of African travel, a subject to which the professor himself had devoted considerable time, and was well prepared to enter intelligently and profitably upon the scheme he had proposed. The plan held out many inducements to Professor Moreton. He was as ambitious of distinction as Ashton himself, and perhaps more so in this particular field. He had given the subject considerable study, and had long desired to rank himself among those daring explorers who had made the wilds of South Central Africa familiar to modern readers. Here was an opportunity such as would never occur again; and had he been obliged to think of himself alone he would not have hesitated to take advantage of it. His studies had made him familiar with the dangers and trials of such an undertaking. For himself he was willing to brave all, but he was doubtful as to the propriety of encouraging his young companions to incur such risks. He argued the matter earnestly with them, setting forth fully all the drawbacks to the undertaking; but the more he argued against the journey the more determined he found Ashton and Houston to undertake it. Philip Lee was rapidly coming to the same conclusion, and Hubbard only waited his father's approval to cast his lot with his companions. By the time the party reached Paris the professor found that he had but one of two things to do,—either to consent to join the expedition or to decline absolutely. He settled the matter by choosing the former alternative, and the African expedition was thus definitely decided upon.

"And now, young gentlemen," said the professor, as they sat at breakfast on the morning after their return to Paris, "as we have decided upon our course, the sooner we put our plans in execution the better. It will require at least two or three months to complete our preparations for such an important undertaking, and during this time you will have the opportunity of seeing something of France, Germany, Switzerland, and Northern Italy. As for myself, I am willing to give my whole time to overseeing the preparations I have spoken of."

We do not propose to relate the adventures of the young Americans in Europe. It is sufficient to say that during the remainder of April and the month of May they visited portions of each of the countries named above. Hubbard wrote to his father immediately upon reaching Paris, and the same mail also carried a letter from the professor to the New York banker. In reply the elder Hubbard sent a reluctant consent to his son's request, and the party was thus complete.

Thanks to the energy of the professor, the arrangements for the expedition were completed by the early part of June. It was decided that the party should proceed to Lisbon, and sail from that port in the Portuguese mail steamer for Saint Paul de Loanda, from which place, or from some neighboring point, the march across Africa was to begin. To the expenses of the expedition each of the party contributed according to his means, but the principal share was borne by Ashton. The total cost of the undertaking was estimated at twenty-five thousand dollars, of which the professor, Hubbard, and Philip Lee each furnished three thousand dollars, Houston contributed six thousand, and Ashton ten thousand. As it was necessary that there should be some one to direct the movements of the party and act as its head, the young men unanimously chose Professor Moreton as their leader, and pledged themselves to obey faithfully and cheerfully such orders as he might give.

While preparing for the expedition the professor and Ashton made several journeys to London, in order to purchase some articles that were needed, and while there obtained valuable assistance from several scientific gentlemen whose acquaintance the professor had made in former years. One or two ex-

RUINED CHURCH NEAR BENGUELA.

perienced African travellers, to whom they were introduced, also gave them many useful hints, and assisted them in procuring the articles needed for their outfit.

At length, everything being in readiness, the party left Paris for Lisbon on the 10th of June to complete their preparations in that city. Professor Moreton and Ashton had made good use of the time that had elapsed since their return from Algiers in studying the Portuguese language, so that upon reaching Lisbon they were able to communicate with ease with the people with whom they had to deal. The remainder of the month was spent in purchasing such articles as would be needed for traffic with the natives of Africa during their journey. Money would be of no use to them in that country, and they converted a large part of their funds into cloth, uniform clothes, beads, copper and brass wire, and ornaments valued by the natives. In these purchases the travellers were greatly assisted by the advice of a merchant of Lisbon, who carried on a large trade with the African coast, and to whom the professor had been furnished by a friend in Paris with a letter of introduction.

The preparations were completed by the 1st of July, and the travellers were astonished to find what an immense amount of *impedimenta* they had accumulated. As they were to pass nearly two years in Africa, it was necessary, however, to provide everything beforehand. They intended that their expedition should not be merely a meaningless walk across the African continent, but that it should be fruitful in observation and research in such branches of science as could be attempted by them. Professor Moreton took upon himself the scientific work, as well as the general direction of the expedition. Ashton was to take command of the natives they might engage for their service, see after them on the march, and look after the proper arrangement and the various details of their camps on the journey; Houston was to have charge of the hunting parties which might be sent out to procure game; Lee was to assist the professor in his scientific work, and take special care of the chronometers and other instruments; and Hubbard was to assist Ashton in his duties.

For the use of the party thus organized a complete equipment had been provided. Each of the travellers was furnished with a trunk of light but stout leather, containing a complete suit of clothing, three changes of linen, an extra pair of shoes, a pair of boots, four bottles of quinine, a small medicine chest, writing materials, fifty cartridges for each firearm, and articles of personal use. Three other trunks were filled with a table service for five persons, cooking utensils, and a toilette set, soap, brushes, mirrors, etc. Ten other trunks were packed with clothing, scientific instruments, tools, and other things needed for the journey. Thirty cases, of the same dimensions as the trunks, were filled with tea, coffee, sugar, dried vegetables, and farinaceous substances carefully soldered in tin. Besides these were numbers of boxes and bales filled with the articles which were to constitute the traveller's money after leaving the African coast.

The instruments selected by the professor were of the finest quality, and were purchased from the best makers in Paris and London. Each member of the party was furnished with a pedometer, a compass, and an aneroid barometer, the use of which was taught the younger members by Professor Moreton. Each was armed with a sixteen-bore rifle of the best quality, a revolver, and a large knife. In addition to these five Winchester rifles, an extra supply of knives, and three double-barrelled shotguns for light game were carried with the baggage.

Everything had been limited to the amount consistent with prudence, but the mass of baggage, when finally gotten together, was so great that our

GOVERNMENT HOUSE AT LOANDA.

travellers were almost hopeless of ever finding carriers enough to transport it across Africa. There were still many things to purchase for barter with the natives, but these were to be procured in the Portuguese colonies on the African coast.

Everything was in readiness at last, however, and on the 4th of July, 1878, the "Young American Expedition to South Central Africa" sailed from Lisbon on board the Portuguese mail steamer "Zaire," bound for Saint Paul de Loanda, on the western coast of Africa.

CHAPTER VI.

INTO THE HEART OF AFRICA.

THE voyage to Saint Paul de Loanda was pleasant and quickly made; and on the 6th of August, 1878, the "Zaire" sighted the entrance to the harbor. The steamer lay to off the bar to wait for a pilot, and soon a small

THE PILOT'S BOAT AT LOANDA.

boat, propelled by two stout rowers, came dancing over the waves towards her. Arrived alongside, a powerful negro clambered to the deck, and, producing his license as a competent pilot, was escorted by the captain to the steamer's bridge. The engines were started again, and the vessel was soon over the bar, and at anchor in the harbor.

The city of Loanda is the capital of the Portuguese possessions in Lower Guinea, and was once a place of considerable importance. These possessions are extensive, stretching along the Atlantic from the Congo River to Cape Frio, and extending inland for three hundred miles. At first the Portuguese began to colonize Angola on an extensive scale. They waged important wars with the natives, fought great battles, and subdued nations. They contemplated establishing an overland route to India, which should extend across Africa, from Loanda to Mozambique, and thus do away with the voyage around the Cape of Good Hope; but the plan was never carried out, and Angola derived its principal importance from the slave trade. The abolition of this traffic

SAN PAUL DE LOANDA.

ruined the merchants of Loanda, and the city is now falling into decay. It possesses considerable trade still in ivory, wax, and coffee, but its glory has departed. The colony is rich in copper, and this source of wealth is being gradually developed.

Loanda possesses a population of about twelve thousand, and is well built, with broad streets, fine stone houses, public buildings, cafés, churches, and jails. It contains the ruins of two cathedrals, one of which was used as a college by the Jesuits during the seventeenth century, but is now a workshop. In the ruins of the other the cattle of the town may be seen grazing. The harbor is spacious and secure, and is protected by three forts. It is formed by an island lying opposite the town, and generally contains a number of vessels riding at anchor. The island which shelters it from the sea was formerly famous for its cowries, a species of shell, which was used as money by the natives of the Congo region. It is now occupied by a hardy race of fishermen, and contains several pleasure resorts, to which the citizens of Loanda repair on their fête days to enjoy the music and dancing, which constitute their principal amusements.

The city is the residence of the governor-general of the Portuguese possessions, who is always a noble of the highest rank. He is jealously watched by the home government, and is recalled after a few years of service, lest he should become ambitious of a crown, and proclaim Angola an empire after the manner of Brazil. Loanda is also the principal convict station of Portugal. The most deserving of the convicts are enrolled among the garrison, and are uniformed as soldiers.

The city looked very white and glaring in the bright light of the African sun, and our travellers surveyed it from the steamer's deck with the deepest interest. It was to be the initial point of their wanderings, the last link that would connect them with Western civilization and home. For the first time they began to realize the magnitude of the undertaking upon which they had entered.

Soon after the steamer came to an anchor the professor and his companions went off to the city in one of the native boats which hovered around the ship, for the purpose of making arrangements for obtaining quarters, and landing and storing their baggage. As soon as they set foot on the quay they were surrounded by the bearers of palanquins, who noisily besought them to avail themselves of this mode of transportation through the city. As a palanquin will hold but one person, they were obliged to engage five.

The palanquin of Loanda is simply a board suspended from two poles, and is borne on the shoulders of two natives. It is covered with a carpet, has a pillow at one end, is curtained at the sides, and is protected by an awning over the top. The person using it must of necessity lie down, as a sitting position cannot be maintained without the risk of being thrown out.

Professor Moreton made his bargain with the owner of the palanquins, and then the young men began to clamber into them. Houston was the first to make the attempt; he climbed clear through the vehicle, and rolled out through the curtains on the opposite side. His mishap was greeted with a shout of laughter from his companions and a crowd of lookers-on who had assembled to witness the landing of the strangers. They were all safely in the palanquins at last, however, and the procession set off at a fast walk, headed by the litter of the professor, which was preceded by the owner of the vehicles, who flourished a large stick with all the gestures of a bandmaster, and at the same time chanted a singular refrain, in which the litter-bearers joined loudly. The words of the song, which were afterwards translated by the professor to his companions, were as follows:

> "Shove them on!
> But are they good men?
> No: I think they are stingy fellows.
>   Shove them on!
> Let them drop in the street, then.
> No! but they have big sticks;
> And they are brave fellows.
>   Shove them on!
> Oh, matar-bicho! matar-bicho!
> Who will give us matar-bicho?"

This was repeated over and over again, as the negroes trotted along into the town. The professor afterwards explained to his companions that "*matar-bicho*" was the Angolese term for "kill-worm," and that the natives supposed that their entrails were constantly tormented by a small worm which it was necessary to destroy by imbibing copious d.aughts of raw spirits. During their stay at Loanda the travellers came to the conclusion that the negroes with whom they were thrown into contact were constant sufferers from this worm, as their demands for "matar-bicho" were unceasing.

The party proceeded at once to the house of Mr. Newton, the American consul, by whom they were cordially received. He had been expecting them, having been informed of their proposed journey through a letter from the American consul at Lisbon, by a previous steamer. The professor at once stated the plans and wishes of his party, and the consul declared his readiness to serve them to the extent of his ability. He advised them to secure quarters in a house near his own, where there was ample room for storing their baggage, and went with them to see the proprietor. They found that the owner of the house had several vacant rooms, but that these were entirely without furniture. He was willing to rent these to them, to store their goods in his house, and to supply them with meals; but more than this he could not do. As they had their camp equipage on the steamer, the professor decided to secure the quarters offered them, and a bargain was at once concluded. The rest of the day was spent in landing their goods from the ship, and getting settled in their new quarters.

The next day they went with the consul to call on the governor-general. His excellency was a courteous gentleman, and received them pleasantly. He expressed his surprise at finding them bent on such an expedition, and gravely assured them that it was an undertaking full of difficulty and danger. He told them it was more than doubtful whether they would be able to begin their journey inland from Loanda, as he feared they would be unable to engage a sufficient number of carriers for the transportation of their baggage, and declared his belief that they would eventually be compelled to proceed to the town of Benguela, where it was easier to procure carriers. Upon looking over a list of the articles they had brought with them, he told them they would need at least three hundred carriers, and was quite sure that so many could not

THE MOUNTAINS OF BENGUELA.

be had at Loanda. He promised to do what he could to assist them in their enterprise, and ended the interview by advising them to make Benguela their starting-point for the interior. From that place they could proceed to the Bihé, or country of the Bihenos, who were friendly to the Portuguese settlements. From that region they could work their way to the Zambezi and the eastern coast of the continent.

"Well," said Ashton, as they left the residence of the governor-general, "his excellency does not give us much encouragement. I suppose we must expect disappointments at every step of our journey; but our business is to welcome them."

Our travellers remained in Loanda during the rest of the month of August. They were cordially assisted by the American consul in their efforts to obtain native carriers, but every day made it plainer to them that these were not to be had. They succeeded in engaging two followers, however. One of these was a native of the Zanzibar country, and was a tall, powerfully made negro, with a calm, resolute face, a pleasant expression, and courteous and dignified manners. When asked his name, he astonished the party by answering in excellent English,

"My name is Charlie." He spoke both English and Portuguese, and was also acquainted with the languages of several of the tribes through whose countries the route of the travellers would lie. He was anxious to get back to the eastern side of the continent, but had no money. He promised to serve the white men faithfully, if they would engage him, and to make their interests his own. After some discussion, the professor decided to engage him in the double capacity of interpreter and overseer of the native carriers they might secure. It was agreed that he should receive his wages in money upon reaching the eastern coast, and the professor promised that if the man gave satisfaction the party would pay his passage from whatever port they might reach on the Indian Ocean to Zanzibar. Charlie expressed himself well pleased with the terms offered him, and assured the professor, with many bows, that he would answer with his head for his fidelity to his trust.

The other person engaged by the professor was an active, bright-faced young negro, a native of the country, named Mombée. He offered his services as carrier and cook, and as he was warmly recommended by Charlie, a bargain was soon concluded with him. He spoke Portuguese and his native dialect, but was ignorant of English.

During their stay at Loanda our travellers were entertained several times by the governor-general and other officials of the colony, and made the acquaintance of some of the merchants engaged in trade with the interior of the country. From all these they received much valuable information and many useful suggestions, but all agreed in representing to them the impossibility of engaging carriers for their baggage nearer than Benguela. Nevertheless the effort was made, only, however, to result in failure; and towards the last of August they decided to leave Loanda by the steamer which was to arrive from Lisbon early in September, and proceed in her to Benguela, from which place they would begin their march across Africa. The governor-general gave them a letter of introduction to the governor of Benguela, in which he requested that official to render to the American travellers such assistance as might be in his power. They were also given, by one or two of the merchants they met at Loanda, letters to their correspondents at Benguela.

The steamer from Lisbon arrived at Loanda on the 4th of September, and lay there for two days discharging freight. On the 6th Professor Moreton and his companions, together with Charlie and Mombée, sailed for Benguela. Charlie watched the transfer of the immense pile of the travellers' baggage to the vessel with great interest, counting each piece as it came on board. When the last package had been safely stowed on the deck he turned away with a sigh.

"Well, Charlie," said Houston, who was standing by, "what do you think of our loads?"

"Me think it take heap of niggers to carry them," replied Charlie, slowly. "Heap niggers to watch, heap to feed, master."

"We can watch them and feed them too, if we can only induce them to go with us," said Houston. "You must do your best to help us to find carriers, Charlie."

"Do all me can," said Charlie; "but nigger man very uncertain."

Benguela was reached on the evening of the 7th of September, but the party did not go on shore until the next morning. Upon going on deck they found the vessel made fast to a fine iron pier, which led directly to the custom-house. During the day the professor obtained permission from the authorities to store the baggage of the party in one of the customs warehouses until it should be needed for the journey into the interior.

Immediately upon landing, Houston was left to look after the baggage until a place for its storage could be found, and the rest of the party accompanied the professor in a visit to Antonio Ferreira, one of the merchants to whom he bore letters of introduction. The Americans were courteously received by the merchant, who offered them the use of a house in the town belonging to him, and promised to assist them in procuring carriers for their baggage. He introduced them to Silva Porto, a trader who had extensive connections with the interior, and who likewise promised them his assistance. In company with the two merchants, the Americans then called upon the governor of Benguela, and presented their letter from the governor-general at Loanda. His excellency invited them to dine with him the next day, when he could discuss their plans with them more at his leisure, and in the mean time gave them permission to store their goods in the customs warehouse during their stay at Benguela. Having obtained this permission, the professor, upon leaving the governor, repaired immediately to the pier, where Houston and the two negroes were watching over the baggage. Such articles as were not needed immediately were stored in the government warehouse, and the remainder were transferred to the house placed at the service of the travellers by Antonio Ferreira. Having made themselves as comfortable as possible in their new quarters, the American travellers repaired to the house of the merchant, who had asked them to dine with him, and spent a pleasant evening.

Professor Moreton and his companions remained at Benguela for two months. They found the town, which was formerly the chief depot in Africa for the Brazilian slave-trade, to be well built. It is a picturesque town, and extends from the shore of the Atlantic to the very summit of the mountains which form the first steps of the lofty plateau of tropical Africa. It is surrounded by a dense forest, even now filled with wild beasts, where excellent sport could be obtained if the Portuguese cared to engage in it. The arrangement of the houses in the European quarter gives to the town a very rural appearance. All are provided with extensive gardens and dependencies. The gardens are carefully tended, and all the vegetables of Europe and many tropical plants are grown in them. The town is provided with large *patios*, or courts, surrounded by overhanging galleries, devoted to the use of the large caravans which descend from the interior to the coast for purposes of trade,

BENGUELA.

and occupy these buildings for three days, during which time they dispose of their wares. The houses of the town are built of unbaked bricks, and are but one story in height. The streets are broad, and are planted with two rows of trees. Several large public squares and a botanical garden constitute the principal resorts of the place. The town is considered very unhealthy, and few Europeans are able to bear the climate. The professor enjoined upon his companions a rigid system of diet, and required them to refrain from all unnecessary exposure, especially at night; and thanks to these precautions, they managed to escape sickness of any kind during their stay in the town.

Two months were passed by our travellers at Benguela. They devoted themselves actively to the work of procuring native carriers, but with indifferent success at first. They needed two hundred and fifty stout men, and these were hard to find. The governor was very active in trying to assist them, but he could do but little. At the end of the first fortnight they had secured the services of fifty men, and were still in need of two hundred more. Antonio Ferreira succeeded in procuring twenty-five more, and the old trader, Silva Porto, was indefatigable in his efforts to obtain recruits. At the end of the first month he despatched several of his own men northward from Benguela to the country of the Bailundos to procure several hundred carriers for his own service. He informed the professor that he intended despatching a caravan of his own to the Bihé in the course of a few months, and agreed to undertake the transportation of the heavier goods of the party to that place along with his own wares. He earnestly advised his "American friends," as he called them, to accept his offer, and set out from Benguela as soon as they had procured one hundred carriers, taking with them such baggage as would be necessary to the journey, and leaving him to send forward the remainder of the baggage.

"You can rely upon me implicitly," said the old trader to the professor. "I am not accustomed to make vain promises. I am an old man, but still tough and strong, and will aid you to the extent of my ability. I have a good house at Belmonte in the Bihé, and you shall occupy it upon your arrival there. I will give you a letter to my agent, placing the establishment at your command. My advice is to proceed to the Bihé as soon as possible, and wait there till you hear from me. If you should find yourselves in the interior surrounded by peril, with all but hope gone, try and hold your own, and despatch me a letter through the natives at any cost. Keep an even mind, and wait; for within the shortest possible time I will be with you, and will bring help and means. I am a man of my word, and will do what I promise."

The professor was deeply touched by this generous offer, and, after reflection, concluded to accept it. The governor told them that he had been exceedingly fortunate in securing the friendship of Silva Porto, who possessed more influence with the natives than any man on the coast. The old trader, he stated, was extensively engaged in traffic with the Bihé, and was in a position to make good his promise. The plan, he admitted, might involve a considerable delay at the Bihé, but it was better than waiting indefinitely at Benguela. A much longer delay there might cause the natives already engaged to become dissatisfied. Once in this frame of mind they would rapidly desert the expedition, and thus all that had been accomplished would be lost. By extraordinary exertions twenty-five additional porters were obtained by the 1st of November, and it was arranged that the expedition should start from Benguela on the 12th of November, and proceed to Quillengues, from which the travellers were to make their way to the Bihé. Silva Porto informed the professor and Ashton that they must be prepared for some desertions along the route, as it was not to be expected that all their men would remain faithful,

NEGRO VILLAGE NEAR BENGUELA.

and the old trader's words were verified on the very morning of their departure by the disappearance of three of the negroes.

Preparations for starting were now pushed forward with energy, the whole party being stimulated by the prospect of a speedy commencement of their journey. Loads were arranged for the carriers, and such articles as were necessary for the march were selected. The remainder of the baggage was delivered to Silva Porto, to be forwarded by him to the Bihé when his Bailundo porters should arrive. The governor now rendered the party a very material service. He was about to despatch a large boat by sea, to convey some stores to the Portuguese post at Dombe Grande, on the Cúio, and offered to send by it the loads that had been selected by the party for the journey.

As Dombe Grande was to be the first halting place on the journey, the offer was gladly accepted, and the loads were promptly transferred to the boat. By the advice of Silva Porto, a considerable quantity of *aguardiente*, a fermented liquor made from a native fruit, was included among the stores of the party. The old trader assured the professor that it would be found very useful, as a present of one or two bottles of it would often cause the success of a negotiation with the natives, where ever; other species of argument would fail.

"Keep it from your own men, and give it prudently to the chiefs you may encounter," he said, "and you will find it better than gold."

Five mules were purchased in Benguela for the use of the Americans, who were resolved to avoid walking as long as possible, and so husband their strength.

The morning of the 12th of November, 1878, found Professor Moreton and the young Americans busy by sunrise, making their last preparations for the start. The negro carriers, to the number of ninety-seven, were assembled in the court-yard of the house occupied by the travellers, and at the gate stood Houston, armed with his rifle, and with orders to allow no one to pass out. The mules, prepared for the journey, were waiting before the house, in charge of Charlie and Mombée. Everything was at last in readiness, and at seven o'clock the governor and Antonio Ferreira arrived, to bid adieu to the party and wish them God speed. A large number of Europeans and natives had assembled near the house to witness the departure, and as the party moved off they were greeted with a loud cheer. Silva Porto, mounted on a mule, accompanied the Americans for several miles, and at length took leave of them with sincere regret.

"Remember," he said, in parting from them, "I will do all I have promised, and I rely upon you to let me know if I can serve you further."

The procession presented quite an imposing appearance as it moved along through the open country, after Benguela was left behind. At the head of the line rode Houston, armed with his rifle, and carrying a small American flag. By his side walked the negro Charlie, armed with an excellent musket, which Ashton, who had taken a great liking to Charlie, had purchased for him at Loanda. The negro was very proud of his weapon, and fondled it repeatedly, glancing at it with admiring looks. Next rode the professor and Ashton, each armed with rifles, and accompanied by Mombée, who bore a shot-gun, purchased for him at Benguela. Then followed the native carriers in double file, while Philip Lee and Hubbard, armed like their companions, rode in the rear, to prevent straggling and desertion. The negroes were in good spirits, and the expedition moved along at a lively step.

The day's march was in a generally southern direction, the route lying parallel with the coast and at a short distance from it. A halt was made towards one o'clock in the afternoon for a lunch, and at night the party bivouacked in a rocky region. They were off by sunrise the next morning, and late in the afternoon reached the Portuguese fort at Dombe. They were most kindly received by the commandant, who, upon reading the letter of the governor of Benguela, lodged the whole party in the fortress. Through his assistance the professor succeeded in engaging a dozen native porters, thinking it prudent to do so, as it was to be expected that some of the Benguela men would desert.

THE VALLEY OF THE DOMBE.

The baggage sent around by sea did not arrive until the 16th, and the party were thus compelled to remain four days at the fort, a delay at which they chafed impatiently. The baggage having arrived, the travellers were anxious to set out the next day, but the commandant informed them that three of the neighboring sovas, or native chiefs, had sent word that they were coming the next day to visit the strangers. He told the professor that it would be necessary to receive the visit, as the chiefs would be seriously offended if they should start without seeing them, and would certainly give them trouble by placing difficulties in their way after they left the fortress, or, perhaps, by inducing their people to desert; so, with a bad grace, the Americans consented to await the coming of the sovas.

The chiefs arrived early on the afternoon of the 17th, accompanied by the dignitaries of their courts. They had meant to impress the strangers with a sense of their importance, and had gotten themselves up in all the splendor at their command. They presented a grotesque appearance as they marched into the fort with stately tread, and it required all the self-command of the young Americans to refrain from bursting into shouts of laughter as they made their appearance.

The principal chief, Sova Brito by name, was dressed in three dirty and rumpled skirts of chintz, of a large flowered pattern, which came down to his knees, with his legs and feet bare. The rest of his attire consisted of an old uniform coat of the Portuguese army, which, being unbuttoned, displayed his naked breast, and a red woollen skull cap, over which was posed an officer's cocked hat.

The second chief was named Bahita, and was also attired in dirty skirts of a woollen material, the uniform coat of a Portuguese admiral, a red night-cap, and the cap of a cavalry officer. The sleeves of his coat came only a little way below the elbows; and as the shoulders of the chief were nearly half as broad again as those of the officer for whom the coat had been originally made, it set upon him in the most ludicrous fashion. His legs were bare from the knees, as were also his feet.

MUNDOMBE WOMEN, VENDORS OF COAL.

Batára, the third chief, was the inferior of his companions in both wealth and power, and his dress consisted of the usual woollen night-cap and a ragged calico skirt; but around his waist was buckled an immense cavalry sabre, very much the worse for wear.

For the reception of the sovas three chairs had been placed in the court-yard of the fort in front of the quarters assigned the Americans, and other chairs were placed opposite them for the commandant of the fortress and his white guests.

The chiefs advanced, preceded by a minstrel playing upon a *miramba*, from which he drew the most doleful sounds. This instrument was formed of two slightly curved sticks about three feet in length, with strings of catgut stretched across the curve. Thin strips of wood placed at intervals along the strings regulated the notes of the scale, and the sound was increased by means of a row of gourds placed below the strings. The commandant received the sovas with grave politeness, and presented them to his white guests, after which all seated themselves, the native dignitaries squatting on the ground around their respective sovereigns. The manner of the chiefs was grave and dignified, but relaxed somewhat when the professor produced a bottle of *aguardiente*, from which each of them drank heartily. Batára was the last to receive the bottle, and, when he had drained it, turned it up with the mouth down, to show that nothing was left. He gazed at it for a moment, and then, with a sigh, placed it on the ground by his side.

A conversation then followed, the chiefs expressing great surprise when they learned that the white men had come into the country only to "look at it," as they expressed it. Sova Brito then commanded his attendants to dance be-

A SOUTH AFRICAN RIVER.

fore the strangers, and similar orders were given to their people by the other chiefs. Immediately the sable dignitaries were on their feet, and some girls, whom the travellers had not noticed before, were brought forward to join in the entertainment. The man with the miramba then struck up a doleful strain, and the blacks commenced a series of capers of the most novel description.

"I say, professor," said Hubbard, "can't we get their majesties to dance? It would be rare fun to see those old fellows cutting such antics."

The professor, nothing loth, repeated the request to the commandant, who acted as interpreter, and that official translated it to the chiefs. They replied in their native tongue, and with the most impressive dignity.

"They say," translated the commandant, "that such a thing is impossible, as it would not be consistent with their dignity to dance before strangers. Nevertheless," he added, "if you really wish to see them dance, I think another bottle of *aguardiente* would overcome their objections."

The fresh bottle was produced, and was speedily emptied. Then there was a consultation among the chiefs in a low tone. It ended by Batára rising gravely and unbuckling his long sabre, which he laid on his chair. The next moment he sprang among the dancers with a yell, followed by his brother chiefs. The dancers fell back to make way for their sovereigns, and manifested their delight at such condescension by rolling over on the ground and indulging in the most violent contortions of body and features. As for the chiefs, they leaped wildly about, shouting and yelling, and manifesting the greatest excitement. Sova Brito declared that he was the greatest warrior in the world, while Bahita improvised a song in honor of the delightful effects of *aguardiente*. Batára was wild with excitement, and vowed he would cut off the heads of all his people with his great sword, in honor of his generous friends. The excitement of the chiefs increased with each moment, and their dancing grew wilder and more grotesque. In about half an hour they suddenly paused and gravely walked back to their seats. They were too much under the influence of the liquor they had imbibed to attempt to carry on any further conversation, however, and soon took their departure, each leaning on the shoulder of an attendant, Batára's long sabre trailing between his legs and threatening to trip him at every step.

The younger Americans were greatly amused by the spectacle they had witnessed, but the professor could not help expressing his regret at having given the sovas too much liquor.

"Oh, you need not regret it," said the commandant. "Drunkenness is a second nature with the natives here, and is considered no disgrace. As long as the fruit from which *aguardiente* is made lasts, which is about three months in the year, these people are never sober."

The Dombe Grande is a fertile valley, extending back from the sea in a southeasterly direction, and is watered by a river known by several names, the principal of which are the Dombe and Coporola. It is thickly planted with manioc by the natives, who annually export large quantities of the flour. Considerable sugar-cane is raised in the valley, and this is converted into rum. The natives understand the use of money, and dispose of their products for cash. The valley forms a part of the province of Benguela, and is in fact the granary of that section.

The delay of the party at Dombe was most unfavorable to the negroes of the expedition. Several of them deserted, and a number sold their clothing to obtain *aguardiente*, while others even went so far as to barter their rations of food for liquor. On the morning of the 18th, it was found that too many were suffering from the effects of drink to allow the expedition to resume its march that day, and it was not until the 21st that the blacks were in condition to take the road again. The professor, in the mean time, had been able to engage a few of the natives to supply the places of those who had deserted, so that when the march was resumed on the morning of the 21st, it was with full ranks. The Dombe was left at eight o'clock in the morning, and for two hours the route lay across the rich plain towards the foot of the Cangemba range of mountains. The professor gave his party an hour's rest before attempting to climb the hills. The ascent was by the dry bed of a torrent, and though the range was not steep, the expedition consumed three hours in marching a thousand yards. Tired and hungry, the men went into camp near five o'clock; the fires were lighted, and rations were eaten for the first time during the day. The mules had proved very troublesome in climbing the hills. They had gotten along very well on the plain below, but when it came to climbing they had to be forced up the ascent, so that the professor and his companions were obliged to make the greater part of the march on foot. The negroes too moved slowly, each man being laden with sixty-six pounds of baggage, besides rations of food for nine days, consisting of manioc flour and dried fish.

MUNDOMBE WOMEN AND GIRLS.

MUNDOMBE MEN.

The camp was pitched beside a well dug in the sandy bed of a rivulet that had run dry. It was a dreary and desolate spot, and Houston declared it gave him the blues to look at it. The well, however, afforded water enough for their wants, and Charlie told Houston that that ought to make him content, as they would doubtless be glad enough to get water of any kind before many days.

The next morning the march was resumed at a little after sunrise, and the expedition managed to cover a distance of twelve miles. Water was scarce, and the pathway difficult and fatiguing. It lay along the dry bed of the river Canga, which was irregular and stony, and very trying to the feet of the negroes. The next day, the 23d, many of the blacks were so lame that it was impossible to prevent straggling. The negroes who carried the provisions of the party were among the stragglers, and were so late in reaching camp that it was nearly eight o'clock in the evening before Mombée was able to prepare supper, the only meal our travellers had eaten since breakfast.

Ashton now called Professor Moreton's attention to a new danger. The negroes had been given rations for nine days, but as soon as the halt for the evening was ordered, they began eating and continued to do so until they went to sleep, regardless of the fact that they were consuming more than had been allotted them for each day. There was serious danger that their rations would be exhausted before reaching Quillengues, the next station of the expedition, and that hunger would follow in a country where it was impossible to obtain food. Charlie was ordered to remonstrate with them, in the name of the White Chief, as the blacks had styled the professor, but his remonstrance produced no effect. Seeing this, the professor decided to urge the men forward as fast as possible during the remainder of the march to Quillengues, in order to reach that place before the lack of food should be too keenly felt.

On the 24th, sixteen miles were made, and on the 25th, eighteen. The road was easier than it had been, lying now through thick forests, in which gigantic baobab trees grew luxuriantly. On the afternoon of the 26th the camp was pitched on the slope of Mount Tama. Scarcely were the tents erected when murmurs of discontent arose from the blacks. Charlie was sent among them to learn the cause, and reported that the men were hungry and demanded food. They had consumed nine days' rations in six days, and were yet three days from Quillengues. The professor caused a ration of rice to be served out to each one, but this did not content them; they wanted dried fish and manioc flour. These were not to be had, as the stores of the white members of the party were very low, and they had been subsisting on one meal a day.

"It is about time for me to begin my duties as huntsman of the expedition," said Houston. "I'll take one of the Winchester rifles and Charlie, and we'll have a stroll in the forest, professor. I may be able to bag some game, and a little fresh meat will satisfy these fellows for another day at least."

Calling Charlie, Houston left the camp with him, and together they plunged into the forest. The undergrowth was thick, and overhead the baobabs reared their lofty branches, and almost shut out the sunlight.

"What you want shoot, Master Hoosey?" asked Charlie.

"Anything those poor black fellows can eat," replied Houston. "What do you think we will find here, Charlie,—an elephant, eh?"

A SOUTH AFRICAN FOREST.

"No, Master Hoosey, no find elephant here, him lib so many miles from here. Maybe find lion, maybe buffalo, maybe antelope. Nigger like antelope berry much."

For over an hour they wandered through the forest without seeing the least trace of game. The sun was rapidly declining, and, as Houston did not wish to be caught in the woods by the darkness, they at length turned their faces towards the camp. Tired and disappointed, they became silent, and moved along slowly. Suddenly Charlie paused and held up his hand warningly.

"Game close by, Master Hoosey!" he exclaimed in a low tone.

"How do you know?" asked Houston.

"Me smell him," replied Charlie. "Wind against him dis time; in our favor. Be quiet and walk softly."

Creeping cautiously through the trees, they came in sight of an opening in the woods, consisting partly of a small level sward of grass, and partly of a slight eminence of rocks. Charlie seized Houston's arm with a powerful grasp, and holding him back, pointed towards the grass-plot, where two fine antelopes were leisurely grazing. At the same moment, the male animal, seeming to scent the danger, sprang up on the rocks, and raising his head, gazed anxiously around in every direction.

"Shoot now," said Charlie in a whisper; "you got him."

Houston silently brought the rifle to his shoulder, took deliberate aim at the antelope, which was clearly outlined against the sky, and fired. Immediately the animal rolled over on the rocks, and the female sprang to its side and gazed at it for a moment. Houston sent a second shot towards her, but with one bound she leaped from the rocks and disappeared in the thicket. With a yell Charlie dashed off in the direction she had taken, and Houston hastened towards the rocks where he had seen the male animal fall. To his delight he beheld the animal lying dead, shot through the breast. As he stood gazing at it with a feeling of triumph, a crackling in the bushes caused him to turn, and he beheld Charlie making his way out of the thicket, literally staggering under the weight of the female antelope. She had been fatally wounded by the second ball, but had made one or two leaps into the undergrowth before falling.

"You good hunter, Master Hoosey," said Charlie, grinning broadly. "We no starve now. You wait here; me run back to camp and fetch some niggers to carry these antelopes."

He hastened off, and was soon back again with four of the blacks. The antelopes were carried to the camp, where they furnished a hearty meal for the men. Houston was warmly congratulated by his companions upon his success, and felt not a little elated by it.

In spite of this addition to their commissariat, the professor resolved to hasten on to Quillengues, as he knew the blacks would soon be hungry again. The march was resumed the next day, and continued with energy; and on the

29th of November the expedition arrived at the fortress of Quillengues, having made over forty miles in less than three days.

They were hospitably received by the *chefe* of Quillengues, Lieutenant Roza by name, an officer in the Portuguese service, and the whole party were given

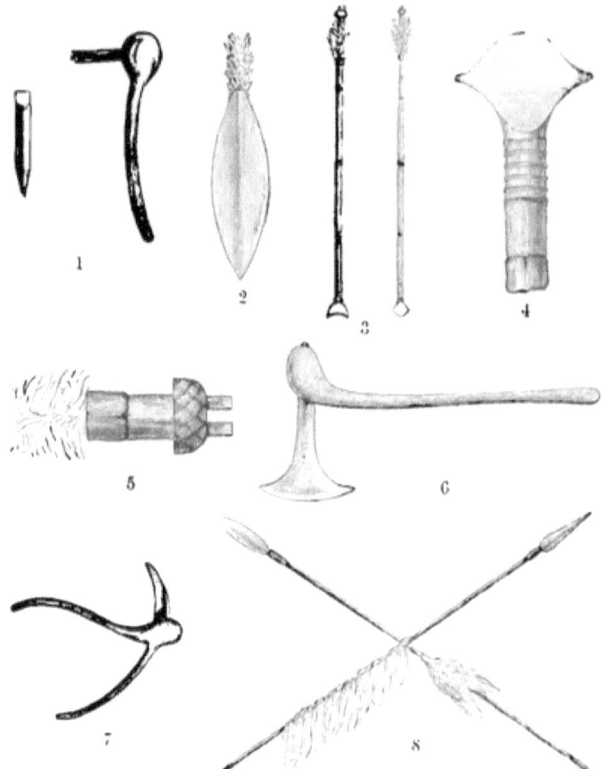

ARTICLES MANUFACTURED BY THE NATIVES BETWEEN THE COAST AND THE BINÉ.
1. Working axe. 2. Arrow-head for war. 3. Arrows. 4. Arrow-head for hunting. 5. Butt-end of arrows. 6. Battle-axe. 7. Hoe. 8. Assegais.

lodgings in the fortress. Provisions were obtained in abundance, and the discontent of the negroes ceased as soon as they saw the prospect of full stomachs.

The professor and Ashton, the day after the arrival of the party at the fortress, distributed among the carriers the first instalment of their wages, which consisted of a certain number of yards of white cloth to each man. This put them in a thoroughly good humor, and they declared their willingness now to go on with the white men, as they saw the latter intended to treat them fairly.

It had been the intention of our travellers to push on immediately from Quillengues to Caconda, and thence to the Bihé, but this plan was frustrated by the sickness of Walter Hubbard. On the morning after the arrival of the party at the fortress, he complained of severe pains and a feeling of lassitude, and before night was down with a sharp attack of the fever peculiar to the country. He was ill for over a fortnight, and it was fully the 23d of December before he was able to walk about the yard of the fortress. He was faithfully nursed

AFRICAN RAT.

during his sickness by his companions, and also by the kind-hearted commandant of the fort and his wife.

During the delay caused by Hubbard's sickness over twenty of the negroes deserted from the expedition. By energetic efforts among the natives of Quillengues Professor Moreton was able to fill their places. The commandant of the fortress also interposed his authority to check the desertions and keep the men faithful to their duties, and much of the trouble that might have been caused by the long halt and consequent idleness of the men was thus averted.

Quillengues is one of the most important of the military posts of the Portuguese in the province of Benguela. The fortress lies in a fertile and well-populated valley, watered by the river Calunga. It is rectangular in shape, and is defended by a strong palisade and four bastions, the latter being constructed of masonry half way up each face. Within the enclosure are roomy barracks which furnish quarters for the commandant or *chefe* and the soldiers.

The natives of the Quillengues valley are both pastoral and agricultural in their habits. They grow large crops of maize, massambala, and manioc; and dwell in huts, circular in form, constructed of the trunks of trees, plastered with mud. The huts are from ten to fifteen feet in diameter, and each has a door or entrance large enough for a man to enter without stooping. The inhabitants acknowledge the authority of the Portuguese, but nevertheless the

TREE-FERNS OF AFRICA.

different chiefs constantly make war upon other native tribes and rob them of their cattle and crops.

The men of Quillengues are tall and powerfully made, very courageous, and fond of war. They are also grossly addicted to drunkenness, *aguardiente* being their favorite beverage. They purchase most of the metal articles in use by them from the Dombe and Benguela, being but little skilled in the manufacture of iron implements. Their villages and the enclosures in which their cattle are kept are surrounded by strong stockades, beyond which are placed abattis of thorns to keep off wild beasts. Thorny barriers also encircle the manioc fields as a protection against small deer, who are very fond of the young leaves of the plant.

Some of the customs of these people proved very interesting to the white strangers. When a native wishes to obtain a wife, they were told, he presents to the father of the damsel he has selected, four yards of cloth from the coast and two bottles of *aguardiente*. If the father consents to the marriage, the bride is sent back with the bearer of the gifts, accompanied by her relatives, and upon her arrival the bridegroom gives a great feast, at which an ox, roasted whole, forms the principal course. When a death occurs, the body is wrapped in a white cloth, rolled in an ox-hide, carried to the grave which has been dug for it, and buried at once. The interment is followed by a feast in the hut of the dead man, which lasts several days, or until the provisions left by the deceased are exhausted. These feasts are elaborate affairs, and render the Quillengues funerals very expensive, as the heir to the estate is required to sacrifice all the cattle of the deceased, in order to do honor to his memory and give peace to his soul. In the case of the death of a chief there is a large sacrifice of cattle.

CHAPTER VII.

ADVENTURES IN THE BLACK MAN'S COUNTRY.

WHILE at Quillengues, Professor Moreton laid in a considerable stock of such provisions as could be obtained, and purchased several oxen and sheep, to be slaughtered on the road; so that when the party started from that place on the 1st of January, 1879, they were well supplied for a portion of their march to Caconda, six days distant from Quillengues. The camp was pitched for the first night at the foot of the Quillengues Mountains, and the next day the party moved through a region of ferns and acacias. No signs of game were seen, and at times not a single note of a bird could be heard; while at intervals throughout the day the route lay through woods which were alive with birds, the cries of which were fairly deafening. The party camped for the night on the bank of a small stream of good water, called the Cuverai, and on the 3d pitched their tents by the brook Quicué. During the night they heard for the first time the repeated roarings of lions in the distance; but as their camp was well protected by a thorny hedge, they paid no attention to the sounds. The next day they halted for the night near the village of Ngóla, in the dominions of King Chimbarandongo.

The next morning, January 5th, Professor Moreton, wishing to devote himself to some scientific observations, despatched Ashton and Houston, with Charlie and Mombée as interpreters, to visit the sable king, and invite him to the camp. The "embassy," as Ashton laughingly styled it, set out immediately after breakfast, and soon reached the village of the king,—a large collection of huts enclosed by a double stockade. The space enclosed is large enough to contain the entire population of the country, which gathers there with its flocks and herds in time of war. A little stream called the Cutota runs through the village, and affords it an ample water-supply in case of a siege.

Ashton and Houston were requested by the negroes on duty at the entrance to the town to wait until their approach could be announced to the king, to whom a messenger was immediately despatched. In about a quarter of an hour they were permitted to enter the enclosure, accompanied by their attendants, and were conducted towards the royal hut.

The king came out of his dwelling at their approach, attended by several

128   OUR YOUNG FOLKS IN AFRICA.

of his wives and a number of his people. He was a tall, powerful man, and was clad in a long waistcoat, over which he wore a leopard skin. His breast

ON THE CUVELAI.

was bare, and a number of amulets were suspended from his neck. His arms consisted of two formidable-looking clubs and an assegai, or iron-headed javelin. He received his visitors in front of his hut, and the interview took place in the broiling sun. The young Americans were each provided with an umbrella to shelter them from the heat, and had brought an extra one as a present for his majesty. This was at once delivered to him by Ashton, and had the effect of putting the sable monarch in an excellent humor. Several other presents had also been sent by the professor, among which were a couple of muskets, a package of gun-flints, and some gunpowder. The king received them graciously, and, coming straight to the point, asked what his visitors desired in return for their valuable gifts. He was profoundly astonished when Ashton informed him that they wished for nothing but his friendship; that he and his white brothers in the camp had heard of Chimbarandongo as a great king, and in passing through his country wished to be good friends with him. When the king was informed that their only object was to cross the continent and reach the great water on the other side, he was still more astonished. He told Ashton that he and his brothers must be brave men to undertake such

KING CHIMBARANDONGO.

a journey, and added that while he would be their friend, they would meet many bad people after they left his country. Ashton then invited him to go with him to the camp to see his companions, and the king at once prepared to accept the invitation. The young men thereupon desired him to bring with him a vessel in which to put some *aguardiente*, and the king brought from his hut an old pint bottle; but Houston told him it was too small, and begged him to bring one that would hold three times as much. The king expressed his surprise at such generosity, and brought out a gourd capable of holding about a gallon.

Chimbarandongo then set off with the young men, accompanied by three of his wives, his daughters, and a number of his people. All were unarmed, to show the confidence with which the young envoys had inspired them.

When they reached the camp the professor was still engaged in his meteorological observations, and the monarch and his attendants were enthusiastic in their admiration of the thermometers and barometers, evidently regarding the use which was being made of the instruments as a species of conjuring.

The king informed the professor that since he had been treated so generously by the white men, he had ordered his people to bring an ox to the camp as a present from himself; and as he spoke two of his men came into the camp, leading a fine ox by a rope. The ox was tied to a tree, and after the instruments had been put away, the king desired Professor Moreton to slay the animal with his own hand. This request somewhat embarrassed the professor, but the animal relieved him from complying with the king's request by breaking loose and making for the woods. At the same moment Houston caught up his rifle and, telling the king he meant to hit the ox between the eyes, fired. The animal fell dead in its tracks, and the king hastened over to it to examine the wound. When he found that the ball had entered exactly between the

ENCAMPMENT OF THE EXPEDITION NEAR CHIMBARANDONGO'S VILLAGE.

eyes, he was wild with delight, and embraced Houston repeatedly, telling him he was a great warrior for so young a man.

The gourd brought by the visitors was now filled with *aguardiente*, and the king, his wives, and his chief attendants proceeded without delay to partake of it, declaring that they were terribly thirsty. During the day they managed to consume the entire gallon, and were consequently very tipsy when the time came for their departure.

During the afternoon a severe thunder-storm, accompanied by heavy rain, broke over the camp, and lasted until nearly dark. The king, his women, and a few of his chief attendants took refuge in the hut of the Americans, and when they were all safely under shelter, Chimbarandongo turned to his followers, and with half drunken gravity made them a speech, telling them that the white men by their conjuring with the instruments they had seen, had caused the rain to fall, and had thus conferred a great blessing on the country, which was suffering very much from the drought. Professor Moreton thereupon endeavored to explain to the monarch that neither he nor any of his companions had any such great powers, but that God alone sent the rain. The king, however, cut him short by declaring loudly that if it stopped raining he would find out the person who was responsible for it, and have him put to death. When the rain finally ceased, however, his majesty was too much under the influence of *aguardiente* to remember his threat. He departed for his home about dark, with the most profuse protestations of friendship for his

THE NEGROES OF THE PARTY CONSTRUCTING HUTS IN THE ENCAMPMENTS.

good friends, the white men. As he was too much intoxicated to walk, he was lifted on the back of one of his followers, who was also half-seas over, and was steadied by two others who walked by the side of his bearer. The whole party reeled about in the most comical manner, and it seemed that the king would be thrown to the ground at every step. They managed to get out of the camp in safety, however, and their shouts and laughter could be heard for some time after they had taken their departure.

The next morning the camp was astir at an early hour, and breakfast was soon despatched. The men were then gotten in marching order, and the journey was resumed. King Chimbarandongo now made his appearance to take leave of his white friends. He was entirely sober, in an excellent humor, and his conversation showed him to be a man of much more wisdom than he had appeared on the previous evening. He told the professor that he was by no means a believer in sorcery, and did not believe that the rain of the previous night was in any way due to the conjuring of the whites; but that it had suited his purpose to appear to do so, as it gave him a firmer hold upon his people, who were very superstitious. He was the good friend of the white men, he said, because it was to his interest to be so. The Portuguese supplied him with the cloth which covered him and the arms and ammunition which enabled him to hold his own against his enemies. "Without the whites," said the king, "we are poorer than the beasts, as they possess the skins we are forced to rob them of; and those blacks are great fools who do not seek to gain the friendship of the white men."

SKELETON OF A HUT.

The travellers parted from the king with much more respect for him than they had felt on the previous evening, and the king assured them that should they need his aid while in his dominions they had but to notify him. He took Houston aside and solemnly gave him a copper coin, which he told him was a "great medicine," and asked him to wear it around his neck, as it would preserve him from harm. When the party had gotten fairly on the march, Houston examined the coin, and found it to be an old and very green American half-cent piece of the year 1800.

Two days' steady marching, on the first of which a deep, swollen river was crossed by a dangerous foot-bridge, the mules and oxen being forced to swim the torrent, brought them to Caconda, the last Portuguese fortress in the interior of Benguela. The fortress was reached late in the afternoon of the 7th, and the travellers were received by the provisional *chefe*, a mulatto, who commanded in the absence of the permanent *chefe*, then on a visit to Benguela. He assigned several huts within the enclosure of the fortress to the Americans and their men, and assured them they would have no difficulty in purchasing food from the natives.

While at Caconda, Professor Moreton fell sick of a slight attack of fever. The disease was much milder than it had been in Hubbard's case, and they were delayed only five days. At the end of that time, although feeling very weak and languid, the professor decided to push on towards the Bihé. Calling his young companions about him on the morning of January 12th, he told them of his intention to resume the march the next day, and urged them to increased vigilance and caution in dealing with their own men, and with the natives they should encounter.

"Heretofore, boys," he said, "we have been to a certain extent under the protection of the Portuguese, and have been travelling among tribes more or less subject to them. We have now reached the limits of the Portuguese authority, and our route hereafter will lie among tribes which possess very bad reputations for treachery and dishonesty. Our own men may be somewhat harder to manage, as they will no longer fear being reported to the white officials. We are now entirely upon our own resources, and dependent upon our prudence and determination for our safety and success."

SPECIMEN OF THE HUTS USED BY THE EXPEDITION.

Two days after leaving Caconda the expedition reached the great village of Quingola. Several native villages were passed on the way, several deep rivers were forded, and on the first day numerous venomous snakes were encountered, and many were killed by the professor and his companions. Quingola was reached on the afternoon of the 15th of January. The native chief received the party kindly, and sent them food, for which payment was made with colored cloth. The professor's fever returned during the 16th, and the march was not resumed until the next day, when the expedition set out again. The professor found it so hard to manage his mule in his weak condition that he decided to ride one of the oxen. Philip Lee and Mombée rode by him to attend to his wants, and the party made several halts during the day to allow the invalid to rest. In this way they were two days in reaching the village of Capôco, the powerful

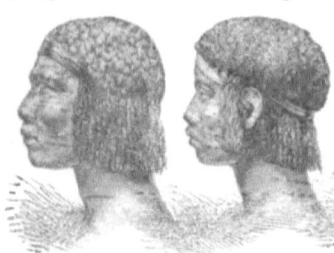

MAN AND WOMAN OF THE HUAMBO.

son of the native chief of the Huambo country. Capôco was the terror of the surrounding country. He was twenty-five years old, in the full flush of health and manly vigor, and had carried his victorious arms in every direction. Two years before the arrival of the Americans in his country he had even ventured to attack Quillengues itself, and had carried off a number of captives from that place. The travellers were, therefore, very uncertain as to the manner in which he would receive them, and upon arriving at his village awaited his appearance with considerable anxiety. To their surprise and delight, he came to meet them with extended hands, and welcomed them cordially. He invited them into his village, and gave up one of his own houses for the use of the

TOMB OF A NATIVE AFRICAN CHIEF.

white travellers, and when he heard that the professor was ill sent him a couple of fowls. In return for this civility, Ashton presented the chief with a couple of pieces of striped cloth and two bottles of *aguardiente*, which pleased him very much. Soon after this a number of young girls brought baskets of food for the negroes of the party. Professor Moreton was not entirely satisfied with the conduct of Capôco, however, as he could not understand why so notorious a freebooter should be so friendly with strangers without apparent cause. He therefore cautioned his companions to be constantly on their guard, and to keep a sharp watch over their men, in order to avoid being taken by surprise in the event of any sudden treachery on the part of the chief or his people.

The result proved that the professor's suspicions were unfounded. Capôco, although a fierce and cruel warrior when on the war-path, was a man of intelligence, and was very moderate in the indulgence of his appetites. He possessed a certain nobleness of character, and could be generous when he chose.

For reasons of his own he chose to be a courteous and generous host to his white visitors, and treated them with great kindness during their stay with him, which, in consequence of the professor's feeble condition, lasted until the 18th of January.

The customs of the Huambo country interested our travellers very much. They found that the language is the same as that spoken by the Nanos, or people of Caconda and the Quillengues. The Huambos are tolerably good workers in iron, and make their own arrows, assegais, and axes, but purchase their other implements from caravans from the coast. The men are well made, tall in stature, and are possessed of great strength, courage, and endurance. They dress their hair very elaborately, the work of arranging it in proper shape often occupying two or three days; but, in compensation for this, these triumphs of the barber's art last for several months. The women adorn their hair with a profusion of glass beads; and as the travellers had these among their stores, they were able to make many friends by judicious presents to the fair sex. The young girls, as long as they remain virgins, wear wooden bangles upon both ankles, or upon the left ankle only.

In the central part of the village was a curious edifice, consisting of a large hut with a thatched roof. In the centre of the building was a stone hearth, on which a fire was kept burning in spite of the extreme heat of the weather. This, the travellers were told, was the "Conversation House," and they were informed that a similar establishment existed in every village of the tribe. In it the inhabitants assembled for gossip and social intercourse, and seated on blocks of wood around the fire indulged in tales of adventure, love, and war.

The travellers noticed that although Capóco was the owner of a very large number of female slaves, he had but a few wives. One day, while conversing with him, Ashton expressed his surprise at this, but the chief told him that he did not think it good for a man to "marry too much." He pointed out a tall, handsome girl among his slaves, and told Ashton that she was the daughter of a chief of Quillengues, and that he had captured her during his attack on that place two years before. He added that he was very much in love with her, and would like to marry her.

"Then why do you not do so?" asked Ashton. "Her fate is in your hands."

CAPÓCO'S SWEETHEART.

"I cannot do it," replied Capóco, drawing himself up proudly. "She is my slave by right of war; but so long as her father shows a disposition to ransom her I must respect her, and she shall be respected, for I intend to deliver her up in the same state in which I took her. When her father ransoms her," he added with a smile, " I will demand her in marriage ; and if he does not give her to me, I will go and take her again."

"But if you are anxious to marry her," said Ashton, " why not propose to her father to relinquish the ransom, if he will give her to you for a wife?"

"That would be bad policy," replied the chief, laughing. "By doing as I intend, I shall get both the ransom and the girl."

In the morning before their departure from Capôco's village, some of the negroes became very much discontented, and demanded their pay, as they declared their intention to leave the expedition. Finally the number of malcontents increased to twenty. Ashton and Houston were unable to overcome the discontent either by argument or authority, and being unwilling to resort to severe measures, sought the professor to ask his advice. Capôco was with the professor at the time, and at once declared he would settle the matter for

ANT-HILLS FOUND BETWEEN THE COAST AND THE BIHÉ.
1 and 2 are a few inches above the ground. 3 and 4 are from three to seven feet high.

his white friends. He advised Ashton to pay to each of the negroes a small portion of his wages in cloth, although they were not entitled to payment until the Bihé was reached. When the cloth had been distributed, Capôco strode out before the blacks, and addressing them in severe tones, reminded them that they had sworn to conduct the white men safe to the Bihé. He told them they must keep their word, and warned them that if any deserted from the expedition, he would have him seized and put to death. This determined course put an end to the trouble for the time.

Before leaving Caconda, Professor Moreton had selected ten of the negroes whom he deemed the most reliable, and had armed them with muskets. He was now well pleased to find that none of these were among the mutineers.

Although the professor was still suffering with the fever, the party left Capôco's village on the morning of the 19th of January, marching in the direction of the country of the Sambo. Towards noon they reached the village of Chacaquimbamba, a petty chief of the Huambo. A considerable crowd of natives had assembled at the entrance to the village; but as Capóco had warned the professor to beware of these people, who, he said, were great thieves, the party passed by the village without halting. They had scarcely gone fifty yards, however, when a commotion was heard at the rear of the column. Charlie was sent back to ascertain the cause, and returned saying that the men of the village had taken away the gun of one of the negroes of their party, who had straggled behind, and had also stolen a she-goat and a sheep, which they had taken into the village.

Not caring to trouble the professor, and firmly resolved upon his course, Ashton ordered the men to move on slowly, and taking with him Houston and Charlie and the nine armed negroes, hastened back to the village, at the entrance to which the natives were still standing. Using Charlie as interpreter, he told the people they must restore the property they had stolen. They answered him with threatening cries and murmurs, encouraged, no doubt, by the fact that they were about two hundred to thirteen. The blood of the young American was thoroughly aroused, however, and he was determined to teach the negroes a lesson. Retaining Charlie and two of the armed negroes, he

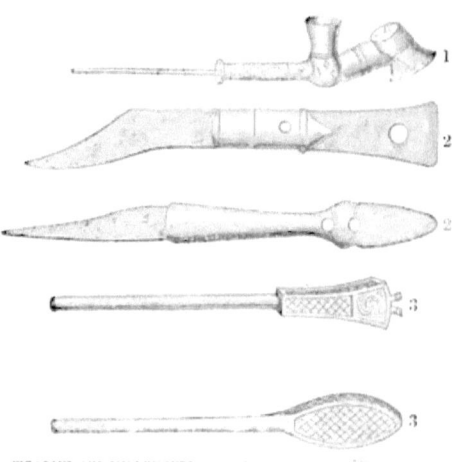

WEAPONS AND IMPLEMENTS OF NATIVE AFRICAN MANUFACTURE.
1. Pipe. 2, 2. Knives. 3, 3. Tomahawks.

ordered Houston to enter the village with the others, and recover the stolen property. Houston needed no urging, and at once dashed into the village at a trot, followed by the seven negroes. At the same time Ashton threw himself with his two men between the natives and the entrance to the town, and the little party with cocked guns stood prepared to cover the movements of their companions. The audacity of the proceeding struck the natives with dismay, and they drew back some distance from the entrance, and contented themselves with angry murmurs. In a short while Houston and his party returned, leading the sheep and the goat; the gun, however, could not be found. Ashton was not willing to expose his men to further risk, and threatening the natives with the vengeance of Capóco if the gun was not returned, hastened back to join the rest of the expedition, which had by this time gotten some distance beyond the village. As soon as he reached the column he ordered Mombée to make a circuit around the place, and to hasten back to Capôco's village and inform him of their adventure. He was then to rejoin them at the town, where they were to halt for the night. Mombée at once set out on his journey, and the party continued their march. At three o'clock they arrived at the village of Quimbungo, the uncle of Capôco, by whom they were hospitably received. When told by Ashton of the adventure at the little village they had passed, the chief begged that his white friends would not let their anger fall upon Chacaquimbamba, and promised that the stolen gun should be returned the next day.

Towards sunset Capôco and Mombée arrived at Quimbungo. The chief was very indignant at the affront that had been put upon his late guests, and assured the professor that not only should the gun be restored the next day, but that the chief of the village should be put at his disposal, in order that he might inflict upon him such punishment as he should see fit.

Capôco was off the next morning before the travellers were up, and about noon returned, bringing with him Chacaquimbamba and the stolen gun. The gun was returned, and the village chief humbly asked pardon of the professor, which was graciously granted. Chacaquimbamba then completed his atonement by presenting to the professor two fine sheep. Then he was suffered to depart, after having been sternly reprimanded by Capôco. In the afternoon Capôco took his leave, after warmly recommending his friends to the care of his uncle. As he shook hands with Ashton he slapped him on the back heartily, and cried,—

"You are a brave fellow. You did right yesterday. Take my advice, and never give way to the black men. You must face them boldly, no matter how great the odds."

The travellers were off the next morning for the country of the Sambo, which they entered the next day, and at three o'clock on the 22d of January they reached the village of the native chief of the Dumbo. This chief, Capôco had told the professor, was a vassal of the king of the Sambo, and was ruler over a number of villages and hamlets besides the one in which he dwelt. Capôco added that he was very treacherous, and advised the professor to watch him closely in all his dealings with him.

Dumbo received the travellers with courtesy, and begged them to accept quarters for their whole party in the village, which offer was promptly accepted. The professor, as soon as he had seen his party in safe quarters, sent the chief a present of three bottles of *aguardiente*. Dumbo accepted the gift, but, contrary to the laws of African hospitality, failed to offer the party any food. The professor and Ashton endeavored to purchase flour, but none of the natives would sell any.

"This is very strange," said Professor Moreton to Ashton and Houston. "It does not accord with the courteous manner of the chief when he received us. It may be that he means to give us trouble; so we had better be on our guard."

"I will caution Charlie," said Houston, "to keep a strict watch over our black people, and keep them in their quarters as much as possible. Hubbard and Lee had better be among them off and on until they go to sleep."

These orders were given, and extra vigilance was observed by the whole party during the remainder of the day and evening.

Towards eight o'clock, the professor and his companions, having partaken of a frugal supper, were gathered in the hut assigned them by the chief. Professor Moreton, though still somewhat languid, was beginning to recover

DUMBO'S WIVES.

from the effects of the fever, and was busily engaged in writing up the journal of the expedition. The other members of the party were lounging about the room, conversing with Charlie, who was relating to them some of his African experiences. Suddenly the door was thrown open, and Dumbo entered, followed by five of his wives, a negro named Palanca, who was his principal adviser, or minister, and another negro, whom he presented as Cassoma, the chief of a neighboring village, who had come to visit him. Although surprised by this unceremonious intrusion, the professor requested the new-comers to be seated, and calling upon Charlie to act as interpreter, entered into conversation with them. Dumbo was courteous for a while, but evidently ill at ease. Cassoma said but little, but regarded the whites with a cold, sinister expression. This attracted the attention of Philip Lee, who leaned over to Ashton, and said in a low tone,—

"Keep your eye on Cassoma, Ashton. I don't like his looks. The fellow means to give us trouble."

"You right, young gentleman," said Charlie, who had overheard the remark. "Me see it in him eye. He one bad man."

Cassoma now interrupted the conversation between the professor and Dumbo, and looking the former full in the face, said coldly,—

"We did not come here to talk, or to waste time about these people's affairs." Then turning to Dumbo, he exclaimed, sharply, "We want *aguardiente*, as you know, so tell the white man to give it to us."

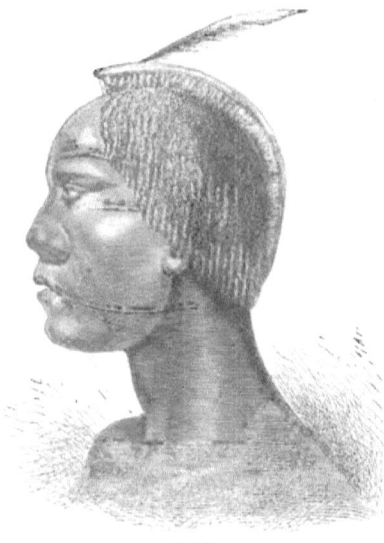

CASSOMA.

Dumbo, who seemed much under the influence of his evil-minded friend, repeated Cassoma's words to the professor.

"Dumbo," said Professor Moreton, sternly, "you have treated us badly. You are the first chief who has let us come into his village and sent us to bed hungry. We gave you three bottles of *aguardiente*, but you sent us no food. Had you done so, I would have given you more liquor; but now you shall not have another drop."

Dumbo was embarrassed by this reply, and endeavored to explain his conduct; but Cassoma cut him short, and pointing to a cask of *aguardiente* standing in a corner of the room, exclaimed,—

"White men, we are many in this village, and you are few. We intend to have what we want, and if you do not give it to us we shall help ourselves."

"You will do so at your peril," said Ashton, coldly, looking him full in the face. "We are not afraid of you, and you will get no liquor here."

Cassoma regarded the young man in silence for a moment. Then, breaking into an insulting laugh, he cried,—

"We are men. You are a boy. If you make me angry I will feed my dogs with you."

Scarcely had Charlie translated this speech, when Ashton was on his feet, with his revolver in his hand. Cocking the pistol, he kicked the cask of *aguardiente* towards the chiefs, and said, sternly,—

"There is the cask. Let me see who will take the first drink."

The negroes hesitated a moment; but Cassoma, springing to his feet, cried to Dumbo,—

"You are king here. You have the right to the first drink. Take it."

Still Dumbo hesitated; but at a word from his friend he rose, threw off his outer robe, and tossed it to Cassoma, saying, with a laugh,—

"Take care the white men do not steal it."

Then, with a hasty glance at Ashton, he moved towards the cask. In an instant the young man raised his revolver to a level with the chief's head and

THE URIVI, OR TRAP FOR SMALL GAME.

fired; but Charlie, who had started to his feet, struck up the outstretched arm, and the ball went crashing into the wall of the hut. With a stern command to Charlie to stand back, Ashton cocked his revolver again, and stood waiting, while his companions, following his example, placed themselves at his side. There was no occasion for a second shot, however. The three negroes retreated to the opposite side of the hut, and stood trembling with fear, while the women set up a chorus of shrill screams. At the same moment there was a burst of laughter from the doorway, and the whites, glancing around, saw Mombée and several of their armed negroes standing at the entrance with cocked guns, enjoying the scene. The faithful fellows had seen the chiefs enter the hut, and, apprehending danger, had come to their employers' assistance.

Charlie now advanced towards the baffled negroes, and speaking to them in a low tone, advised them to leave the hut at once. He told them the white men were terrible in their anger, and that they had better go away without saying another word, as he might not be able to save their lives a second time. The blacks at once took his advice, and filed out of the cabin in deep silence. When they had gone, Charlie turned to Ashton, and said, with a smile,—

"You brave man, Master Ashton, but you too quick. You kill Dumbo, his people kill us."

"That is true, Charlie," said Professor Moreton. "You have done us a great service. In saving the chief's life you have saved all of us from massacre. Dumbo's people would surely have avenged his death."

"Oh, yes," replied Charlie; "they bound to do that. They too many for us. They scared now, though. We safe to-night."

"That may be," said the professor; "but we must be prepared for them, at all events."

"Now look here, professor," said Ashton. "I've gotten you into this scrape, and I'll get you out of it. You are not well enough yet to worry about these matters. I insist upon your lying down and getting some sleep. The rest of us will keep watch; and if anything happens during the night you shall be called in time to give us the benefit of your counsel."

GANGUELLA, LUIMBA, AND LOENZ WOMEN.

The other young men joined their entreaties to Ashton's, and the professor, who was still quite feeble, consented to lie down.

"I say, Ashton," said Houston, when the professor's heavy breathing announced that he had fallen asleep, "I don't think you were so rash, after all. It might have been bad for us if you had killed that nigger, but it never would have done to let them take the *aguardiente*. They would have been drunk and furious very soon, and there is no saying what trouble they might have given us. As it is, you have kept them sober, and I think they are all pretty badly scared."

A careful watch was kept during the night, and several times Charlie was sent out to ascertain the state of affairs. He reported that all was quiet, and that their own people were asleep. Ashton was not blind to the danger which surrounded his party. They were in a fortified village, the inhabitants of which outnumbered them ten to one; and in case of trouble the natives would certainly receive aid from their people in the neighboring villages. He resolved, therefore, to leave the inhospitable place at the earliest moment in the morning. Towards midnight a heavy tempest, with violent lightning and thunder, broke over the village, and lasted until daybreak. Charlie assured Ashton that this was much in their favor, as the negroes were not apt to attempt anything against them in such unpropitious weather.

Breakfast was served for the party at a little after daybreak on the morning of the 23d, and this over, Ashton sent word to Dumbo that he would like to see him as soon as possible. The chief came at once, looking very meek, and apologized humbly for the occurrence of the previous night. He threw the whole blame on Cassoma, who, he said, was a bad man, and had led him to do wrong. He added that he had sent him away from the village. Ashton received the chief's excuses coldly, and told him that his party intended to leave the village at once. He warned him that while the white men and their followers desired to be on good terms with the people of their village, they would sternly punish any effort made to molest them. Dumbo humbly declared that the whites had nothing to apprehend from himself or his people, who would thenceforth be their good friends.

AFRICAN WOMEN POUNDING MAIZE.

Dumbo was left at eight o'clock, and that night, although in the neighborhood of another large village of the Sambo, the chief of which urged them to accept his hospitality, our travellers resolved to camp in the open country, rather than enter the village. After the camp was pitched a number of negro girls made their appearance, offering Indian corn and corn-meal for sale, supplies which were promptly purchased. On the 25th the Cubango River was crossed on a well-constructed bridge, and the expedition encamped for the night on the left bank of the stream, near the village of Chindonga, in the vicinity of which they noticed some valuable iron mines from which they were told the natives obtain a considerable quantity of ore. The Cubango forms the boundary between the territories of the Sambo and the Moma tribes, the latter of which are a branch of the Ganguella race. On the 27th the Cutato, a tributary of the Cubango, was crossed, and on the banks of this stream the travellers noticed thousands of small hillocks, rising often to a height of from thirteen to fifteen feet, and lying so closely together that they resembled a miniature range of mountains. These they found to be nothing more than gigantic ant-hills. Some of these were cultivated by the Ganguellas, and others were covered with trees and vegetation. On the left bank of the Cutato our travellers were surprised to see large and carefully cultivated fields of maize, beans, and potatoes. These, they learned, belonged to the people of Moma, the principal village of that part of the country. On the 29th they

BRIDGE OVER THE RIVER CUBANGO.

reached the village of Camenha, the son of the captain of the Quingue, where they were hospitably received.

Camenha had but recently returned from a successful war with one of the neighboring tribes, and was in an excellent humor. He readily provided the party with food, and urged them to stay several days with him. This they consented to do, as the professor saw at a glance that the Caquingue people were much superior to the tribes they had been travelling among, and he was anxious to study their customs. They had no reason to repent their decision, for Camenha proved a courteous and attentive host, and readily supplied them with food in return for cloth.

The Caquingue country is bounded on the north by the Bihé, on the east and south by other tribes of the Ganguella race, and on the west by the Moma territory. The Ganguellas of the Caquingue country are commonly known as the Gonzellos. They constitute a single kingdom, under one monarch, to whom each of their chiefs, or captains, owe direct allegiance. They cultivate the soil, engage in trade with neighboring and even distant nations, and are good workers in iron. They make all the iron weapons and implements needed for their own use, and also sell large numbers to the tribes with which they trade. They have many fine traits of character, but are very superstitious, believing thoroughly in sorcery and having no conception of a supreme being by whom all things are governed.

A recent writer thus speaks of some of their customs: "During the coldest months, that is to say June and July, the Gonzellos miners leave their homes,

ANT-HILLS ON THE BANKS OF THE RIVER CUTATO OF THE GANGUELLAS.

and take up their abode in extensive encampments near the iron mines, which are abundant in the country. In order to extract the ore, they dig circular holes or shafts of about ten to thirteen feet in diameter, but not more than six or seven feet deep. . . .

"As soon as they have extracted sufficient ore for the work of the year, they begin separating the iron. This is done in holes of no great depth, the ore being mixed with charcoal, and the temperature being raised by means of primitive bellows, consisting of two wooden cylinders about a foot in diameter,

10

hollowed out to a depth of four inches, and covered with two tanned goat-skins, to which are fixed two handles, twenty inches long and half an inch thick. By a rapid movement of these handles a current of air is produced, which plays upon the charcoal through two hollow wooden tubes attached to the cylinders, and furnished with clay muzzles.

CIQUINGUE BLACKSMITHS' TOOLS.
1. Bellows. 2. Clay muzzle. 3. Anvil. 4. Hammer.

"By incessant labor, kept up night and day, the whole of the metal becomes transformed by ordinary processes into spades, axes, war-hatchets, arrow-heads, assegais, nails, knives, and bullets for fire-arms, and even occasionally fire-arms themselves, the iron being tempered with ox-grease and salt. I have seen a good many of these guns carry as well as the best pieces made of cast steel.

"During the whole of the time that these labors last no woman under any pretext is allowed to go near the miners' camp, for fear, as they say, of the utter ruin of the metal.

"So soon as the metal is converted into articles of trade, the miners return to their homes laden with their manufactures, which they subsequently dispose of by sale, after reserving what they require for their own necessities.

"It is curious that none of these people admit the existence of natural causes of disease or death. If any among them should fall ill or die, the cause is attributed either to the souls of the other world (one among the spirits being specially designated), or to some living person who has compassed the evil by sorcery or witchcraft. On the death of a native, should no relatives be upon the spot, they are at once summoned, and, pending their arrival, the corpse is suspended from a stout pole, planted at a distance of some two or three hundred yards from the entrance of the village.

"On the assembling of the relatives, divination is at once resorted to in order to learn the cause of death. For this purpose the corpse is fastened to a long stake; a man seizes each end of it, and the body is thus conveyed to the place set apart for the divination, where the diviner is in attendance, together with a concourse of people standing in two rows.

"The diviner then taking in his right hand a piece of white coral, commences operations.

"After no end of mummery and discordant cries, during which the corpse is made to sway about,—the people all the while believing it does so without human intervention,—the diviner declares that it was the soul of such a person, male or female, whom he mentions, that occasioned the death; or he avers that it was this or that *living* person who slew the defunct by sorcery. In the former case, a grave being dug in the neighbouring wood, no spot in particular being selected for the purpose, the body is interred without more ado, and stones, wood, and earth are heaped over it; but in the latter case the person designated by the diviner as the sorcerer is seized, and must either pay to the nearest of kin the value of the life he is deemed to have taken or forfeit his head, an account of the event being subsequently given to the ruling chief, together with a female goat as a fee for listening to the case.

"An accused person has fortunately the right to deny his supposed crime, and to furnish a defence. He applies for such purpose to a medicine-man (by

CAQUINGUE BLACKSMITHS.

way of advocate), who, in presence of the people, proceeds to prepare his proofs, in the shape of an ordeal, to establish either the guilt or innocence of the accused. For instance, in sight of the latter's kinsfolk and of the general public, he composes a poisonous draught, to be taken both by the accused and the nearest relative of the dead man. This draught produces a species of temporary madness, and he who suffers most from its effects is deemed the more guilty, and has sentence of death passed upon him.

"If this sentence fall upon the accused, he either pays the life of the deceased or forfeits his own; if it fall upon the other man, he has to indemnify the accused for the accusation made by giving him at once a pig, to pay for the trouble in seeking a medicine-man, and subsequently, whatever else the accused may claim, namely, a couple of oxen, two slaves, or a bale of goods.

"The medicine-man is defined by the name bestowed upon him. He pre pares medicaments. He has some knowledge of medicinal herbs and roots which he invariably employs empirically, and makes great use of the cupping glass; but as regards science, he has little or none. The medicine-man never makes a diagnosis of any disease, but deals freely in prognostics. His doses of medicinal plants are always empirical, and the most absurd and useless components enter into his pharmacopœia. It is true that among ourselves the use of antidotes does not go very far. The medicine-man, who is at the same time a compounder of drugs, employs during their preparation a certain number of ceremonies and words without which they would lose their virtue. He makes a great secret of the plants and simples he uses, and puts on a very sapient air when questioned upon the subject. The medicine-man is a person of great importance, and many solemn acts require his presence. He decides many great questions, his opinion prevailing over that of the diviner, and he

ANT-HILL THIRTEEN FEET HIGH, COVERED WITH VEGETATION, ON THE BANKS OF THE RIVER COTATO.

never pronounces it without a preliminary flourish, in the shape of remedies and ceremonies, performed now with plants, now with the blood of human creatures, or beasts, and on which are bestowed the name of *medicinal rites*.

"The diviner, on the other hand, deals in divination and nothing else. In the case of any one falling sick, the diviner is first called in to divine whether the attack is due to spirits of another world, or to sorcery, and it is after his work is done that the medicine-man is applied to.

"These two personages always perfectly understand each other.

"The diviner is not consulted solely in cases of disease or death, he is appealed to in all conceivable matters of moment, and nothing is done without his being first called in.

"In questions of consultation, he takes up his stand in the centre of a circle formed by the people, who must be seated. He brings with him a calabash and a basket. The calabash contains large glass beads and dried maize; the basket is full of the queerest odds and ends, such as human bones, dried vegetables, stones, bits of stick, the stones of fruit, birds' and fishes' bones, etc.

"He begins by shaking the calabash about in the most frantic way, and during the rattle consequent on the operation he invokes the *malignant spirits*; the basket is then shaken up, and in the articles that appear uppermost he reads what his hearers are desirous of learning of the past, present, or future."

On the 1st of February, Professor Moreton being very much better, the party resumed their journey. Five days of steady marching carried them into the Bihé country, and on the 6th the expedition arrived at Belmonte, the village belonging to the old Benguela trader, Silva Porto. They were courteously welcomed by the agent of the trader, to whom the professor at once delivered the letters he had brought from Silva Porto. These directed the agent to place the whole establishment at the disposal of the travellers, and to render them every assistance in his power. The professor and his companions were accordingly lodged in Silva Porto's own house, and the blacks were made comfortable in some of the out-buildings.

CHAPTER VIII.

FROM THE BIHÉ TO THE ZAMBEZI.

ONE of the first acts of Professor Moreton after reaching Belmonte was to pay and discharge the negro carriers who had come with the party from Benguela. As they had all been faithful in the main, each man received, in addition to his stipulated wages, a handsome present, consisting of cloth, beads, and other articles which represented current money in the regions they had to

VIEW OF THE EXTERIOR OF THE VILLAGE OF BELMONTE IN THE BIHÉ.

traverse on their return to their homes. The professor also issued ten days' rations to them, to supply them with food on the first part of their homeward journey.

On the morning of the 8th of February the carriers set out on their return to the coast, loud in their praises of the generosity of their white employers. Five of the black gun-bearers, however, remained with the expedition. They had become much attached to the professor and the young men, and had declared their intention to remain with them until the end of the journey. The professor and his companions were well pleased with this arrangement. Although quartered in Silva Porto's village, and nominally under his protection, they were still in the midst of a country unknown to them, and peopled by savages who were famous for their treachery and dishonesty. They knew they could depend upon the negroes who had decided to remain with them, for their fidelity had been proven at every stage of the march from the coast. Their presence would be an additional guarantee of the safety of the whole party, since it would enable the professor, as leader of the expedition, to reckon upon the aid of eleven armed men in case of danger. Charlie and Mombée

SILVA PORTO'S HOUSE AT BELMONTE.

were much pleased with the arrangement, and the former told the professor that he could rely implicitly upon the faithfulness of the blacks.

"You trust them, Master 'Fessor," he said; "they no fool you. Me know niggers well. These men lub all the white gentlemen, and when time comes will fight well."

When the carriers started for the coast the professor allowed the five armed negroes who wished to return to Benguela to retain their guns, and distributed five more muskets to as many men, who were recommended by the negro who was to lead them back to the coast. He also entrusted to the leader letters to Silva Porto, the governor of Benguela, and Antonio Ferreira. He urged the old trader to hasten forward the goods left in his hands, if he had not already done so, and enclosed to him letters from himself and his young companions to their friends at home, which he requested Silva Porto to forward by the mail steamer from Benguela.

When the carriers had set out he called the young men about him.

"Boys," he began, "we have now accomplished the first stage of our journey in safety. We have reached the Bihé, and are in good quarters. We have gotten through the easiest and safest part of our journey, hard as it has been. What lies beyond us I know not. One thing is certain, however, we must remain here until the goods we have entrusted to Silva Porto arrive. We cannot go on without them. I think we had better make up our minds to stay here a considerable time. That Silva Porto will keep his promise to us I do not doubt; but it may be weeks and even months before his men reach us. In the mean time we must do our best, maintain the strictest discipline among ourselves and our negro followers, and try to cultivate friendly relations with the people around us. Should we come to the worst, we must try to make our way back to Benguela."

"That we will never do, professor," said Ashton. ".We have set out to cross Africa, and we intend to do so."

"By all means," said the professor, "if we can. But we must still keep open the way for a safe retreat, should such a step become necessary. As we shall certainly make a lengthy stay here, we shall have ample time to decide upon our movements after leaving this place."

The sojourn of our travellers at Belmonte was much longer than they had anticipated, and lasted until the latter part of April. During this enforced delay Professor Moreton recovered his health, and by strict attention to diet and avoidance of exposure the remainder of the party continued well. They had an abundant store of sulphate of quinine with them, and found among Silva Porto's stores a considerable quantity of good coffee, which Ashton purchased from the old trader's agent, giving his draft upon his bankers in London, as had been arranged between himself and Silva Porto at Benguela. Whatever supplies were needed during their stay at Belmonte were purchased in this way. Silva Porto's agent, who was a mulatto and a man of great intelligence, showed the strangers great attention, and managed on the whole to make their stay very comfortable.

The sojourn of our travellers at Belmonte was not passed in idleness. The professor and Philip Lee busied themselves in making scientific observations, and in writing up the journal of the expedition. Ashton and Hubbard took charge of the negroes, and looked after the general management and discipline of the quarters, and Houston was kept constantly occupied in providing the table with game, which was abundant in the neighboring country. In all such expeditions, Charlie was his constant companion, and sometimes one or more of the armed negroes accompanied them. Each evening the professor and his companions assembled, and all gave an account of their doings during the day, which was duly reduced to writing by Professor Moreton or Philip Lee.

The village of Belmonte had been established some years before by Silva Porto as a depôt for his traffic with the tribes of the interior; and as in former times the old trader had often made it his residence, he had chosen the site with a view to its healthfulness as well as its defence. It stood upon the

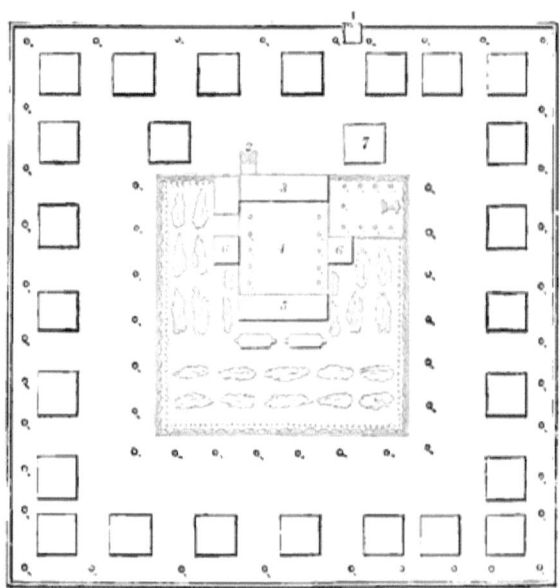

PLAN OF THE VILLAGE OF BELMONTE IN THE BIHÉ.

α Sycamores.   ▬▬ Strong wooden stockade.   ▭▭▭ Garden palisade covered with ever-blooming rose-trees.   ↟↟↟ Pomegranates.   ⬭ Orange-trees. ⬭ Gardens.   ⬬ Cemetery.   ☐ Negroes' houses.

1. Entrance of the village. 2. Entrance into Silva Porto's house. 3. House. 4. Interior pateo or court-yard. 5. Kitchen and store-room. 6. Servants' houses. 7. Warehouse.

highest portion of a rising ground, the northern declivity of which sloped gently down to the bed of the river Cuito, which flows eastward into the Cuqueima. It was enclosed by a strong stockade, which was still further strengthened by a row of enormous sycamore-trees, which extended entirely around the settlement. The space thus enclosed comprised considerable ground, and contained, besides the buildings of the village, an orange orchard, which was in full bearing at the time of our travellers' visit, and excellent gardens.

WOMAN OF THE BIHÉ, DIGGING.

The buildings were neatly and substantially constructed. They consisted of a large central building with a thatched roof, which comprised the dwelling-house of the old trader and his private store-house. This was surrounded on three sides by a grove of orange-trees, and in front of it stood the principal warehouse of the settlement and the dwelling of the agent in charge. Rows of huts, neatly constructed and well thatched, were built around the four sides of the enclosure, immediately within the stockade. The whole settlement had an air of neatness and prosperity in marked contrast with the native villages through which our travellers had passed. The view from the village across the open country was very fine, and the situation being high was both dry and healthy.

The Bihé, so called from the founder of the reigning dynasty of the country, comprises that portion of South Central Africa bounded on the north by the country of the Andulos, on the northwest by the Bailundo, on the west by the Moma country, on the southwest by the Gonzellos of Caquingue, and on the south and east by the free Ganguella tribes. The country, though small in extent, is thickly populated for Africa, containing in an area of about two thousand five hundred square miles between ninety thousand and one hundred thousand inhabitants.

The government is an absolute monarchy. Five generations ago the country was covered with a dense jungle abounding in elephants, and containing a few scattered hamlets of the Ganguella race. At this time the Sova or king of the Gamba country, which lies north of the Bihé, was named Bomba. He had a beautiful daughter, named Cahanda, who was his pride and delight. When she came to womanhood, the princess obtained her father's permission to visit certain relatives in the village of Ugundo, the only place of importance in the Bihé region at that time. While there she met a famous elephant hunter named Bihé, the son of the Sova of the Humbe, who was hunting in that region with a numerous suite. The young people at once fell in love with each other, and the princess soon became the elephant hunter's wife. Bihé thereupon founded the town of Cobongo, which still remains the capital of the country, proclaimed himself king of the region, to which he gave his name, and by degrees established his authority over the scattered Ganguella tribes. King Bomba soon after became reconciled to the marriage of his daughter, and allowed a considerable emigration of his people to the new state. Many of the huntsmen who had come into the country with Bihé married Humbe women, and their descendants now constitute the nobility or wealthier class of the country. The lower classes are the issue of the marriages of several races.

The Bihenos are very little given to agriculture or manual labor of any kind. All the work is done by the women, the men confining their exertions to hunting and travelling. The men are natural traders, and do not hesitate to make long journeys in any direction, wax, ivory, and slaves being their principal articles of traffic, though they have no objection to dealing in any kind of wares that promise a fair profit. Their roving disposition is their chief characteristic. Benguela is the principal outlet for their wares, with the exception of slaves. Their caravans penetrate into the interior with goods purchased at Benguela, collect ivory, wax, and other articles of trade, and return with them to the Bihé, from which they are despatched to the coast by caravans of Biheno carriers. Many of the principal merchants are natives

BIHENO CARRIER ON THE MARCH.

of the country. While our travellers were at Belmonte one of these, Chaquingunde by name, who had formerly been a slave of Silva Porto, arrived from the interior, where he had traded to the amount of over seventeen thousand dollars. So accustomed are the Bihenos to take long journeys from their homes that they regard them as a matter of course. "If they only had the power of telling where they had been and describing what they had seen, the geographers of Europe would not have occasion to leave blank great parts of the map of South Central Africa. These people have a certain emulation among one another as travellers, the most experienced priding themselves on having gone where no others had ever been, and which they call *discovering new lands*. They are brought up to wandering from their very infancy, and all caravans carry innumerable children, who, with loads proportionate to their strength, accompany their parents or relatives on the longest journeys; hence, it is no uncommon thing to find a young fellow of five-and-twenty who has travelled in the Matianvo, Niangué, Luapula, Zambezi, and Mucusso districts, having commenced his peregrinations at the age of nine years."

The Bihenos have no religious faith of any kind, adore no gods or idols, but are grossly addicted to sorcery. They have, however, a belief that the soul exists after death in a sort of purgatory "until such time as the survivors are enabled to fulfil certain precepts or perform certain acts of vengeance on behalf of the dead."

The government of the Bihé, as has been said, is an absolute monarchy, and the customs of the country are strongly feudal in their character. The Sova or king is surrounded by a certain number of *saculos* or nobles, who constitute a sort of council, to which the king always submits his resolutions. Their approval follows, as a matter of course, but the sovereign is free to act

Simple Palisade.   Palisade bound together with Withes.   Palisade with forked Uprights.
PALISADES USED FOR THE DEFENCE OF AFRICAN VILLAGES.

without it, or to disregard it. The members of the council are styled *macotas*, and many of them possess *libatas*, or fortified villages, in which they assume the airs of sovereigns, requiring their people to address them as *Ná cóco*, or "Your majesty."

"In addition to the macotas, there are three negroes who are in attendance on the Sova, and who, when he gives audience, squat upon the ground near him, and carefully gather up the royal spittle, to cast it out of doors. There is another, who carries the royal seat or chair, and there is the fool, an indispensable adjunct of the court of every Sova and even of opulent and powerful seculos. To the fool is assigned the duty of cleaning the door of the Sova's house, and the space all around it."

From Silva Porto's agent our travellers learned much that was curious concerning the customs of the country. The ceremonies attending the death of a king and the proclamation of his successor struck them as very remarkable.

"The decease of the Sova is of course known to the macotas, who keep the matter a profound secret. They give out to the people that their king is ill, and therefore does not appear. Meanwhile they lay out the corpse on the bed within the hut and cover it with a cloth—at least, this is the custom in Caquingue, but in the Bihé country they hang it up by the neck to the roof

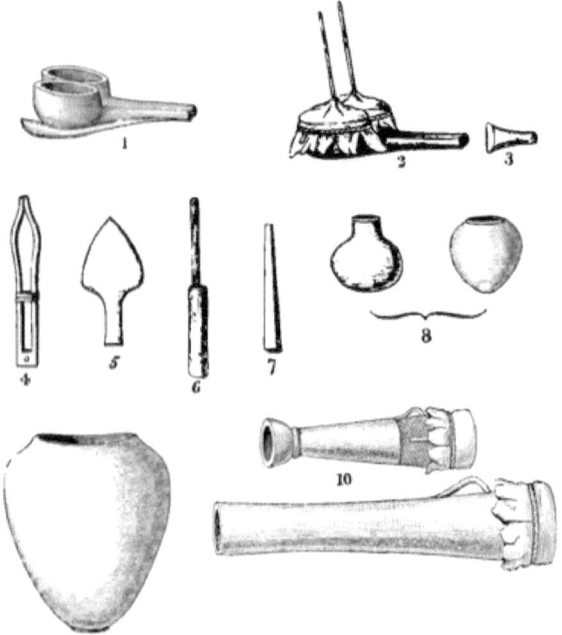

ARTICLES MANUFACTURED BY THE BIHENOS.

1. Bellows. 2. Bellows ready mounted. 3. Earthenware muzzle. 4. Pincers. 5. Large hammer. 6. A fragment of a musket with a wooden handle used by the smith to remove small pieces from the furnace. 7. Small hammer. 8. Kitchen pots. 9. Large pipkin for capata. 10. Drums.

of the hut. The body so remains until putrefaction and insects have left the bones bare; or until, as in the Bihé, the head drops from the body. It is when this occurs that they announce his death and proceed to the interment of his remains. The bones are placed within an ox-hide and deposited in a hut which exists within the *lombe*, and serves as the mausoleum of all the Sovas. The hut in which the corpse putrefied is demolished, and the material of which it is composed is carried out of the enclosure and scattered about the jungle.

"It is scarcely necessary to say that the death of a Sova is always produced by sorcery or witchcraft, and that some unfortunate has to pay with his life, not for the sorcery, which he never committed, but the private vengeance of one of the macotas. No sooner is the death of the Sova announced than the people rush madly about, and for some days not only strip and pilfer all persons who are met with in the neighborhood of the capital, but make captives of the strangers themselves, and subsequently dispose of them for slaves.

"The macotas then seek out the rightful heir and accompany him to the *libata grande* or capital; on his arrival, however, he does not at first penetrate the *lombe* or inner enclosure, but takes up his residence among the people, living for a time as one of them. No sooner, however, has the heir-apparent entered the libata than two bands of huntsmen issue forth, one in search of an antelope and the other of a human victim.

"An antelope being started, a member of the former of the two bands fires at the animal and at once takes to flight, his companions rushing forward to cut off the creature's head; for should this be done by the huntsman who shot it down, he would be at once assassinated, and none might say by whose hand.

"The other troop, in pursuit of human game, seize the first poor wretch (man or woman) who falls in their way, and hurrying the victim off to the jungle, cut off the head, which they bring back with great care, abandoning the body where it fell. On arriving at the libata they wait for the troop on the hunt for the antelope, as it is always much easier to find and kill a man than to find and kill any particular animal.

"Having put the two heads into one basket, the medicine-man appears and begins to perform the proper *remedies* to enable the new Sova to assume the reins of government; and his tomfoolery being at an end, he declares that the sovereign may enter the lombe. Attended by the macotas, the Sova enters accordingly, in the midst of loud acclamations and a great expenditure of gunpowder.

"The first step taken by the Sova on attaining to power is to select from among his women the one he chooses to make his wife, who is styled *inaculo;* the others still continue to reside in the lombe, but not within the precincts of the royal residence."

Polygamy, however, is one of the most firmly established institutions of the Bihé.

The Bihenos, like all the natives of this part of Africa, are greatly addicted to drunkenness. Their favorite liquors are *aguardiente, capata* (which is also called *quimbombo* or *chimbombo*), *quiassa,* and *quissangna*. *Capata* is a species of beer made from Indian corn, and is not very intoxicating. Quiassa is made by adding honey to *capata*. This produces considerable alcoholic fermentation, and in the course of a few days the *capata* is converted into almost pure alcohol, and is very intoxicating. *Quissangua* is made from the root of an herbaceous plant, called by the natives *imbuadi*. It ferments rapidly, and is intoxicating.

The food of the Bihenos is almost entirely vegetable. They possess but few cattle, and rarely eat meat; when they do, it is generally the flesh of a

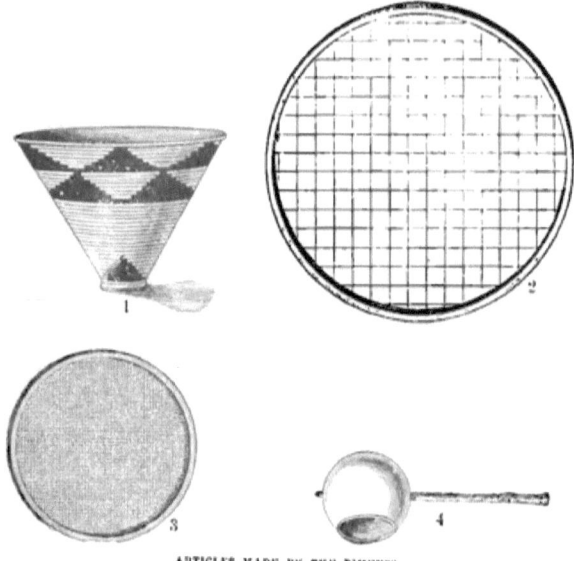

ARTICLES MADE BY THE BIHENOS.

1. Quinda, or straw basket which will hold water. 2. Large sieve for drying rice or maize flour. 3. Sifting sieve. 4. Ladle for watering the capata.

pig. They are fond of meat, however, and will readily eat it when offered to them, preferring it in a state of putrefaction. They fatten dogs for food, and eat the flesh of lions, jackals, hyenas, crocodiles, and all flesh-eating animals. Though not positively cannibals, they sometimes devour human flesh. The Sovas frequently hold a grand festival at the capital, called the "feast of the quissunge," at which are immolated and devoured five persons, namely, one man and four women. The victims are beheaded, their heads cast into the jungle, and their bodies carried into the enclosure of the royal residence, where they are quartered. An ox is then killed, and its flesh is cooked with the human flesh, partly by roasting and partly by boiling in *capata*, so that everything which appears at the banquet is mixed with human blood. When this disgusting meal is ready the king causes it to be proclaimed throughout the capital that he is about to begin the *quissunge*, and the inhabitants flock in crowds to the entertainment.

The Bihenos are also passionately fond of white ants. They destroy their habitations and eat them raw by the handful.

As carriers, and when engaged on a journey, the Bihenos are scrupulously honest and faithful to their duties. At home they are thorough thieves, and steal everything that comes in their way. They have a singular custom by which all crimes save that of murder are tried before the person offended, who thus becomes both prosecutor and judge. Offences are generally punished by the imposition of a fine. Should the convicted criminal refuse to submit to an adverse decision, an appeal is had to the king, whose decision is final. Should the accused submit, however, the sentence is not only imposed, but is carried out by the injured party.

"The word which strikes most terror in the Bihé is *mucano*, a word which does not merely express a crime committed, but an idea that expresses both the crime and the payment of a fine. When a wealthy person upon whom a *mucano* is pending refuses to pay, the party injured, if he be powerful, makes a seizure of some of the other's property for a far higher value than the amount of the fine, and the property so seized remains in deposit, to be subsequently sold or appropriated by the person effecting the seizure. Should, however, a seizure be held unjust, the party committing it is compelled by the Sova to make restitution, and give a pig by way of solace to the party prejudiced. This system offers a premium to extortion, and not a day passes without the most stupendous *mucanos* being put forward. If a man under the charge of a *mucano* should die, the unfortunate wretch who heedlessly takes up his quarters in the dead man's house becomes responsible for the former tenant. The mode in which justice, so called, is administered in the Bihé is an enormous obstacle to trade, and the source of most serious losses to the Benguela houses."

A BIHÉ HEAD-DRESS.

Such are some of the customs of the Bihenos, as revealed to our travellers partly by observation and partly by the accounts given by Silva Porto's agents and native traders with whom they met while at Belmonte.

The months of February and March passed slowly away, and yet no news came from Silva Porto. By the 1st of April the weather was excellent and the country in good condition for travelling. The anxiety of the professor increased daily, and many were the consultations he held with his young companions as to the course they should pursue if their goods failed to reach them. The agent of Silva Porto was firm in his confidence that their property would reach them in good time. His employer had promised it, and they could rely upon his word. They must remember that in Africa a few months was but a short time; and since they were in comfortable quarters, what mattered a few weeks more or less of delay? This argument had but little comfort in it for the impatient travellers, and it must be confessed that, as April advanced and their goods did not arrive, their faith in the old trader's promise began to grow weak. Their supplies were also running low, as were those of Silva Porto's people, and a very much longer delay would find them without the means of purchasing food from the natives. The country around Belmonte abounded in partridges, but of large game there was none. Houston and Ashton were engaged for several hours every day in shooting partridges and wood-pigeons on the banks of the Cuito; but as their stock of powder was getting low, they were obliged to confine their efforts to killing such game as was absolutely necessary for the wants of the party.

One source of constant anxiety to the professor was the dread that some of the negroes would get into trouble with the natives, and thus bring upon them a claim for a *mucano*, which in their impoverished condition they would not be able to pay. He was firmly resolved not to submit to extortion in any claim of the natives, but was aware that resistance to even the most unfounded claim for damages would involve the party in serious trouble with the Bihenos. Situated as they were, with scanty supplies of stores, food, and ammunition, they were in no condition either to pay a *mucano* or to successfully resist it. Silva Porto's agent told the professor that he was very much surprised that no such claim had been made by the natives, as it was their custom to fleece every stranger arriving in their territory. Even Silva Porto himself had been compelled at times to pay heavy damages for preposterous claims.

"It may be," said the agent, "that they think you too well armed to be trifled with."

"Suppose a *mucano* was laid upon us, and we refused to pay it," asked Ashton, "what would they do? Would they attack us?"

"They might do so," replied the agent; "but it is more likely they would seek to give you trouble after you leave this place; or, they might think you too well armed to be molested. In that case they will wait, perhaps it may be for years, until the next white man comes along, and if he is not strong enough to resist, will compel him to pay your *mucano*."

"That's a queer idea of justice," said Houston; "but if we are troubled with a *mucano*, I think we shall let the next white visitor here pay it."

During their stay at Belmonte our travellers were visited by many of the natives, and managed to preserve friendly relations with all. As they kept their property well housed, and under strict guard, they suffered no loss from thieves.

One morning towards the last of April a number of Bihenos came into Belmonte in company with a medicine-man, who wished to sell to the whites a liquid which he assured them was "a great medicine." He declared that whoever drank it would be rendered impenetrable to bullets. He produced a small pipkin of earthenware, which held about a pint of a dark-colored liquor, and exhibited it to the whites.

"Have you ever tried it yourself?" asked Ashton.

Charlie translated the question, and the medicine-man answered that he certainly had done so, and was in consequence proof against all kinds of firearms.

"Tell him," said Houston, "that I will give him four yards of white cloth if he will let me fire at him with this rifle."

When these words were translated to the medicine-man, he glanced nervously at Houston and then at the rifle, and drew back quickly a few paces. Immediately the people who had come with him burst into a roar of laughter. This nettled the man; and he came forward again, and holding up the pipkin declared that so far from Houston being able to put a ball through him, he could not even strike the vessel containing the liquor.

"Tell him," said Houston to Charlie, "that if he will put up his jug as a target I'll put a ball through it at once."

The fellow hesitated, then burst into a laugh, and answered that it would be useless for the white man to attempt such a feat, as the best shots among the Bihenos had repeatedly struck the vessel without doing it any injury. Nevertheless Houston insisted that the medicine-man should prove his sincerity by allowing him to fire at it, and agreed to give him a bottle of *aguardiente* if he failed. The Bihenos who had come with the medicine-man also demanded that the trial should be made, and the man was forced to set up the vessel as a target. He took care to place it at a distance of about eighty paces, thinking, no doubt, that the young American would find it impossible to hit so small an object at so great a distance; and then, smiling calmly, stood by to watch the result. The Bihenos leaned forward in eager silence, with their eyes fixed upon Houston.

"You must hit it, old fellow," said Ashton to his companion. "Aim carefully. To fail in this would lose us our credit with the negroes."

"It is not difficult," replied Houston, quietly. "I think the loss of credit will be on the part of that impudent juggler. He'll not find it so easy to humbug the natives after this."

Houston stepped forward amid a profound silence, took deliberate aim at the vessel, and fired. The pipkin flew into a dozen pieces, and the magic liquor flowed over the stump of the tree. The Bihenos greeted the successful shot with a perfect storm of applause, while the discomfited medicine-man gave one anxious look at Houston and then ran out of the village as fast as his legs could carry him, followed by the laughter of his countrymen.

"He scared bad, Master Hoosey," said Charlie, laughing. "He 'fraid you shoot him next. No like to stay too close to that gun."

May day came, bright and smiling, and with it the end of our travellers' suspense and anxiety. The first detachment of the caravan despatched from the coast by Silva Porto arrived at Belmonte, bringing with them a considerable quantity of goods on the trader's account, and a portion of the property belonging to the travellers. The remainder arrived by the 5th, and the promise of the old trader was at last fulfilled. Upon examining the packages turned over to them by Silva Porto's agent, they found that the trader had not remained content with merely keeping his promise to forward their goods; he had sent them, as a present from himself, ten excellent guns, with a liberal supply of ammunition, and a quantity of articles of prepared food for use on their journey. He also wrote to the professor, offering to be of still further assistance if his aid should be needed.

As soon as the first load of goods was received, and he was assured that the rest were close at hand, the professor set about engaging carriers for the journey beyond the Bihé. He needed one hundred and fifty men, and in order to secure them he applied to several pombeiros, or contractors, as we should call them. Five of these men engaged to furnish him with thirty carriers each, to accompany him as far as the Zambezi, and to have their men in readiness by the 20th of May.

The Biheno carriers form themselves into parties, under the command of one among them who becomes their chief; this chief is called the pombeiro. He manages the negotiations for the services of his men, and is responsible for their good conduct. "He eats and sleeps with them, and in fact may be looked upon as their captain. The pombeiro carries no load, but in the event of the sickness or death of one of his men he takes his place as temporary carrier. During the march his place is at the tail of the train, and if a carrier lags behind he is there to look after or assist him. The men are never paid in advance, and in regular trading journeys their recompense is very small. The pombeiros never undertake a venture for any determinate time, and their gains are the same for the shorter as well as the longer period. They are employed, in fact, by the job, for it is well known that in Africa the negroes make no account of time."

When the goods were all safely in hand the professor and his companions set to work to arrange them into loads for the carriers, and made a list of the contents of each package, so as to be able to lay their hands at once upon any desired article. Among the articles received were three mackintosh or india-rubber boats, which would be of great service to them in crossing the large and deep rivers which lay in their path eastward. When not in use each of these boats, which had a capacity for carrying five persons, could be folded into a convenient package, which could be borne on the head of a single carrier. When needed for use the package could be unfolded, and the boat made buoyant by inflating its "skin" with air by means of a hand-bellows. Should the bellows be lost on the journey, the lungs of a strong negro would answer the same purpose.

Silva Porto's agent now urged the professor to leave Belmonte as soon as possible. He told him it was known to the natives that the party had received a large supply of goods from the coast, and that it was very certain the Bihenos would endeavor to get possession of some of them by laying a *mucano* upon him, as the head of the expedition. He urged him to impress upon his companions and upon his black followers the necessity of increased caution in their conduct, so as to give the natives no hold upon them. Our travellers had themselves been apprehensive of this, and recognized the force of the agent's reasoning. The work of preparing for their departure was, therefore, pushed forward with all speed, and by the 15th of May all was in readiness for the carriers when they should make their appearance.

As has been stated, our travellers held many councils during their stay at Belmonte for the purpose of deciding upon their route after leaving that place. The result of their deliberations was the determination to march from Belmonte direct to the Upper Zambezi, following the lofty ridge of the country in which the rivers of that part of Africa take their rise. On arriving at the Zambezi they were to follow that stream to the Zumbo, from which they would proceed eastward by Tete and Senna to Quillimane, a town and military station in the Portuguese territory of Mozambique. Should circumstances prevent this, they would seek to reach the Transvaal and the British possessions on the Indian Ocean. The main object was to reach the falls of the Zambezi. Should they succeed in that, they would then be able to decide upon the remainder of their route.

On the 19th of May three of the pombeiros arrived at Belmonte with ninety carriers. They were confident that the others would arrive with their men in time to begin the journey the next day, but the 20th passed, much to the disgust of the Americans, without any increase in the number of carriers. Two days more passed away, and the matter began to look serious. Sixty carriers were still needed, and how to obtain them was a problem. The pombeiros who had fulfilled their contract to furnish men were indignant at the failure of the others. They advised the professor to leave Belmonte at once, and establish a camp a few miles beyond the village. This, they said, would show that he had begun his journey, and might induce carriers to volunteer their services.

This advice pleased the Americans very much, and was warmly supported by Charlie, who had, from the first, declared his belief that the other pombeiros were only waiting to see if the party really intended to start. Accordingly, on the 23d of May our travellers bade farewell to Belmonte, and set out on their march. As the professor intended to halt in the Cabir woods less than a day's march from the village, he succeeded in inducing some of Silva Porto's people and a number of the natives of the vicinity of Belmonte to carry the extra loads to the place selected for the camp. It was reached early in the afternoon, and the negroes were at once set to work to construct the encampment. This was finished before night, as the labor was not very great, and the next day the camp was enclosed with a stockade as a protection against the visits of wild beasts and the intrusion of the natives. The encampment was composed of conical huts made of the trunks of small trees, each hut measuring ten feet in diameter at the base by eight feet high. In the centre of the camp were five huts of larger size for the professor and his young companions. The huts of the negro carriers were built in a circle and formed the outer line of the camp, and between each hut, and connecting them, was a stockade or stout hedge of thorny trees. Immediately behind the huts of the white men were those of Charlie, Mombée, and the five armed negroes. To guard against fire the professor had all the huts covered with green boughs instead of dry grass. This was the manner in which the encampments of the expedition were constructed throughout the journey.

On the 25th one of the pombeiros arrived at the camp, bringing with him the thirty men he had promised. He made no explanation of the cause of his delay, and, as the professor was heartily glad to secure the additional men, he was asked no questions. The four pombeiros now exerted themselves to obtain the remaining thirty men needed for the journey, and by the 28th they were successful.

On the 30th of May the camp in the Cabir woods was broken up, and the march was resumed towards the eastward. On the 31st the party halted for the night in the vicinity of the village of the famous trader, José Antonio Alves, whose character has been so graphically sketched by Lieutenant Cameron in his account of his journey across Africa. Our travellers, who were familiar with Cameron's description of the man, were rejoiced to find that Alves was away on a trading expedition; and so the next morning they pushed on again towards the Cuanza River. They were anxious to get out of the Bihé territory as soon as possible, so as to be beyond the reach of the dreaded *mucano*. A march of a few hours brought them to the village of Cassamba, near which they encamped.

The village was situated in the midst of a dense forest, which seemed to promise an abundance of game, and as soon as the huts were finished Houston and Lee started out with their guns in search of food. They succeeded in

CROSSING THE CUQUEIMA.

shooting only a few guinea-fowls, and returned to the camp about nightfall, much disappointed.

Early the next morning, June 2, the route was resumed, and for over a couple of hours lay across a marshy plain, where progress was difficult and slow. Towards noon they reached the left bank of the river Cuqueima, which at that point pursued a northerly course. It was a swift, wide, and deep stream, and the pombeiros said was infested with crocodiles. None of these were seen by the party, however.

The professor waited on the bank of the river until the entire party had come up. Then the mackintosh boats were brought out, inflated, and safely launched upon the stream. Each boat would carry five men and their loads, and the passage of the river was at once begun. Houston and Lee were sent over with the first boats, to keep the men in order and look out for the loads after they were landed on the opposite shore, the professor, Ashton, and Hubbard remaining on the Bihé side to direct the movements of the boats. The passage of the river consumed several hours, but about the middle of the afternoon the entire party were safe on the opposite side of the stream.

"Well, boys," said the professor, as the last of the mackintosh boats was folded and strapped, ready for the carriers, "we are out of the Bihé territory at last, and I breathe freer. We have passed through that region without any quarrel with the people, or suffering any *mucano*."

He had scarcely spoken when the party were startled by a loud shout from the opposite bank; and looking across the river they beheld two men standing at the water's edge, shouting and gesticulating with great earnestness. Charlie, who spoke the language of the Bihenos, was ordered to answer their hail. In reply to his demand to know their business, they shouted that they had an important message for the white men from the king of the Bihé, and asked to be taken across the river. As he translated the reply, Charlie shook his head doubtingly.

"Him no good, Master 'Fessor," said he. "We got no business with Bihé Sova now. We out his country."

"Still," replied the professor, "they may have something of importance to say to us. Shall we ferry them over, boys?"

"It can do no harm to hear what they have to say," answered Ashton. "There are but two of them, and we have nothing to fear from them."

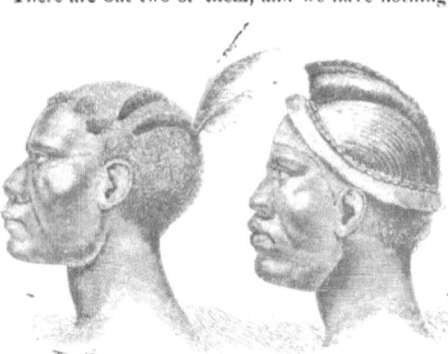

QUIMBANDE MAN AND WOMAN.

Charlie again protested that it would be better to leave them where they were, but the professor decided to bring them across. One of the mackintosh boats was again inflated and launched, and sent over the stream in charge of Ashton and Houston, who volunteered for the service, deeming it best not to trust it to any of the negroes. The men were soon brought over, and the boat was prepared again for the carriers.

The two men now came forward to where the professor and his companions were standing. One of them was a Biheno, with a villainous countenance, and the other a powerfully-made man, dressed in the Biheno costume, with a red woollen cap on his head. He was as dark-skinned as a native, but his features and beard were evidently those of a European. He was as villainous looking as his companion, and came forward with a dogged, insolent air.

"That man no nigger, Master 'Fessor," said Charlie, in a low tone. "Him Portygee. Me keep my eye on him."

"He is very likely an escaped convict from one of the Portuguese settlements, who has cast in his lot with the natives," said Ashton. "I don't like his looks either, Charlie, and I am sorry now we brought him over."

The professor fixed a searching glance upon the man, and then, addressing him in Portuguese, asked him his business. The man answered sullenly in the Bihé tongue that he did not understand Portuguese; but the professor cut him short, and told him sternly that they knew him for a European, and that he must answer in Portuguese or leave the party at once. Seeing that further deception was useless, the man then said that he was a Biheno by adoption, and had become a person of great importance in that country. His companion, he said, was a native of rank, and had been injured by some of the white men's party, who had stolen a pig from him. The matter had been laid before the Sova of the Bihenos, who had sent them to demand payment for the pig, and damages for the wrong his subject had suffered.

"And how much do you demand?" asked the professor.

"Four pieces of striped cloth and three bottles of *aguardiente*," replied the man.

"Suppose we refuse to pay?" asked the professor.

"Then," replied the man, "we will go to the village just beyond here, and order the chief, in the name of the Sova of the Bihé, to collect the *mucano*."

"We owe you nothing," said Professor Moreton, "and we will pay you nothing. We know that we are no longer in the territory of the Sova of the Bihé, and that he has no authority here. You are an impudent fellow to come to us with such a demand, and I warn you to go back to your adopted country at once. You will get nothing from us."

"Then we will go on to the next village," said the man, insolently, "and give the king's message to the chief."

"You will do nothing of the sort," said Ashton, sternly. "Both you and your companion will at once go back across the river. You do not pass one foot beyond this bank."

"Then," exclaimed the man, angrily, "I will command your carriers, in the name of their king, to drop their loads and return with me. I will tell them you intend to carry them to the sea, and there sell them into slavery. I will——"

His speech was cut short by a powerful blow from Charlie's fist, which sent him sprawling upon the ground. At the same instant both he and his companion were covered by the revolvers of the whites.

"That was well done, Charlie," said the professor, laughing.

"Me know him one bad man," said Charlie. "Me stop him talk. He make trouble if he talk to niggers."

The fallen man had now raised himself on his elbow, and was glaring at the whites with suppressed rage, while his companion stood by trembling with fear. The carriers grouped around, looking on with deep interest, but not a sound came from them.

"We must settle this matter at once and finally, professor," said Ashton. "I'll not hurt the fellow if he goes away promptly; but we must prevent his saying a word to the Bihenos at any cost. Sustain me in what I do."

"Very good," said the professor; "settle the matter. I see you have made up your mind what to do."

"My fine fellow," said Ashton, addressing the European in Portuguese, "you are in our power. Attempt to utter one word to our carriers and I'll put a bullet through your brain. You shall give us no trouble, and if you attempt the slightest resistance to us you shall surely die. You see we are armed, and prepared to carry out our resolution."

"What do you intend to do with me?" asked the man, sullenly.

"Send you back to the Bihé," replied Ashton. "Both you and your companion will at once walk down to the river and swim across to the opposite shore. Once there you will leave the river as quickly as possible; for if we see you hanging about the bank we shall send a rifle ball after you."

"The river is wide and swift, and there are crocodiles in it," said the man. "You surely will not force me to swim it."

"You will do as I say," said Ashton, sternly. "We have seen no crocodiles, and we don't intend to unpack our boats again. Get on your feet at once, and start."

"I will call out to your men that I am the Sova's servant, and that you are trying to murder me," said the man, rising, and looking at Ashton doggedly.

"A single word to them will be your death," said Ashton. "Charlie, explain to that Biheno fellow what I have said to his comrade. Now," he continued, taking out his watch, "I give you just three minutes to decide. If you are not in the water at the end of that time I shall shoot you."

The man still hesitated; but as soon as Charlie had translated Ashton's words to the Biheno, the native gave a howl of dismay, ran towards the river, sprang in, and struck out lustily for the opposite shore. The Portuguese hesitated no longer, but jumping into the stream, swam after his companion.

"Now, professor," said Ashton, "get the men out of earshot as rapidly as possible, while Houston and I stay here for a while with our rifles, and see these fellows safely across. We can't afford to let them speak a word to our men."

The carriers were at once put in motion, and marched from the river, while the two young men remained on the bank watching the swimmers. The swift current carried them down the stream some distance, and by the time they reached the opposite shore the professor had gotten his men far enough from the river to prevent the shouts of the baffled villains from being understood.

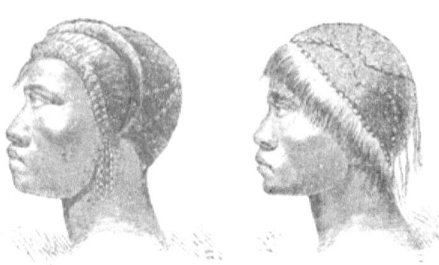

QUIMBANDE GIRLS.

Upon reaching the Biheno shore the Portuguese and his companion moved up the bank to a point opposite the young men. Shaking his clinched fist at them, the Portuguese broke into a storm of oaths, and threatened them with a dire vengeance.

"We had better send a shot or two after them," said Houston, "to start them back from the river."

"All right," answered Ashton; "aim to strike near them, but not to hit them."

The young men fired simultaneously. Ashton's ball struck the ground within a foot of the infuriated Portuguese, and Houston's cut a twig from a tree close by the head of the Biheno. The fellows at once ceased their shouts, and started back from the river at a run. The young men watched them until they were out of sight, and then set off to rejoin the professor.

Having reached a point sufficiently removed from the river to be out of hearing of the men they had driven away, the professor halted his party, and caused Charlie to explain to the negroes that the men who had been dealt with so summarily were merely thieves, who had endeavored to rob them of their property under the pretext of levying a *mucano* upon them. The pombeiros unanimously declared that the fellows had been served perfectly right, and their men endorsed their opinion by nods of approval.

Perceiving a village a short distance in advance, Professor Moreton asked one of the pombeiros its name, and was told that it was the village of the Sova of the Ganda, who was the chief of a Ganguella tribe, and was well disposed towards travellers. As the ground between the village and the river was too marshy for a camp, the party proceeded in the direction of the village, and one of the pombeiros was sent on in advance to ask the chief to provide the huts in the village for the entire party for the night. The chief not only granted the request, but came out of the village to meet his guests. He was greatly surprised by everything the white men possessed, and presented them with a fine ox, which was slaughtered for the evening meal. In return the professor gave him a piece of striped cloth and a few charges of gunpowder, with which he was highly delighted.

On the 3d of June, Ganda was left behind, and that evening the camp was pitched about a mile west of the village of Muzinda. During the afternoon the chief of Muzinda visited the camp, bringing with him an ox as a present. He was given a piece of cloth and some gunpowder in return. The next day's march brought the party to the left bank of the river Cuanza, where they camped, about one mile from the village of Liuica. As food was plentiful in the region, and the natives were disposed to sell, the 5th of June was passed in the camp and in purchasing provisions. The chief of Liuica presented the professor with an ox, for which he was rewarded as the others had been.

On the 6th the party crossed the Cuanza, using the mackintosh boats and several small canoes, which were loaned them by the chief of Liuica. The passage of the stream occupied a couple of hours, and then the march was resumed, the route leading into the country of the Quimbandes, a Ganguella tribe. The villages of Muzeu and Caiaio were passed, and the party went into camp at a spot about two hours' march from the latter village, and near the source of a little stream called the Mutanga, which runs northwest into the Cuanza.

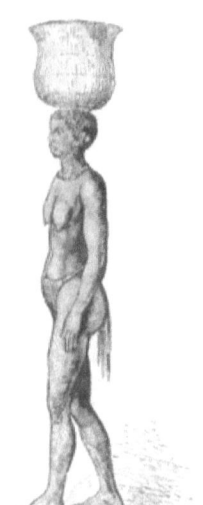

QUIMBANDE WOMAN CARRYING HER LOAD.

The pombeiros informed the professor that the village of the Sova Mavanda was but a short distance beyond the camp. The Quimbandes, they told him, form a confederation, their country being divided into small states, which always unite for their common defence. The villages in the neighborhood of the camp were subject to the Sova Mavanda, who was, in his turn, a vassal of the Sova of Cuio or Mucuzo, a town some distance to the northward.

Our travellers noticed while in the country of the Quimbandes that their villages were not as strongly fortified as those of the Bihé. They were struck with the singular fashion in which the women of the country dressed their hair. Cowries, or small shells, were used for ornaments of the hair, which was plastered and kept in shape by a red cosmetic made of a resinous powder and castor oil. Some of these head-dresses looked for all the world like a European woman's bonnet, and others were shaped like a Roman helmet. The natives prepare castor oil in considerable quantities, but use it entirely for such purposes, having no knowledge of its properties as a medicine. The dress of the women is certainly economical, consisting simply of a cloth worn about the loins. The men cover their nakedness with two aprons of small antelope skins, one before and the other behind, which are suspended from a broad belt of ox hide. The Sovas only use leopard skins for this purpose.

As soon as the camp was constructed, Professor Moreton despatched a small present to the Sova Mavanda, who returned his hearty thanks for it. He begged the professor to send him a shirt also, as he was greatly desirous of possessing such a garment, and the present was accordingly forwarded to him.

Early the next morning a message was received from the Sova. He stated that he was about to march with his army to attack a neighboring village, where one of his subjects had rebelled against his authority. He was anxious that the white men should see his army, and would march by their camp about midday.

Near the appointed hour the sound of drums announced the approach of the Sova and his forces, and the professor drew up the entire party in front of the entrance to the camp to watch the sable warriors pass by.

First marched two stout negroes beating war drums, and uttering the most horrible yells. These were followed by a color-bearer, who bore a lofty staff from which floated a faded Portuguese flag. Then came two men carrying on their shoulders a long pole, from which an enormous powder-chest was slung by ropes. Behind these marched the Sova and his principal officers, and after them about six hundred warriors marching in single file. Eight of the men were armed with muskets; the rest carried bows and arrows. They marched by at a quick step, and soon disappeared in the distance.

Towards sunset the army returned, victorious, without having struck a blow, as their appearance so inspired the rebels with terror that they surrendered at discretion.

Upon reaching the camp of our travellers the army halted, and the Sova sent one of his officers to say that he would put his men through a sham fight in order that his white visitors might witness his mode of attacking a village. At a sign from the Sova the bowmen spread out into a long thin line, having the flag in the centre, and behind it the monarch and the powder-chest. The line then began to surround an imaginary village, contracting and growing more compact as it enclosed the threatened place. Then, at a sign from the Sova, the men dashed forward upon the village, bounding in the air, brandishing their weapons, and uttering the most terrific cries. The battle over, they returned to the position they had occupied before the attack, formed in line, and marched off towards their town.

During the evening the Sova sent word to the professor that he would pay him a formal visit the next day, and although the travellers were anxious to be on the march again, they could not decline to receive the visit. The Sova's friendship might be valuable to them, and would be well purchased by a delay of a day.

It was near noon on the 8th of June when the Sova Mavanda made his appearance at the camp surrounded by his court.

"We shall certainly be able to boast of one thing, if we ever get home again, professor," said Houston, as the royal party approached. "We can say we have seen the greatest man in Africa."

"He is a giant," said Ashton; "by far the largest human being I ever saw."

Mavanda was indeed a man of tremendous size. His height was enormous, and his body was of phenomenal proportions, besides which, he was extremely fat. In spite of this, he moved as actively as a much lighter man could have done, and walked with a certain dignity that commanded the respect of the strangers. His dress consisted of three leopard skins hung from a cloth twisted around his waist, and around his huge neck was a collar of beads, from which were suspended several amulets.

He was received with formal courtesy by the professor, who presented his young companions, Charlie acting as interpreter. Mavanda expressed his pleasure at seeing them, and declared that he would be glad if more white men would visit his country. He added that he had brought with him a fine ox as a present to the strangers. The animal proved to be as enormous in its proportions as its donor, and was a welcome gift indeed. The usual compliments then passed between the professor and the king, when the latter, turning abruptly to the professor, said he had come to ask a favor of him. This was to give him a "medicine" to save his cattle. His animals, when sent out to pasture, strayed away into the woods, and did not all return to their shelter at night. Many of them fell victims to wild beasts, and others were never seen again, so that, on the whole, he was a loser to a considerable extent. He had heard the professor was a great "medicine-man," and he would like him to give him a "medicine" such as was used in the white man's country.

In reply the professor advised him to put his cattle in charge of a herds- man, who would look after them and prevent their straying. The idea impressed the king very forcibly, and he declared that he would adopt it, although it was not the custom in his country to watch the herds. Still the plan was a good one, and he would try it at once.

In return for the ox the professor presented the king with a gun and some charges of powder. He also gave him a number of small articles, among them a box of lucifer matches, which greatly delighted the sable monarch, who declared that he could now make fire whenever he wanted it. He was much interested in the rifles of the whites, and declared he would give half of his kingdom if he had an army equipped with such weapons.

"With such guns," he declared, "I could bring great countries under my rule."

The Sova remained in the camp until twilight, when he departed with his

THE SOVA MAVANDA, MASKED, AND DANCING IN THE CAMP.

people, greatly pleased with his visit. As he was taking leave he told the professor that the greatest desire of his heart was to possess a pair of trousers, and asked if he could not give him a pair. The professor replied that he had none sufficiently large for his majesty, but would make him a pair, and send them to him the next day.

During the evening Professor Moreton, with the aid of Houston and Charlie, managed to cut the desired article from a large piece of figured calico. Charlie undertook to sew them up the next morning, as he avowed himself a proficient with a needle and thread. He made quite a creditable "job" of the trousers, which were certainly large enough, as they contained five yards of calico. They were despatched to the king the next morning, and he was so much pleased with them that he sent back his thanks to the professor by one of the highest officers of his court. This dignitary also stated that the king had commissioned him to say that as it was a time when his people kept high festival, he would do his white friends the honor to come to their camp in the afternoon, masked, and dance before them. This, the officer added, was the highest honor the Sova could grant his friends.

Early in the afternoon a number of the attendants of the king arrived at the camp, accompanied by a large concourse of people. Half an hour later Mavanda himself appeared, presenting such a comical appearance that our travellers could scarcely refrain from bursting into laughter at sight of him. His head was thrust into an enormous gourd, painted white and black, and over his body he wore a frame of osiers covered with grass-cloth, also painted white and black. He also wore a sort of coat made of horse-hair and the tails of animals, which came down over his knees.

As the Sova drew near, his men formed in a line, behind which the atten-

DITA-SOA—FISH OF THE RIVER ONDA.

dants ranged themselves, while the women and children withdrew to a distance. The attendants and men then stood upright, with motionless bodies, and began a singular, monotonous chant, which they accompanied with a clapping of hands. Mavanda then took his place about thirty yards in front of the line, and began a remarkable performance, in which he acted the part of a wild beast torn with rage. He leaped about and capered with a lightness and suppleness surprising in a man of such enormous size, and was greeted with shouts of applause from his own people and from the negroes of the expedition. The performance was kept up for about half an hour, and then the king suddenly darted out of the encampment at full speed, followed by his people. In about an hour he returned, clad in his ordinary dress, and spent the remainder of the day with the professor and his companions. He proved himself to be a man of more than usual good sense, and many of his ideas would not have shamed a more civilized potentate.

The night which followed the Sova's visit was very cold, and the entire party suffered considerably from the sudden change of temperature.

The next morning they were on the march at an early hour. They passed by Mavanda's village, where the king was waiting to take leave of them, and parted from him with genuine regret.

"You will come back to me," were his last words. "You will never reach the Great Water the way you are going. It lies behind you. I would like

TREE-FERNS ON THE BANKS OF THE ONDA.

you to come and live with me. Then I would give you wives and cattle, and make you happy."

Four hours' steady marching brought the party to the river Varea, which they crossed on a tolerably good bridge of timber. They had no sooner gotten over, however, than they received a visit from the chief of the little village of Divindica, situated on the left bank of the Varea, who came to demand payment for the use of the bridge, on the ground that the structure was the property of his people. The pombeiros advised the professor to give the man something, but not all that he claimed, and the fellow was forced to content himself with four yards of cloth. The march was then resumed, and about three o'clock the camp was pitched on the left bank of the river Onda, opposite the large village of Cabango, the capital of the East Quimbande tribes.

The country of the Eastern Quimbandes was found by our travellers to be much more thinly populated than that they had left behind them. The people are also different in characteristics. They are lazy and shiftless, doing no work, carrying on no trade, undertaking no journeys, and going almost naked. They are very poor, gathering only a little wax, which the Bailundos take from them in exchange for cowries and beads; but even this traffic is so slight as to be scarcely worth mentioning. The women are the most industrious part of the population. They cultivate the ground; and the soil, being very rich, yields abundant crops, chiefly of manioc and gingerba.

On the 11th the party crossed the Onda, and encamped about three miles from their last resting-place, beyond the village of Cabango, the Sova of which sent word that he would visit the strangers the next day. This necessitated another delay, but there was no help for it. During the night the party suffered very much from cold, the mercury falling at half-past three o'clock to zero, a change which the half-naked Africans felt keenly.

The next morning the Sova of Cabango arrived, with about sixty of his people, including several of his wives and a number of the dignitaries of his court. They were all in an almost complete state of nudity, but their hair was dressed in a singular and elaborate manner. The Sova brought with him a fine ox, which he presented to the professor, and received in return a gift of cloth and beads, with which he seemed satisfied at the time. His appearance was not pleasing, and inspired the whole party with distrust, so that they were careful not to show him any more of their property than was necessary.

CABANGO WOMAN'S HEAD-DRESS.

King Chaquiunde—for such was the name of the Sova—departed in an hour or two with many professions of esteem for the strangers; and as they intended to push on the next day, our travellers hoped that they had seen the last of him. He returned in the afternoon alone, however, and, after a somewhat lengthy conversation with Professor Moreton, began to put in a claim for sundry articles, declaring that he had sent another ox to the camp, and was entitled to payment for it. The professor checked him promptly, telling him that he had sent them but one ox, for which he had been well paid, and requested him to leave the camp, as nothing more would be given him. The king, seeing the white man was firm, at once changed his tone, and apologized for the attempted trick, declaring that he had been put up to it by his macotas, or principal men, who intended to divide among themselves whatever he could succeed in extorting from the whites. The professor treated him very coldly after this, and the Sova soon took his departure, very much crestfallen.

KING CHAQUEENDE.

The morning of the 13th of June was bitter cold, the mercury at six o'clock registering but two degrees above zero. The march was begun about eight o'clock, and continued until noon, when the party encamped once more on the banks of the Onda. The men were heavily laden, and showed some disposition to straggle, so Professor Moreton thought it best to make an early halt.

Soon after the camp was constructed, the professor, Houston, and Lee started out to examine the country. Leaving the forest, they soon came across a village of ants, located in an open tract near the river. The "village," as Houston termed it, consisted of a number of hills with rounded tops, looking like stumps of trees covered with hemispherical cupolas, about forty-two inches in diameter at the base, by about the same in height. They examined the hills carefully, and found them constructed of the stiffest clay, which the insects, by a peculiar process, had rendered nearly as hard as stone. Houston fired his rifle at one, and found that the ball would not penetrate more than four inches into it.

"These hills," said the professor, in reply to a question from Philip Lee, "are the habitations of the species of white ants known as *termites*. Though they resemble the common ants in their social habits, they belong to a different order. They are one of the scourges of all tropical climates, and devour everything that comes in their way save iron and stone. They increase with almost incredible rapidity, a single female having a capacity of laying as many as eighty thousand eggs in twenty-four hours. Wood and timber of all kinds are attacked by them; and in some countries, so great is their industry, so rapid their operations, and so incredible their numbers, that they will consume all the woodwork of a house in a night or two. They have a great aversion to light, and invariably work under cover; hence, in attacking a tree, a post,

LAKE LIGURI.

a rafter, or a table, they eat out the interior, leaving the thinnest possible layer of the outer wood remaining. It frequently happens that after their depredations have been committed no indication of the work appears to the eye; but the least touch is sufficient to bring down the apparently solid structure, like a house of cards, amidst a cloud of blinding dust. They manifest a most remarkable instinct in some things. While a pillar, or the supporting posts of a house, or any incumbent weight has to be sustained, they guard against the crash which would involve them in ruin by gradually filling up the hollowed posts with a sort of mortar or cement, leaving only a slender way for their own travel. Thus the posts are literally changed from wood to stone, and retain their solidity."

"Have you noticed," asked Houston, "how closely this settlement of ants resembles a Quimbande village?"

"Yes," replied the professor; "the shape of the houses of these open-country ants is very different from those of the forest ants we have encountered, which are built in the form of true cones."

In a little more than an hour after leaving the camp the professor and his young companions passed from the open country, and entered a noble forest, the ground of which was covered with a soft, green turf. Through the wood ran several brooks, tributaries of the Onda. Crossing the last of these, they wandered on, and suddenly came upon a beautiful lake. The water was as clear as crystal and very deep, with a bottom of fine white sand. The lake was bordered with magnificent trees, the luxuriant foliage of which was reflected in the clear waters. Hundreds of birds chirped in the branches and skimmed lightly over the surface of the lake. The whole made up the most beautiful scene our travellers had witnessed in Africa. This was Lake Liguri, of whose beauties they had heard from the pombeiros, and also from the Sova Mavanda.

A LUCHAZE OF THE BANKS OF THE RIVER CUITO.

The next day the march lay along the right bank of the Onda, through a dense forest. It was necessary to force their way through the thick growth, and as the ground was marshy, the progress of the party was difficult and slow. They were glad when they turned their backs upon the Onda, and found more solid footing. They went into camp about three o'clock in the afternoon on the banks of a small rivulet called the Bitovo, and were well disposed to enjoy a rest after their hard tramp of six hours.

On the 14th of June they followed the course of the Bitovo for a while, and then passed through a forest, which brought them to the valley of the Chiconde, a small, rapid rivulet, along which they moved until they reached the river Cuito, where they encamped.

Soon after reaching the Chiconde, Hubbard, who had, contrary to his custom, been silent for a while, suddenly called out,—

"Professor, only look at the stream!"

"What is there remarkable about it?" asked Professor Moreton, in surprise.

"Its waters are flowing in an opposite direction from those we have been following," replied the young man.

Leaving the party to proceed, Professor Moreton, Hubbard, and Ashton lingered a while beside the brook to determine its course, and found that it was indeed flowing to join the Cuito. Hitherto all the streams they had encountered sent their waters towards the Atlantic, but this one followed an opposite course.

"Your discovery is an interesting one, Hubbard," said the professor, at length. "It shows that we have snapped the last tie that binds us to the west coast of Africa. We are indeed in the heart of the continent."

The Cuito was crossed on the 16th, and the party entered the country of the Luchazes. Our travellers found the land tolerably well cultivated, with both men and women working in the fields. The principal crops were the massango, or canary seed, manioc, beans, castor-oil plant, and cotton, but all these were grown upon such a small scale that they were scarcely sufficient to supply the wants of the people. The Luchazes work in iron, which is found in their country, and make all such implements as they use. They collect wax from the hives of the wild bees of the forest, and barter it for dried fish, which the Quimbandes bring into their country. They are but little given to travelling, rarely leaving their villages except to hunt the antelope, which they value for its skin. Our travellers were much struck with their mode of producing fire, which they obtain by using a flint, steel, and tinder. They obtain their flints from the Quibôcos or Quiôcos, paying for them with wax; but manufacture the steels themselves out of wrought iron, tempered by cold water, into which the iron is thrown while red hot. The tinder they prepare by mixing raw cotton with the crushed kernel of the stone of a fruit called *micha*.

LUCHAZE TINDER-BOX, FLINT, AND STEEL.

The camp was pitched for the night at the edge of a forest not far from the Cuito, and on the 17th the march was continued to the village of Bembe, on a stream of the same name, on the banks of which the expedition went into camp.

Soon after the work of cutting down wood for the encampment began, the blacks were suddenly seized with a panic, and fled in all directions, howling lustily. The professor and Ashton hurried forward to see the cause of the alarm. On the very spot chosen for the camp they beheld issuing from the earth millions of the terrible ant known to the Bihenos as the *quissonde*, and to science as the *termites bellicosus*, or warrior ant. At the same moment Charlie came running up, crying out excitedly,—

"Must move the camp at once, Master 'Fessor. Them very bad ants; kill us all if we stay here. Kill elephant sometime!"

The professor did not need any urging, and at once gave orders to remove the loads and pitch the camp a mile farther on. The order was obeyed with an alacrity which showed how much the Bihenos dreaded an encounter with their diminutive enemies.

"Is this ant as dangerous as the negroes consider it?" asked Houston of Professor Moreton, when the blacks had begun the construction of the camp at the new site selected for it.

"They are dangerous to animals," replied the professor; "but it is a disputed point whether they are fatal to a human being in good health. Their bite is very painful, however, and they attack in such overwhelming numbers that resistance is useless. Safety lies in flight alone. They cling with such tenacity to the objects they attack that they will suffer themselves to be torn to pieces before they will relax their hold. It is said that they will even kill an elephant by swarming into his trunk and ears. However, we are well rid of them now, and I trust will see no more of them."

A LUCHAZE WOMAN ON THE ROAD.

As soon as the camp was begun the professor despatched messengers to the village of Bembe to purchase food; but these returned with the announcement that the chief had ordered his people to sell no provisions to the strangers. Whether this was from churlishness, or because the natives did not have food to spare, it was impossible to tell. The next morning, however, the chief had the assurance to send several of his people to the camp to ask for presents. They were dismissed promptly by the professor, with a message to their master which was more forcible than courteous. Immediately after leaving camp, on the 18th of June, the party forded the Bembe, and for several hours marched across a marshy plain towards a mountainous region, at the foot of which they encamped on the bank of a brawling torrent.

Early the next morning Charlie informed the professor that several of the natives had seen the tracks of buffaloes or some other large game leading past the camp towards the water. As the whole party were anxious to obtain fresh meat, which is always scarce in Africa, the professor decided to remain at the camp during the day, and allow the young men to indulge in a buffalo hunt. A hasty breakfast was despatched, and then the four young men, with Charlie and two of the armed negroes, started out. They soon found the trail, which led them to the stream at some distance from the camp. Proceeding cautiously along the water-side, they at length sighted five large buffaloes, grazing at the outskirts of a dense forest, and totally unconscious of their presence.

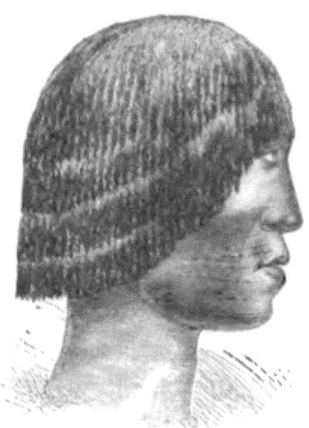

LUCHAZE WOMAN OF CAMBUTA.

In a low tone Charlie cautioned the young men and the negroes not to speak, and they continued to creep stealthily through the undergrowth until they reached a point within eighty yards of the animals. Here they paused, almost holding their breath for fear of frightening their game. Fortunately for them, the wind was from the direction of the buffaloes. Had it been otherwise, the keen scent of the animals would have warned them of the presence of human beings. Ashton now directed the whole party to aim carefully at the buffaloes, and fire when he gave the word.

"We can't afford to indulge in sport," he whispered to Houston. "We need the meat, and must do our best to get it."

The guns were carefully aimed, and at Ashton's signal seven loud reports rang out upon the air. Two of the animals fell dead, a third staggered madly about, while the other two bounded off into the forest. With a shout Houston sprang forward, and at the same moment the wounded buffalo, a large bull, perceiving him, made a dash at him. The movement was so quick that Houston was taken by surprise, and for a moment was in danger. His companions shouted to him to run and leave them to settle with the beast; but, recovering his self-possession, the young Californian raised his rifle and fired a second time. As he did so he sprang aside, just in time to avoid the infuriated animal, which tottered for a moment and then fell heavily to the ground, when a shot from Ashton's rifle finished him.

"Well done, Houston!" cried Hubbard. "I thought the fellow had you."

"It was a close shave," said Ashton. "Only your quick hand saved you, my boy. You might try it again with worse luck."

One of the negroes was now sent back to the camp for men to assist in cutting up the animals. They soon arrived, and the buffaloes were quartered, and then the party returned to the camp, well satisfied with their morning's

SOUTH AFRICAN BUFFALO.

work. During the day the negroes held high festival over their share of the flesh.

In the afternoon some of the carriers brought in a lot of wild honey which they had found in the woods, and also a quantity of a fruit which they called *atundo*, which grows upon a stunted herbaceous plant. The fruit-stalks spring from the stem very close to the ground, and the fruit is as much below as above the surface of the earth. Our travellers tasted it, and found it palatable enough, but the professor was inclined to doubt its being nutritive.

The camp was astir betimes the next morning, which was cold and raw, and the travellers were soon on the road. A march of a couple of hours brought them to a rapid stream about twelve feet wide and as many feet deep, with steep banks, and a fierce, rapid current. It was too deep and swift to be forded, so they were forced to bridge it. This was done by cutting down some large trees, and throwing them across the stream, and on this primitive structure the entire party passed over in safety. A short distance below where they crossed the stream, the name of which they afterwards learned was Nhongoaviranda, they encountered a rivulet flowing into it from the eastward, and following this for a couple of hours, they halted for the night on the banks of another stream, the Cambinbia, opposite two Luchaze villages, and not far from a village of the Quiôcos.

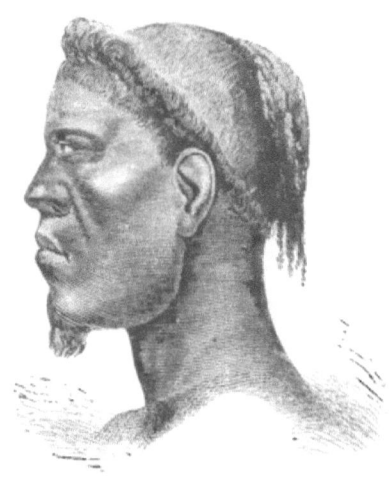

LUCHAZE MAN OF CAMBUTA.

They were visited during the afternoon by a number of the people of the last village, from whom they learned that the Quiôcos, or Quibôcos, as they are sometimes called, had but recently emigrated to the Luchaze country. They said they had left their own country, farther to the north, on account of a pestilence and lack of food, and that their people were good travellers and bold huntsmen. They reported the region in which they were then located as deficient in provisions, but added that beyond the mountain ridge towards which the travellers were journeying, and which was not far from the camp, there were several Luchaze villages, at which they would find an abundance of food.

On the 21st of June the expedition left the Cambinbia and marched towards the Serra Cassara Caiéra, the lofty mountain they had seen for several days, and beyond which, according to the Quiôcos, they were to find an abundance of provisions. The ascent of the mountain was begun about two hours after starting, and was quite fatiguing. As they toiled up the steep, the carriers broke into a loud, monotonous chant, which Charlie translated as follows:

> "The cobra has no arms,
> No legs, no hands, no feet;
> And yet he climbs the mount!
> Why should we not get up as well,
> With arms and legs and hands and feet?"

Our travellers found that the mountain formed a table-land, with tolerably steep slopes, attaining, as the barometer showed, a height of five thousand two hundred and ninety-eight feet above the sea, and four hundred and fifty feet above their camp of the previous day. Upon reaching the summit, they followed it for about an hour, and then came to the descent on the eastern side, from which they beheld the finest panorama they had met with on their journey. The view was very extensive, stretching from northeast to northwest, and embracing a large part of the vast water-shed of the Lungo-é-ungo, a tributary of the

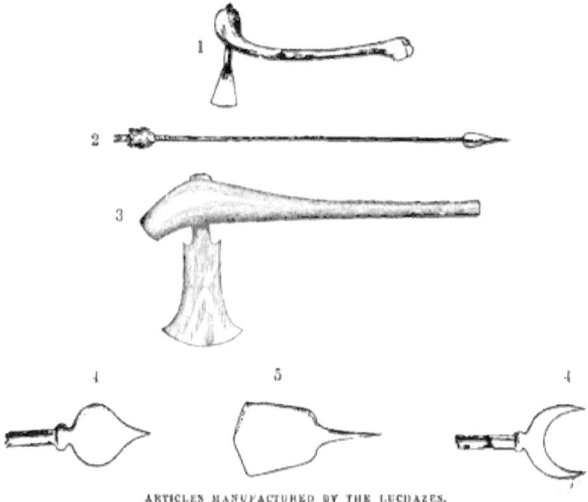

ARTICLES MANUFACTURED BY THE LUCHAZES.
1 and 3. Hatchets. 2. Arrow. 4, 4. Arrow-points. 5. Spade.

Zambezi, and the entire course of the Cuango, which empties into the former river. Descending the eastern slope of the mountain, they reached the source of a rivulet called the Cansampoa, the first water they had met with during the day's march.

On the opposite side of the rivulet were five Luchaze hamlets, all subject to a petty chief named Cassangassanga, who came into the camp soon after it was pitched, bringing with him a kid as a present. He was suitably rewarded, and the professor succeeded in purchasing from him a quantity of massango for the men. The chief told him that at the village of Cambuta, a day's march farther on, he would find food in plenty. Thus encouraged, the expedition pushed on the next day, and, after a march of four hours, camped on the Bicéque, close to the village of Cumbuta.

The Sova of Cambuta was absent on a hunting expedition, but the strangers were kindly welcomed by his wives, who expressed their willingness to sell

VILLAGE OF CAMBUTA, LUCHAZE.

them food. They even urged the professor to lay in a considerable store of provisions, as the country he would traverse beyond the river Cutangjo was a waste, unpopulated region, in which it would be impossible to obtain food. This decided the travellers to pass the 23d of June at Cambuta, for the purpose

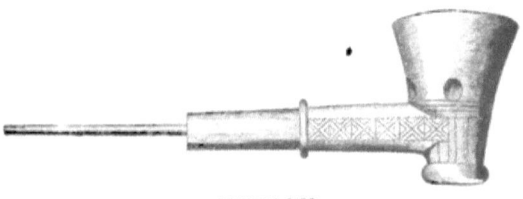

LUCHAZE PIPE.

of obtaining supplies. A considerable quantity of massango was purchased, this being the only food to be had. It did not add to the burdens of the carriers, for the long journey had greatly lightened many of the loads, and the provisions thus purchased were assigned to the carriers whose burdens had grown less.

Cambuta was left at nine o'clock on the morning of the 24th, and at noon the Cutangjo was crossed by fording it. Immediately after crossing the river the camp was pitched on its right bank, near the village of Chaquissembo. The travellers were much interested by their visit to this village, which they found to be well constructed and clean. The houses were made of the trunks of trees, four feet in height, which was the height of the walls, the space between each upright being filled in with mud or straw. The roofs were thatched, the framework bending inwards. The granaries were little more than enormous water-proof baskets perched upon a framework at a considerable height from the ground. They were made entirely of straw, and were reached by means of a ladder.

LUCHAZE FOWL HOUSE.

In the centre of the village our travellers found a building used as a conversation house, or place of meeting. Here several men were squatted around the hearth, on which a fire was burning, making bows and arrows. They received the strangers politely, and offered them a drink of a liquor made of water, honey, and powdered hops, which they mix in a calabash and allow to ferment. They called it *bingundo*, and assured Charlie, who as usual acted as interpreter, that it was very good. Professor Moreton tried it, and declared that it was as near pure alcohol as the most hardened tippler could desire.

On the 25th the march was exceedingly difficult, as it lay through a dense jungle for the first three hours; but this was left behind at last, and early in the afternoon the camp was built on a slope of rising ground bordering an extensive marsh in which the Cuando, one of the principal tributaries of the Zambezi, takes its rise. The night was very cold, and the next morning the mercury registered only two degrees above zero. The entire party were aroused at daybreak by the shrieking of thousands of paroquets, which filled the trees around them, and fairly deafened them with their cries. They were soon on the road again, following the course of the Cuando for a couple of hours. At the end of this time they crossed the river by an improvised bridge of felled trees, which was easily built, as the stream was but seven feet wide. They camped at night on the left bank of the river, and the next day followed the stream again until noon, when they went into camp.

The halting-place was in the midst of a grove of enormous trees, which the negroes called *cuchibi*, and which they hailed with delight. The fruit produced by the trees resembles a French bean, and consists of one bright scarlet seed enclosed in a dark-green husk. The seed is steeped by the natives in water, and after a few hours the scarlet envelope softens and is removed, leaving a white kernel, which is very oleaginous, and is highly esteemed as food by the natives, who also extract from it the oil with which they moisten their food. Close to the *cuchibi* trees another species of fruit-tree was found. It was of medium size, and was called by the natives the *mapoleque*. The fruit, to which they gave the name *mapole*, resembled an orange both in size and color, and hung vertically from the tree by a long stalk.

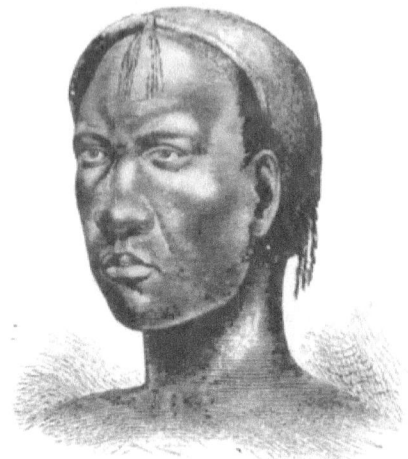

LUCHAZE WOMAN OF CUTANGJO.

The husk is so hard that it can be broken only with a strong hatchet. It contains a mass of thick and coagulated liquid, full of seeds like the stones of small plums. The liquid is of an acid-sweet taste, and when taken in any quantity is purgative. The pombeiros assured the professor, however, that it was exceedingly nutritive, and that a man could live on it for several days without other food.

On the 28th the march was in an easterly direction, towards the sources of the Cubangui. The first part was across a troublesome marsh, through which the progress was slow; and once over this, the travellers began the ascent of a spur of mountains running north

THE CUCHIBI.

and south. The ridge was crossed by noon, and at two o'clock the camp was located on the border of a marsh in which the river Cubangui has its source. The next two days were spent in following the right bank of the river, and on the afternoon of the 30th of June the camp was built on the river shore, by a small rivulet called the Linde, in the neighborhood of several Ambuella villages, from which a small supply of massango was obtained.

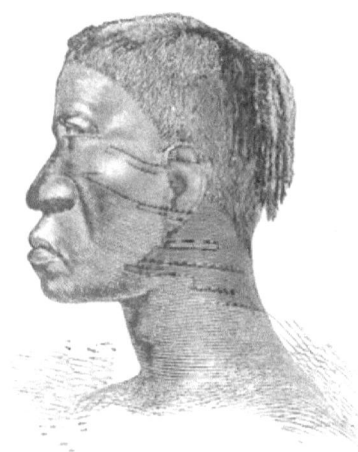

LUCHAZE OF THE CUTANGJO.

The march of July 1st brought the expedition to the village of the Sova of Cangamba, and the camp was built a short distance beyond it. The professor at once despatched a present to the Sova in the shape of an old uniform coat gayly trimmed with gilt braids, and with a profusion of buttons. This so delighted the monarch that he gave prompt orders to his people to sell the strangers all the food they wished to purchase. The only thing that could be obtained, however, was massango, of which the whole party had begun to be heartily tired; but as there was no escape from it, they had to make the best of it.

The pombeiros reported that some of their men were footsore, and were sick from the effects of the food they had been subsisting on, and begged the professor to remain in camp the next day to allow them to rest. This was agreed to, and the 2d of July was spent at Cangamba. Finding that the natives had stores of dried fish and manioc, the professor succeeded in purchasing three days' supply for his party, and the change of diet was greatly enjoyed by the blacks as well as by the whites.

During the day a band of elephant hunters from the north arrived, and camped near the halting-place of the expedition. This was the first time our travellers had heard of elephants since their departure from Benguela, and they were eager to obtain information concerning them. The hunters told them that the elephant country was still six days' march to the southward, and that none of the animals were ever seen in the country through which the travellers were journeying.

In the afternoon the party had a visit from the Sova of Cangamba, a fine-looking negro, named Moene-Cahenga. He brought with him a large basket of massango and four chickens, and was rewarded with some cloth and beads. He was dressed in the uniform sent him by the professor, to which he had added several leopard skins hung from a belt around his waist. In his hand he carried an instrument made of antelopes' tails, which the young men were at first inclined to think a sort of sceptre or badge of authority; but which they found was meant for the humbler office of keeping off the flies.

From the Sova our travellers obtained much interesting information respecting his people. He told them that the fields were cultivated by both men and women, and that they grew massango, manioc, a little cotton, and a still smaller quantity of sweet potatoes. His people were good workers in iron, which was procured from mines on the right bank of the Cubangui to the north of Cangamba; the men also made baskets and the women mats. The cotton grown in the country was woven by rude looms into cloth, which our travellers found to be of an excellent quality, though the pieces were only as large as an ordinary towel. The arms of his people, the Sova told them, consisted of bows and arrows and small hatchets; they had no guns, though he would be glad to procure a few.

MOENE-CAHENGA, SOVA OF CANGAMBA.
1. Fly-flap.

On the 3d of July the party set out again, camping for the night on the right bank of the Cubangui. The next day the river was crossed by means of the mackintosh boats, and the march was continued in a southeasterly direction, through an uninteresting and depopulated country. All through the next three days the party pushed on, and on the 6th of July encamped on the right bank of the Cuchibi River.

The country along this part of the Cuchibi was entirely unpopulated, but was very interesting. The river flowed through a long valley, enclosed by gentle slopes of mountains covered with a dense forest. The valley was perfectly dry, and the stream flowed in long, gentle curves, so that at a distance it seemed almost straight. Game was more plentiful, and Houston and his

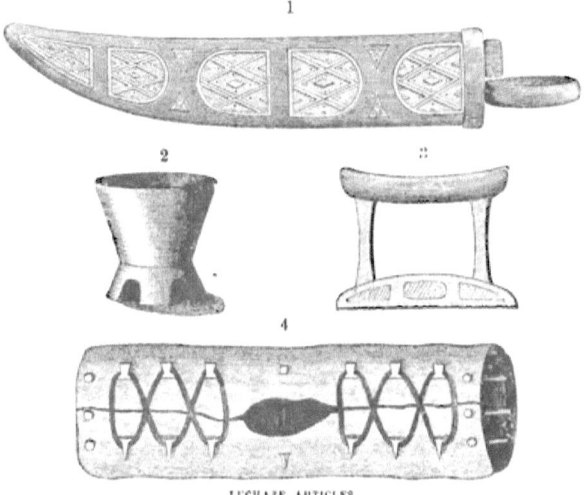

LUCHAZE ARTICLES.
1. Knife-sheath. 2. Basket. 3. Wooden bolster. 4. Bee-hive.

companions succeeded in bringing down half a dozen antelopes, which furnished a meal for the party. Rats were also plentiful, and the Biheno carriers succeeded in catching a number, which they ate with a keen relish.

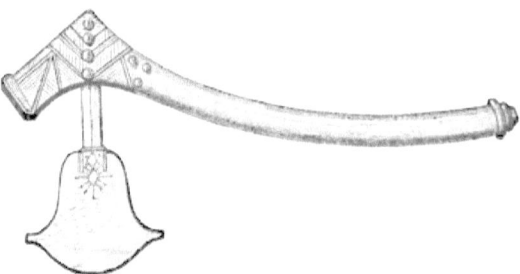

HATCHET OF THE AMBUELLAS OF CANGAMBA.

Four days of steady marching succeeded the halt on the 6th, the route lying along the right bank of the Cuchibi, and on the 10th the camp was built near the Ambuella village of Cahu-heú-úe, where the Sova of the Cuchibi country had his residence.

The pombeiros were well pleased to reach this point, which they said was a station on the regular route of the Biheno caravans to the Zambezi.

Scarcely had the camp been completed when a stranger came in and asked to see the white chief. He was brought before the professor, and stated that he was a Biheno, and had been left at the village on account of sickness, by a caravan three years before. He begged to be taken into the service of the white men, in order that he might be able to return home with his countrymen when they left the party. As the loads were growing lighter daily, in consequence of the withdrawal from them of the goods necessary for the purchase of food and for presents to the chiefs along the route, there was no actual necessity for engaging the man ; but the fellow was so eager, and looked so pitiful, that the professor summoned several of the Bihenos, and told them the man's story. Several of the men recognized him as a fellow-countryman, and two knew him by name. Having secured this identification, Professor Moreton consented to engage the stranger, who was wild with joy at his good fortune.

AMBUELLA PIPE.

The man brought news, however, which caused our travellers considerable anxiety. He told them that there had been a revolution in the Baroze country, to which they were journeying, and that the native king, Manuauino, had been expelled, and another made king in his place, of whom nothing was known. The professor had learned from Silva Porto and from his agent at Belmonte that although Manuanino was very ferocious and cruel to his own people, he was very hospitable to strangers. They had counted upon his assistance to enable them to descend the Zambezi, and they had no means of judging what their reception at the hands of his successor would be.

The professor now sent a present to the Sova of Cahu-heú-úe, consisting of some cloth and three yards of copper wire, which Silva Porto had told him was used by the Ambuellas for making bracelets. The Sova was much pleased with the present, and sent back a number of his people with provisions and a considerable quantity of Indian corn. The latter was gladly received, as the change from massango was a pleasant one. The Sova also sent word that he would visit the camp the next day.

Our travellers were informed by the pombeiros that the people of the neighborhood were the pure Ambuellas, while those they had hitherto met were very much mixed with the Luchazes. They were struck with the peculiar manner in which the villages were constructed. These are situated either on

THE QUICHOBO.

islands in the rivers or upon piles driven down into the stream. As the inhabitants possess the only canoes in the country, they are thus secure from invasion, and have but little fear of their enemies.

The next morning the Sova Cahu-heñ-ñe arrived at the camp with a number of his people. As Houston declared, he was "the most respectable-looking darkey" they had met with during their journey. He was well advanced in years, and very black, but with an intelligent and kindly face. He was better dressed than any of the native chiefs had been thus far, and in addition to an old uniform coat wore a large cloak of white linen, with a handsome colored handkerchief around his neck. On his head was a cap of red and black woollen stuff. He carried an accordeon or concertina in his hands, and as he advanced towards the whites drew from it the most doleful sounds. He brought with him an additional present of maize, manioc, beans, and fowls, which the professor returned with some copper and brass wire and a small quantity of gunpowder, the last being the most valuable gift that could be offered in the Ambuella country.

During the conversation which followed, the old king agreed to sell the party supplies of corn, manioc, and beans, but stated that it would take several days for him to collect what was wanted and send it in. When questioned as to the change of sovereigns in the Baroze country, he said he knew but little about it. He paid tribute to the monarch of the Baroze, he said, in order to avoid war, though it was an unjust claim; but as

THE SOVA CAHD-HEŌ-ĈE.

the time for payment of the tribute had not yet come, he had heard nothing of a change of sovereigns. He took his departure about noon, well pleased with his visit; and during the stay of our travellers in his territory he called upon them frequently, bringing them presents of food, and receiving in return a little gunpowder, which he regarded as ample payment.

Soon after the visit of the Sova some of the negroes of the expedition brought into the camp two Mucassequeres, whom they had captured in the forest. The fellows were perfect savages in appearance, though they seemed harmless enough, and spoke a dialect which was very different from any the travellers had yet heard,

AMBUELLA WOMAN.

and much harsher. Fortunately they knew a few words of the Ambuella tongue, and by means of an interpreter the professor managed to communicate with them. They were badly frightened, and expected either to be put to death, or to be kept in slavery for the rest of their days. Professor Moreton reassured them, however, by returning their bows and arrows which had been taken from them, and telling them they were free, and might return to their people. He also gave them something to eat, and presented them with a string of beads apiece for their wives. Their surprise knew no bounds at such unexpected kindness, but was manifested more by signs and gestures than by words.

THE KING OF AMBUELLA'S ELDEST DAUGHTER.

They told the professor that they belonged to a village situated in the forest, not far from the camp, and that they were engaged in searching for roots in the woods when captured by his people.

As the Mucassequeres were so different from any of the tribes he had yet met, Professor Moreton was anxious to see more of them, and asked the men if they would conduct him and his companions to their village. The men hesitated for a while, but after discussing the matter between themselves, answered that they were willing to conduct the professor and two of his companions to their village, but no more. Their people, they added, had but little to do with strangers, and if they brought many into the village they would draw down upon themselves the anger of their countrymen.

Professor Moreton chose Ashton and Houston as his companions in the visit, and taking with him a few strings of beads as presents, set out with the savages for their homes. Upon leaving the camp, they plunged at once into the forest, walking so rapidly that the professor and his companions had hard work to keep up with them. An hour's walk at this pace brought them to the village or camp of the Mucassequeres, which was situated in the centre of a patch of cleared ground.

The camp was of the rudest description, consisting merely of five huts formed of the branches of trees bent over, and interlaced with others. The inmates were fifteen in number, three other men, seven women, and five children, all nearly naked, their only covering consisting of small monkey skins.

They presented a most wretched and revolting appearance, and were the ugliest human beings our travellers had seen in Africa. Their eyes were small, and out of the right line; their cheek-bones very high and far apart; the nose flat to the face, with enormously wide nostrils; the hair, which was crisp and woolly, growing in separate patches, the thickest being on top of the head. Around their wrists and ankles they wore strips of the hair of some animal, but whether as an ornament or charm the professor and his companions could not tell. The men were armed simply with bows and arrows. A fire was burning in the camp, but there were no signs of cooking utensils. The food of the people consists of roots and fragments of flesh roasted on wooden spits. Salt is unknown to them.

THE KING OF AMBUELLA'S YOUNGEST DAUGHTER

As they could not speak to the Mucassequeres, the visitors made their stay a short one. The professor gave each of the women a few beads. They received them in a listless, indifferent way, manifesting neither pleasure nor gratitude. The whole appearance of the people was so utterly wretched that the pity of the visitors was aroused. After remaining in the village half an hour they managed to make their guides understand that they wished to

CUCHIBI CANOE AND PADDLE.

return. A walk of another hour through the woods brought them to their own camp, the guides leaving them abruptly, and without a word or sign, on the verge of the forest.

During their stay on the Cuchibi, the travellers learned that the Mucassequeres occupy, jointly with the Ambuellas, the territory lying between the Cuando and the Cuchibi, the former dwelling in the forests and the latter on the rivers. "They hold but little communication with each other, but, on the other hand, they do not break out into hostilities. When pressed by hunger, the Mucassequeres will come over to the Ambuellas and procure food by the barter of ivory and wax. Each tribe would seem to be independent, and not recognize any common chief. If they do not fight with their neighbors, they nevertheless quarrel among themselves; and the prisoners taken in these conflicts are sold as slaves to the Ambuellas, who subsequently dispose of them to the Bihé caravans. The Mucassequeres may be styled the true savages of South tropical Africa. They construct no dwelling-houses or anything in the

DRUM USED AT AMBUELLA FEASTS.

likeness of them. They are born under the shadow of a forest-tree, and so they are content to die. They despise alike the rains which deluge the earth and the sun which burns it, and bear the rigors of the seasons with the same stoicism as the wild beasts. In some respects they would seem to be even below the wild denizens of the jungle, for the lion and tiger have at least a cave or den in which they seek shelter, while the Mucassequeres have neither. As they never cultivate the ground, implements of agriculture are entirely unknown among them; roots, honey, and the animals caught in the chase constitute their food, and each tribe devotes its entire time to hunting for roots, honey, and game. They rarely sleep to-day where they lay down yesterday. The arrow is their only weapon; but so dexterous are they in its use, that an animal sighted is as good as bagged. Even the elephant not unfrequently falls a prey to these dexterous hunters, whose arrows find every vulnerable point in his otherwise impervious hide. The two races which inhabit this country are as different in personal appearance as they are in habits. The Ambuella, for instance, is a black of the type of the Caucasian race; the Mucassequere is a white of the type of the Hottentot race, in all its hideousness."

On the morning of the 12th the king of Ambuella sent three canoes with a message to the professor, asking him to visit him at his own village of Cahuheú-úe, and to bring his "sons" with him. Leaving Hubbard—who was not feeling well—to look after the camp, the professor and the other young men set out to visit the monarch, taking Charlie with them as interpreter. Proceeding to the river they found the canoes, each in charge of a female rower. As the little boats were insufficient for the entire party, Charlie was sent back to the camp for one of the mackintosh boats. The professor and Ashton undertook

FROM THE BIHÉ TO THE ZAMBEZI.

the navigation of the mackintosh, while Houston, Lee, and Charlie embarked in the canoes. They were soon out in the stream, and the girls proved themselves so expert with their paddles that the white men found it difficult to keep up with them. A row of about an hour brought them to a number of marshy islets situated in a bend of the river. The islands were separated by numerous canals, which formed a perfect labyrinth, winding among the thick reeds which grew in the marshy soil. A sudden bend in one of the canals brought the boats to the royal village, which consisted of some twenty or more huts of

AMBUELLA CHIEF.

AMBUELLA HUNTER.

cane built upon piles, and elevated about six feet above the ground. The roofs of the huts were composed of thatch, and were pointed. On one of the islands somewhat larger than the rest were a dozen huts, which comprised the royal quarter. One hut was occupied by the Sova himself, four more by his four wives, and the rest were storehouses. In front of the king's hut was a rustic trophy consisting of the skulls and horns of animals and other spoils of the chase. The huts were small, badly constructed, and afforded but a poor shelter to their occupants.

The Sova received his guests at the landing-place, accompanied by two of his favorites, and conducted them to a cleared spot in front of his dwelling, where the people of the village were gathered in silence. Pieces of matting were spread on the ground, and upon these the monarch and his favorites seated themselves, and invited the guests to do likewise. No sooner were the strangers seated than the favorites commenced clapping the palms of their hands together vigorously, after which they scraped up a little earth, rubbed it on their breasts, and repeated rapidly and many times the words *bamba* and *calunga*, again clapping their hands, but not so vigorously as before. This was the Ambuella mode of opening a conversation with the sovereign.

After some remarks had passed, the king desired to see the boat that had

ROYAL VILLAGE OF CABU-HEÉ-ÚE, ON THE CUCHIBI.

brought the professor, and made a short excursion in it on the river. He was profoundly astonished at its construction and floating power, and begged the professor not to sell any like it to the other tribes, as he and his people would be lost if he did, their only safety consisting in their monopoly of the canoes of that region. The professor assured him that he had nothing to fear, as the white men had no more such boats than they needed for their own use on their journey.

Upon returning to his island the king sent for a calabash of *bingundo* and a tin cup. Filling the cup with the foaming liquor, he allowed a few drops to fall upon the ground, and, covering the place with earth, tossed off the contents of the cup at a draught.

He then offered the liquor to his guests; but upon being told by Charlie that the white men drank water only, he passed it to his favorites, who soon finished what was left.

Some further conversation followed, and in about an hour the professor and his companions took their leave, and set out on their return to their camp, which was reached early in the afternoon.

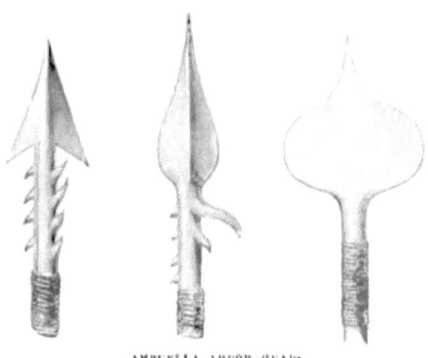

AMBUELLA ARROW-HEADS.

Upon reaching the camp they found it alive with merriment. A number of Ambuella women and girls had arrived, and were dancing with the negro carriers to the music of native instruments. As the sport was good-natured, and there was no carousing, the professor did not interfere with it.

Late in the afternoon a couple of large cobras and several venomous scorpions were killed in the camp, but not before a few of the negroes had been

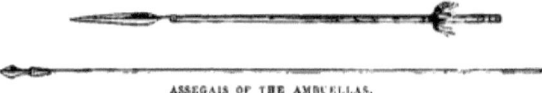

ASSEGAIS OF THE AMBUELLAS.

bitten by the latter. The bites were not fatal, however, and resulted only in painful swellings and inflammation of the parts attacked.

During the next three days the Sova kept his word, and sent in supplies of maize, manioc, and beans, for which the professor paid in cloth, gunpowder, and copper and brass wire.

The provisions being all in and prepared for transportation by the night of the 15th of July, the professor and his companions resolved to resume their journey the next day. Accordingly they left Cahu-heñ-úe early on the morning of the 16th, following the banks of the stream for a couple of hours until they came to a ford, where they crossed it. The water was breast-high and the current very swift, so that the passage consumed two hours more. The whole party was so fatigued by the operation that soon after passing the river they went into camp near the village of Lienzi. They were cordially welcomed by the inhabitants of the village, who brought out a large number of fowls for sale. These were purchased, and every man in the camp supped that night off chicken. The next day they made a painful march of six hours through a tangled forest, where not a drop of water was to be had, and in the afternoon reached the right bank of the Cuchibi, sorely parched with thirst. During the night they were kept awake by the roaring of lions and leopards, which roamed around the camp all through the hours of darkness; but the

FORDING THE CUCHIBI.

next morning not a trace of an animal could be seen. The march of the 18th of July was very trying. The Cuchibi was crossed by a bridge left by some former caravan, but beyond the stream was a marshy plain which the party traversed with difficulty, the men often sinking in the bog up to their waists. The river was found to be full of fish, and several small crocodiles were seen. The men were so fatigued by the journey across the morass that, upon reaching a suitable place in the forest beyond it, the professor ordered the camp to be built.

On the 19th a small rivulet was forded soon after leaving the camp, and then the party came upon a lake a couple of hundred yards wide, across which they were obliged to wade, with the water up to their waists. The camp was pitched by a small, sluggish stream, called the Combule, an affluent of the Chicului; and on the afternoon of the 20th the party halted at the source of the river Ninda, after a difficult march through a thorny forest, through which they had literally to cut their way. The pombeiros informed the professor that the Ninda was noted for the number and ferocity of the wild beasts that haunted its banks, and advised him to enclose the camp with a much stronger stockade than usual. The advice was taken, and the camp was protected by a stockade and abattis, which rendered it impenetrable to any attack of the denizens of the forest. Nor were these precautions useless, for our travellers were

FISH OF THE CUCHIBI.

much disturbed during the night by the loud roaring of lions, to which were added the yells of a pack of hyenas near morning.

The men had suffered so much from the march through the thorny forest that Professor Moreton decided to remain in camp during the day, in order to give them a rest. As they had now reached the first stage of their journey where elephants appear, he sent out several of the men during the day to see if they could discover any traces of them, but nothing could be found but some old tracks. Houston and Lee went out with their rifles in the afternoon, and succeeded in killing a fine buffalo, which furnished the party with fresh meat for their evening meal.

During the next three days the journey lay along the right bank of the Ninda; but on the 25th a deviation from the river became necessary, as the reeds and cane which lined its bank were impenetrable. The camp that night was pitched near the village of Calombeu, a sort of advanced post of the sovereign of the Baroze country.

The people of the village proved very inhospitable, and refused to sell any provisions. This was very annoying, as a number of the Biheno carriers fell sick, and the party was detained in camp for the next two days on their account. The provisions laid in on the Cuchibi were running low, and the professor was anxious to push on. The camp was also pitched in a most uncomfortable region, the vast plain of the Nhengo lying three thousand nine hundred feet above the level of the sea. Though apparently dry, the ground was but little better than a sponge, yielding slowly but surely to the weight of the body, the water oozing up and filling every depression thus made. This peculiarity caused the professor to be extremely anxious for the health of his young companions and his men, and he resolved to push on on the 28th, if only for a few miles.

On the evening of the 27th of July he was sitting in the door of his tent, conversing with the young men, when a stranger, followed by a boy and a woman, suddenly entered the camp, and, coming rapidly forward, seated himself at the professor's feet.

The new-comer was a negro, tall and powerfully made, but dressed in rags. What had once been a mantle hung in tatters from his shoulders, and a ragged cap adorned his head. The rest of his clothes were torn and soiled, and his whole appearance indicated a recent experience of hardship. His weapons were borne by the boy, and in his hand he carried a stout stick. His face was

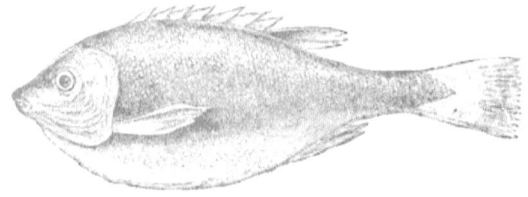

CHIPULO OR NHELE.

a remarkable one, indicating determination, firmness, and a high order of intelligence, and his manner was quick and decided.

"Who are you, and what do you want of me?" asked the professor, sternly, speaking in the Biheno tongue, of which he had mastered enough to carry on a short conversation.

The man looked him calmly in the eye, and answered simply,—

"I am Caiumbuca, and have come to seek you."

In an instant the whole party were on their feet, with hands outstretched to the stranger, in whom they beheld the man they had most wished to see in Africa. He was indeed Caiumbuca, the old pombeiro of Silva Porto, and the boldest and most daring of the Bihé traders, whose name was known from Nyangwe to Lake Nyami. Before leaving Benguela, Silva Porto had repeatedly said to the professor,—

"On reaching the Bihé seek out Caiumbuca, engage him in your service, and you will have the best assistant you can meet with in all South Central Africa."

On reaching the Bihé the professor had sought him in every direction, but without success. "He is gone into the interior, and nobody knows where," was the unvarying answer to his inquiries. Caiumbuca now explained that he was on the Cuando, just below the confluence of the Cuchibi, when the expedition reached the Ambuella country. Hearing of the presence of white men from Benguela, he had hastened across the country with the woman and boy to join them.

A long conversation followed, and ended by the professor engaging Caiumbuca to join the party as confidential adviser. He spoke all the languages of the region, and knew the country well from actual experience, and promised to be of special service to them in their dealings with the monarch of the Baroze country.

On the 28th of July the carriers were better, and the party made a forced march of six hours, camping on the right bank of the river Nhengo, which is in fact the lower Ninda. The party remained in camp the next day, and the professor sent out a number of men to the neighboring villages to purchase food; but the natives would neither sell them provisions nor have anything to do with them. This was now a serious matter, as the provisions were running low, and it was absolutely necessary to procure food somewhere.

By the advice of Caiumbuca, the professor sent one of the negroes ahead to the capital of the Baroze monarch, to inform him of the arrival of the white men in his country, and of their intended visit to him. The man was one of the most trustworthy

THE MALANCA.

fellows in the command, and was promised a handsome reward if he would push on quickly, and return as soon as possible, the professor informing him of the route the party would pursue after leaving their present camp.

During the afternoon several of the negroes, who had ventured some distance from the camp, came rushing into the enclosure, hotly pursued by a couple of lions. The young Americans caught up their rifles to have a shot at the beasts, but the latter gave up the chase as they drew near the camp, and, wheeling, bounded off into the forest.

On the 30th a forced march of eight hours, away from the river, brought the party to the banks of a lake, near a collection of villages, which Caiumbuca called Cacapa. The professor at once sent Caiumbuca with several of the negroes to the villages to procure food, while the rest set about building the camp. Towards nightfall the messengers returned, and reported that the inhabitants, who were a part of the Ganguella race, held in subjection by the Luinas or Barozes, had not only refused to sell them food, but showed a decided disposition to hostilities. Caiumbuca was indignant at the reception he had met with.

"They have a plenty of sweet potatoes and manioc," he said to the pro-

ANT-HILLS OF THE SHENGO.

fessor; "but they are surly fellows. If these were my men, and I had as many guns as you, I would go there to-morrow and take what I wanted."

"But we should have to fight for it," said the professor.

"Your guns will scare them," continued Caiumbuca. "You need only fire a few shots, and they will surrender to you."

During the evening the professor had an anxious consultation with his young companions. It was certainly necessary to procure food at once. The provisions brought from the Cuchibi would last only one day longer, and they were ignorant of what was in store for them beyond. Ashton and Houston were in favor of adopting Caiumbuca's suggestion, and compelling the people to supply the needed provisions; but the professor hesitated to resort to violence. Finally, as the matter admitted of no delay, it was resolved to make another offer to purchase food the next morning, and, if this were refused, to seize the town, take what they needed, and then pay for it. This decision was communicated to Caiumbuca, Charlie, and the pombeiros, and was heartily endorsed by them.

At daybreak on the 31st of July, Caiumbuca and several of the blacks were sent forward to the villages to make another effort to procure food peaceably, but were driven off with insults and threats of violence. Upon their return to the camp the professor called his people together, and told them that as all his attempts to procure provisions had been repulsed by the ill-natured villagers, he had resolved to attack the place, and compel the people to supply what they needed. He was answered with a shout of approval. Guns and ammunition were issued to Caimbuca, the pombeiros, and several of the Biheno carriers who had proved themselves most trustworthy on the march, so that the professor found himself at the head of twenty-four men, white and black, armed with guns and rifles, and about sixty blacks bearing bows and arrows and assegais. Mombée and three of the carriers were left in charge of the camp, with strict orders to remain in the enclosure, and to allow no one to enter it until the return of the attacking party.

About nine o'clock the march was begun towards the villages. Arriving near them, they found all the entrances closed, and about two hundred blacks, armed with bows, arrows, assegais, and hatchets, assembled about the central village, which was the residence of the chief. Bringing his men into line, the professor ordered them to open fire on the chief's compound, but to aim over the heads of the natives, in order to avoid shedding blood, as he wished to frighten rather than injure the blacks.

Three volleys were fired in quick succession, and were answered by a flight of arrows. As the smoke from the third volley cleared away, the natives set up a howl of terror, threw down their arms, and huddled together in confusion. Professor Moreton thereupon ordered his men to cease firing, and advanced rapidly with them to the terror-stricken blacks. The chief at the same time came forward and held up his hands to show that his people had surrendered. He was seized by order of the professor, and the victors entered the village, leaving a small guard at the entrance to keep the natives in check. Proceeding to the general storehouses, which were in the chief's compound, the professor found an ample supply of sweet potatoes and manioc. He took enough to supply the expedition for four days, and then set out on his return to the camp, carrying with him the chief and half a dozen of the villagers as prisoners.

Upon reaching the camp Professor Moreton paid the chief in cloth and beads for the captured provisions, and then ordered the prisoners to be released, telling them they were free to return to their homes. He gave them a sharp lecture upon their folly in refusing to be friendly with white men, and told the chief he would report the affair to the king of the country upon his arrival at the capital. The chief was astounded at the generosity of the whites, and humbly begged the professor not to get him into trouble with the king, promising that his people should sell him provisions whenever he might need them. The professor, who had no idea of bringing the matter to the notice of the king, consented to be silent in consideration of the chief's promise of good behavior in the future; and the latter soon after took his departure, with many expressions of gratitude and promises of friendship.

A LUINA HUNTER.

On the 1st of August camp was broken and the march resumed, the halt for the night being near Canhete, the first village occupied by the Luina race. The inhabitants proved very friendly, and provisions were brought into the camp in considerable quantities for sale.

Soon after nightfall the negro Cainga, who had been sent on to the king to inform him of the arrival of the expedition in the country, returned in safety. He was accompanied by several chiefs, who brought with them six oxen as presents from the king. These were a very Godsend to the travellers, who had been so long without meat, and were gladly welcomed.

Cainga reported that the king of the Baroze seemed highly pleased at the prospect of a visit from so many white men, and intended giving them a splendid reception. With a view to displaying his greatness, he had ordered a number of canoes to be gotten in readiness at the point where the expedition would cross the Zambezi, in order that the whole caravan might pass the stream at once. The king, Cainga said, was a young man of about twenty years, and had been much pleased when he heard there were four young men in the party, declaring that he was sure they would become friends. The Luina chiefs, who had come from his majesty, brought a cordial message of welcome, and urged the professor to resume his march the next day, in order that they might reach the royal city as soon as possible.

Still the professor was not entirely reassured. He was sufficiently aware of the treachery that underlies the character of African monarchs not to place too much reliance upon the king's messages. They were better, however, than a hostile reception, and there was nothing left but to go on and trust in Providence for the future.

Canhete was left on the morning of the 2d of August, and in the afternoon the party encamped near the village of Tapá. On the 3d a fresh start was made at eight o'clock, and in an hour the route brought the travellers to the right bank of the Nhengo, which they followed for another hour, when they reached its confluence with the Zambezi.

The entire party greeted the great river with enthusiasm, and a general halt was made upon the shore to enjoy a view of it. The river flowed with a dull, sluggish current, but gave evidence of being very deep. Some distance out in the water a group of hippopotami were resting, with their large heads above the surface of the stream. Houston raised his rifle and fired at one, and they instantly disappeared, but the crimson tint of the water showed that the ball had been well aimed. An enormous crocodile, basking in the sun on an islet in the stream, lifted his head lazily, and glanced around, and a second shot sent him scampering into the water.

The emotions of the professor and his young companions as they gazed upon the mighty river, which was slowly rolling its waters towards the Indian Ocean, are hard to describe. They felt a thrill of triumph at having carried their enterprise successfully thus far, but at the same time could not repress a feeling of misgiving for the future. A piece of wood thrown into the slowly moving current of the Liambai, as the upper Zambezi is called, might, in time, reach the far-off sea; but would they be so fortunate? Who could tell?

They were aroused from these thoughts by a shout, which announced the arrival of the canoes sent by the king to ferry the party across the river. The preparations for the passage were soon made, and by noon the travellers were on the left bank of the Zambezi. The march was then resumed in an easterly direction, and two hours later a wide but shallow branch of the Zambezi was forded. On the opposite bank our travellers found a large number of Luinas, who had been sent by

LUINA SHIELD.

the king, waiting to receive them. These fell into line in advance of the party, and all hastened on eastward, passing several lakes which had to be avoided, and about five o'clock in the afternoon arrived in front of the town of Lialui, the great capital of the Baroze, or kingdom of the Lui.

CHAPTER IX.

ADVENTURES IN THE LUI COUNTRY.

HALTING for a short time to enable his men to close up well, the professor led them towards the town, which was surrounded by a strong stockade. At the entrance the travellers were met by one of the dignitaries of the court, accompanied by thirty attendants, who welcomed them in the name of the king. They were then conducted through parallel lines of warriors extending from the gate of the town to the quarters set apart for the strangers. Before reaching these the whites, with Caiumbuca as their interpreter, were conducted to a large court-yard, at one end of which was a sort of raised platform or dais, on which they were requested to seat themselves to receive the compliments of the court.

In a little while four of the king's councillors, headed by a dignitary named Gambella, who, Caiumbuca informed the professor, was the president of the king's councillors, arrived and seated themselves before the strangers. Then began on both sides a series of compliments and many protestations of friendship, with expressions of welcome on the part of the dignitaries. Gambella, a stern, resolute-looking man, with a cold, haughty manner, was profuse in his welcome, and, as Houston declared, "rather overdid the business." He informed the professor that the king would see and converse with him and his companions the next day, and that in the mean time they would be comfortably quartered in the town. The dignitaries then retired, and their places were taken by others, who went through the same ceremonies, giving place in turn to others still, until the whole court had welcomed the strangers. By this time it was dark, and our travellers were glad when the ceremonies came to an end, and they were permitted to withdraw to the houses assigned them.

"Well, professor," asked Ashton, when they were alone, "are you satisfied with our reception here?"

"So far as it has gone we have nothing to complain of," replied Professor Moreton; "but, to be frank with you, I am anxious for the future."

"We can only wait and see what will happen," said Ashton. "We had best keep our people together as well as possible, and be prepared for any treachery."

"If treachery comes," said Houston, "it will be through that fellow Gambella. Mark my words, professor, in spite of his fine speeches he is not pleased to see us, and he may try to give us trouble."

"You right, Master Hoosey," exclaimed Charlie. "Me no like him eye. He one bad man. Me watch him."

"We shall know something of what is in store for us very soon, I suppose,"

LUINA HOUSES AND HOES.

said the professor. "We have an audience with the king to-morrow, and he will probably make known his intentions concerning us."

"One thing struck me during the interview with the court to-day," said Philip Lee; "these people take us for Englishmen."

"I noticed it also," said the professor; "and I think it will be better to allow them to continue under this impression. They know of England and respect her, as she has large possessions on this continent. Besides, Dr. Livingstone once visited these regions, and left a very favorable impression behind him. Our own country is not known in this part of Africa, and we shall probably enjoy more consideration as Englishmen than as Americans."

"After all," said Ashton, "we can only wait and hear what the king has to say."

The position of the professor and his companions was indeed one that demanded the greatest caution and tact upon their part. They were in the Upper Zambezi, in the large city of Lialui, the new capital, founded by King

Lobossi, of the kingdom of the Baròze, Lui, or Ungenge, "for by all these names is that vast empire of South Tropical Africa known to the world." The king, whom they were to meet on the morrow, was by far the most powerful sovereign they had yet encountered, and reigned over a vast portion of South Central Africa, having relations with both the Portuguese on the West Coast and the English at the Cape of Good Hope. It will be well, therefore, before proceeding further, to present to the reader a view of the kingdom and its people. This we do in the words of the latest explorer of this region:

"We learn from the descriptions of David Livingstone," says Major Serpa Pinto, "that a warrior coming out of the South at the head of a powerful army, by name Chibitano, a Basuto by origin, crossed the Zambezi close to

LUINA PIPES FOR SMOKING BANGUE.

its confluence with the Cuando, and invaded the territories of the Upper Zambezi, subjecting to his sway the whole of the tribes who inhabited the vast tracts of country thus conquered.

"Chibitano, the most remarkable captain who has ever existed in Central Africa, started from the banks of the Gariep with the nucleus of an army formed of Basutos and Betjuanos, to which he went on adding the young manhood of the peoples he vanquished, and as he drew nearer to the North, he organized his new phalanxes till they became as terribly successful in the conquest of the Upper Zambezi as in the defence of the subjected countries. On this army, formed of different elements and of peoples of many races and origins, their commander bestowed the name of Cololos, hence the designation of Macololos, which became so well known throughout Africa. In the Upper Zambezi Chibitano met with many distinct peoples, governed by independent chiefs, who could not, separated as they were, oppose any serious resistance to the Basuto warrior's arms.

"Chibitano turned out to be as wise a legislator, and as prudent an administrator, as he was a redoubted warrior; and he succeeded in uniting the conquered tribes and causing them to regard each other as brethren in one common interest. The said tribes might be grouped in three great divisions, marking three distinct races. In the South, below the region of the cataracts, were the Macalacas; in the centre the Cangenjes or Barôzes, and in the north the

IRON IMPLEMENT USED AS A HANDKERCHIEF BY THE LUINAS.

Luinas, a more vigorous and intelligent race than either of the other two, and which was destined in the course of time to take the place of the Macololos in the government of the country. The reins of government have been indeed centred in the country of the Barôze or Ungenge, since the time of Chicrêto, the son and successor of Chibitano, and while all the tribes of the West bestow upon the vast empire the name of Lui or Ungenge, those of the South distinguish it by the designation of Barôze.

"The political organization of the kingdom of the Lui is very different to that of the other peoples of Africa. It possesses two distinct ministries, that of war and foreign affairs, the last being subdivided into two sections, each having a minister of its own. One of them has to do with Western, the other with Southern affairs, so that while the former deals with the Portuguese in Benguela, the latter has to treat with the English at the Cape."

At the time of our travellers' visit Gambella was president of the king's council and was also minister of war and Southern foreign affairs, while the Western foreign affairs were managed by a minister named Montagja.

"The empire, so powerfully sustained by the iron hand, wisdom, prudence, and policy of Chibitano, began visibly to decline under the reign of his son Chicrêto. Of the natives who came from the South with Chibitano, viz., the Macololos, few now remain, they

LUINA MILK-POT.

having been decimated by the fevers proper to the country, which do not even spare the natives themselves. Drunkenness and the too free use of *bangue*, joined to the unruliness of the chiefs, little by little deprived the invaders of all their usurped authority. On the death of Chicrêto, he was succeeded by his nephew Omborolo, who was to reign during the minority of Pepe, a younger brother of Chicrêto and son of the great Chibitano. The Luinas conspired, and Pepe was one day assassinated. Omborolo ere long shared the same fate, and the Luinas, having organized what amounted to another Saint Bartholomew's, slew without mercy the remnant of the former invading warriors, of whom only a handful escaped, who, under the command of Siroque, a brother of Chicréto's mother, fled westward and crossed the Zambezi at Nariere. The Luinas, after this sanguinary act, proclaimed their chief Chipopa, a man of ability, who took measures to prevent any dismemberment of the country, and managed to keep the empire in the same powerful condition that it boasted in the time of Chibitano. Chipopa reigned many years, but treachery was soon at its old work, and in 1876 a certain Gambella caused him to be assassinated and proclaimed his nephew Manuanino, a youth of seventeen, king in his stead. The first act of Manuanino's exercise of authority was to order Gambella, the man who had brought him to the throne, to be beheaded; and, not content with this, he deposed from office all the relatives and friends of his father, who had assisted to procure him his dignity, and collected about him only his maternal kinsmen. The former conspired in turn, and made a revolution, with the object of assassinating him in March, 1878; but Manuanino, learning of his danger through some who were yet faithful to him, succeeded in escaping, and fled towards the Cuando, where he assailed and devastated the village of Mutambanja.

"Lobossi, having been proclaimed king, despatched an army against him, and Manuanino had to retire from his new quarters, and repassing the Zambezi at Quisseque plunged into the country of the Chuculumbe, which he crossed and joined a band of whites (elephant-hunters), who were encamped on the borders of the Cafucue. Lobossi, apparently conscious that his own safety depended upon the death of Manuanino, sent a fresh army against him.

"The Lui or Barôze, properly so called,—that is to say, the country lying to the north of the first region of the cataracts,—is composed of the enormous plain through which courses the river Zambezi, stretching from one hundred and eighty to two hundred miles from north to south, with a varying width of from thirty to thirty-five miles; a plain raised to some three thousand three hundred feet above the sea-level, and rising still higher in the eastward, where numerous villages are seated whose plantations flourish in the open. It likewise consists of the enormous valley of the Nhengo, through which runs the river Ninda. The Nhengo district is separated from the bed of the Zambezi by a ridge of land upwards of sixty feet in height, running parallel to the river, and in which many villages are situated that are out of reach of the greatest floods. During the rainy season the plain of Zambezi becomes inundated. The Luina people, who in great part reside in the plain, repair to the mountainous region during the inundations. On the retirement of the waters they return to reoccupy the villages abandoned during the inclement season, and cover the country with their enormous herds, which, to say truth, do not find a very luxuriant pasturage at any portion of the year, as the meadows are for the most part formed of rushes and canes. Cultivation is carried on more upon the right than on the left bank of the Zambezi, and always near the rising ground. The inundation leaves upon the extensive plain an immense number of small lakes, which form the beds of aquatic vegetation, and become so many sources of miasma and swamp fevers, so that there are portions of the year when the aborigines themselves suffer greatly from zymotic diseases. The lakes abound in fish, and are the homes of multitudes of frogs. It is from these lakes, also, that the natives draw their supplies of drinking-water, but it is necessary to explain that they only drink it when converted into *capata*.

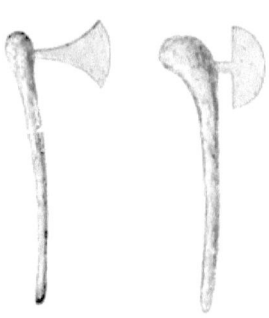

LUINA WAR-HATCHETS.

"The Luinas are no great tillers of the land, but they are great rearers of cattle. Their herds constitute their chief wealth, and in the milk of their cows they find their principal nourishment. A Luina's property may be said to consist of cows and women. Few countries in Africa have carried further than the Luinas the practice of polygamy.

"The basis of their food is milk, either fresh or curdled, and sweet potatoes. Maize flour is used to make *capata*, mixed with the flour of *massambala*, the chief article of cultivation in that country.

"The people work in iron, and all their arms and tools are manufactured at home. They use no knives, and one cannot fail to admire their wood carvings. In the Lui they employ but two implements; the rough work is done by the hatchet and the fine by the assegai. The iron of the latter performs all wonders; the benches on which they sit, the porringers out of which they eat, the vessels that contain their milk, and all their other wooden articles are wrought by its means. There is one utensil upon which generally the greatest care is bestowed, and that is the spoon. Living, as he does, upon milk, the Luina cannot do without his spoon, but he dispenses with the knife.

"Ceramic manufacture is limited in the Baróze to the making of pipkins for cooking purposes, pans for *capata*, large jars for the preservation of cereals, and moulds for the confectioning of pipes in which to smoke *bangue* (Indian hemp). The Luina smokes nothing but *bangue*. Tobacco is cultivated to a considerable extent, but it is used exclusively as snuff, and both men and women make great use of it in that shape.

"The people are tolerably well covered. It is rare to see either an adult male or female naked from the waist upwards. The men wear skins fastened to a girdle, which hang behind and before, and reach as low as the knees. A fur mantle with a cape covers the shoulders, and falls to about the middle of the leg. A broad leathern belt, independent of that to which the skins are fastened, completes the attire. The women wear a petticoat of skins, reaching in front to the knee, and behind to the calf of the leg. They also have a broad girdle about the waist, adorned with cowries. A small fur mantle, a great many beads round the neck, and several bangles on the wrists and ankles form the usual costume of the country. It is no uncommon thing to see females substituting European stuffs for skins, and wearing cotton counterpanes for mantles. The women of the upper ranks, and generally the rich, grease their

LUINA EARTHENWARE.
1. Kitchen jugs. 2. Jar for wheat. 3. Pipe-bowls.

bodies over with beef-suet mixed with powdered lac, which gives the skin a vermilion lustre, and at the same time a disgusting smell.

"Many of the Luinas possess percussion muskets of English manufacture, conveyed thither by the traders from the south, and others flint ones, made in Belgium, obtained from the Portuguese at Benguela. The natives prefer percussion guns, and there are even some who seek after rifles. They do not use cartridges, like the Bihenos and their immediate neighbors, but carry their powder loose in little horns or calabashes. The arms of the country are assegais, clubs, and hatchets. Bows and arrows are not in use. By way of defensive arm they employ large oval-shaped shields of ox-hide over a wooden frame. Every man carries, as a rule, from five to six assegais for throwing. The irons of these assegais, although not poisoned, are none the less very terrible weapons, owing to their being barbed in every direction, so that where they run into the body there is no extracting them, save by the death of the wounded.

"All goods are acceptable in the Lui, the best being preferred. Brass wire, about the eighth of an inch in diameter, is valuable, and all ready-made clothes, coverlets, percussion arms, powder, lead in pigs, and articles of the chase are quoted at a high figure. Throughout the country trade is carried on exclusively with the king, who makes a monopoly of it; to him belongs all the ivory obtainable within his dominions, as well as all the cattle of his subjects, from whom he obtains them whenever needed. He makes presents to his hunters, chiefs of villages, and courtiers of the goods, arms, and other articles which he obtains by barter.

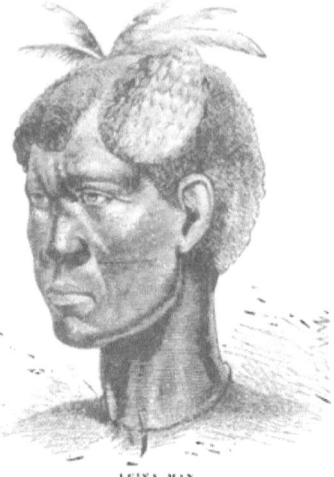

LUINA MAN.

"Women enjoy within the territory a good deal of consideration, and the nobler among them do literally nothing, passing their lives seated upon mats, drinking *capata*, and taking snuff. They possess many slaves, who are for the most part Macalacas, who wait upon them and attend to their wants."

Such was the country, and such were the people, in which our travellers now found themselves. What would the morrow bring forth?

Early the next morning Professor Moreton was informed that King Lobossi was ready to receive his white visitors. The travellers thereupon arrayed themselves in their best clothes, and repaired to the great square of the town, where the audience was to be held.

They found the square full of people. King Lobossi was seated in a high-backed chair in the middle of the square, and behind him stood a negro shielding him from the rays of the sun with an umbrella. Our travellers were surprised to find the king so young a man. He was about twenty years old, very tall, and proportionately stout. He was better dressed than any African sovereign the party had yet encountered. He wore a colored shirt, over which was thrown a cashmere mantle, and around his neck were several amulets in place of a cravat. His trousers were also of cashmere, and his feet were encased in a pair of clean white stockings and neatly polished low-quarter shoes. He held in his hand a curiously carved wooden stick into which were stuck bunches of horse-hair. This he waved to and fro with great gravity during the interview, to keep off the flies.

Gambella was seated in a lower chair on the king's right, and the three councillors were on the opposite side. Back of the monarch stood fifty armed warriors, who remained as motionless as statues during the interview. About one thousand of the native nobility squatted on the ground in a semicircle, displaying their rank by the distance at which they were placed from the king.

KING LOBOSSI.

As the professor and his companions approached, the king rose, and his example was followed by the councillors, and then by the nobles. A pressure of the hand was exchanged by each of the travellers with King Lobossi and Gambella, but to Matagja and the other councillors they simply bowed. The king and his people then resumed their seats, and the whites were requested to seat themselves on the ground near the monarch and Gambella. Caiumbuca, who had accompanied the party as interpreter, was given a seat by the professor.

The interview opened with an exchange of compliments which would not have shamed an European court. The king expressed his great satisfaction at seeing so many white men in his country, and hoped they would find their visit pleasant. Professor Moreton then told him that he and his companions were not merchants, but were children of the great white king whose country lay far beyond the sea. They were on their way to join the whites on the Indian Ocean, and in order to do so had to pass through his majesty's dominions. They felt themselves honored by being permitted to see and converse with so powerful a monarch, and hoped he would prove their good friend, and help them on their journey.

Lobossi replied that he knew and understood that the white strangers were not traders, and that the reception he had given them on the previous evening ought to convince them of this. He added that the strangers were his guests, and that, as he hoped they would remain some time at his court, they would have plenty of time to talk about affairs. Some more conversation in a similar strain followed, and then the interview came to an end.

Upon returning to their quarters our travellers found the court-yard occupied by thirty oxen, which the king had sent them as a present. Caiumbuca informed the professor that although the oxen were nominally for the sole use of the party, the proper thing to do was to cause them all to be slaughtered at once, to send the best leg of beef to the king, and distribute the remainder of the flesh between the courtiers and the men of the expedition. The professor, therefore, gave orders to Charlie to have the animals slaughtered. When this was done, a choice quarter of beef was despatched to the king with the professor's compliments, and others to Gambella and the three councillors. The rest was divided into two parts, one of which was retained for the use of the expedition, and the other distributed among the courtiers. The hides of the animals, which are highly valued by the Luinas, were presented by the professor to Gambella and Matagja.

In the afternoon the king sent a message to the professor that he would like to converse with him again, and that gentleman, taking Caiumbuca with him as interpreter, repaired to the royal residence. The house in which the monarch received him was semi-cylindrical in shape and of large dimensions, being about sixty feet long by twenty-five wide, and correspondingly high.

GAMBELLA.

The king was seated near the centre on a stool, and opposite him, on a bench, were the four councillors. Several of the higher nobles of the court were present, and among them was an old man, with white hair and beard, and tall and vigorous frame, who frequently regarded the professor with glances of kindly interest.

A large pot of *quimbombo* was placed in the middle of the room, and from it the king and his attendants drank copiously. The professor was asked to take his share, but replied that he drank only water.

The king opened the conversation by asking the professor how large his country was, and was astonished at the reply. He then asked the professor to repeat something in English, that he might hear how it sounded. Professor Moreton repeated one of Hamlet's soliloquies, which so pleased the monarch that he declared that English sounded like music, and was very sweet to his ears. The conversation which followed was unimportant, and the professor perceived that the time had not yet come to lay his plans before the king. The interview soon came to an end, and the professor was dismissed with many words of friendship from King Lobossi. One thing impressed him unfavorably, however. During the whole audience Gambella preserved an unbroken silence, though he did not cease to regard the professor with cold and sometimes unfriendly glances.

When the party had collected in their hut after nightfall, Charlie suddenly turned to Professor Moreton and asked,—

"Master 'Fessor, why you take Caiumbuca to talk for you?"

"Caiumbuca understands what the king and his people say, and I do not," replied the professor. "He can tell me what they say."

"You trust Caiumbuca?" asked Charlie, after a pause, during which he appeared to be thinking earnestly.

"I have no reason to distrust him," replied Professor Moreton.

"Me no trust him," said Charlie, energetically. "Caiumbuca one bad nigger, Master 'Fessor. He talk too much with Gambella when you no see him. Me see him talk. Bimeby Gambella buy him, and he sell us all."

"Then we shall be in a sad plight," said Ashton. "He is the only one among us who speaks the language of this country."

Charlie burst out into a hearty laugh, which greatly surprised his hearers. Then turning to Ashton, he said, quietly,—

"No, no, Master Ashton, Charlie talk Luina tongue like Caiumbuca. Lobossi and Gambella talk to you in Sesuto. That Macololo tongue,—only used by the king and the nobles. Common niggers here talk Luina tongue. Me talk both."

"How did you learn them?" asked Ashton, quickly.

"Me been in Luina country before," replied Charlie, smiling. "Not this place,—another part. Stay there long time, and learn very quick."

"Then you shall be our interpreter, Charlie," said Professor Moreton. "You shall talk to the king for us."

"No, no, Master 'Fessor," said Charlie, laughing. "That spoil all. They not know Charlie understand them. Me tell you what to do. You take Charlie with you when you go see Lobossi. Me no talk; me listen, and tell you if Caiumbuca talk all right what you say to Lobossi."

"That's an excellent suggestion, professor," said Ashton. "Charlie is faithful to us, we know; and he will act as a check upon Caiumbuca should he meditate treachery against us."

After some discussion it was agreed to adopt Charlie's suggestion, and the faithful black, encouraged by his success, now turned to the professor and asked,—

"Me tell you 'nother thing, Master 'Fessor. You think you safe here?"

"The king seems very friendly to us now," replied Professor Moreton. "I don't think we are in any danger just now."

"No danger now," said Charlie, earnestly. "Lobossi like you now. Gambella no like you. Bimeby he turn Lobossi against you. Maybe you have to fight. What chance you got here, Master 'Fessor?"

"None in this town," replied the professor. "We are at their mercy. What do you advise, Charlie?"

"Me tell you," said Charlie. "Next time you see Lobossi, you tell him you want to build camp where you can keep your niggers together. He ask Gambella. Gambella glad to get you out of the town. He no want you too near Lobossi. He tell Lobossi to say 'yes.' Then, Master 'Fessor, you build strong camp in the woods. You have to fight, you got good camp, and not shut up here."

"Charlie's advice is good," said Ashton, emphatically. "We must not lose a moment in acting upon it."

The professor was of the same conviction, and it was determined that at the next interview they would ask permission to build a camp in the vicinity of the town.

On the morning of the 5th of August our travellers received a visit from the old man whom the professor had noticed at the audience of the previous afternoon.

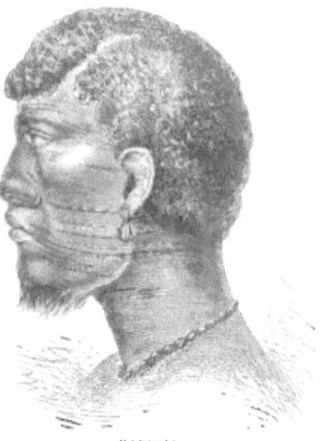

MATAGIA.

He proved to be Machauana, the former companion of Dr. Livingstone in the journey which the great explorer made from the Zambezi to Loanda, and who is mentioned so highly by the doctor in his journals. He had conceived a warm friendship for Livingstone, and now desired to extend it to those whom he supposed to be the countrymen of his friend. He spoke a little English and a little Portuguese, and by means of these was enabled to carry on a long conversation with the professor about his former companion. He was greatly distressed to hear of Dr. Livingstone's death, and declared he was the best man he had ever known, and that, for his sake, he would always love the English. As he was leaving he told the professor he would be his friend with the king.

"But," he added, "beware of Gambella. He is the true king here, and he does not like you. Watch him."

In the afternoon Professor Moreton received a message from the king, through a confidential slave, that he would like to see him at his house that night. At nine o'clock the professor set out for the royal residence, taking with him Caiumbuca, as usual, and also Charlie, who carried a present intended for the king. This consisted of the second-hand uniform of a Parisian *gendarme*, and had been purchased in Paris by the professor for a mere trifle. It included the white cotton epaulets and the cocked hat with its tall tri-colored plume, and was altogether the handsomest costume our travellers had brought with them. They had reserved it for some negotiation of more than usual importance, and now, as so much depended upon King Lobossi's good will, they felt that the time had come to make use of it.

Professor Moreton found the king in one of the inner houses of his quarter, seated upon a stool near a large fire, burning in an open brazier. Behind him ranged in a semicircle were twenty stalwart men, armed with assegais and shields, who stood silent and motionless during the conference. The king greeted the professor cordially, and in a few minutes Gambella came in, and the conference began.

The professor opened the interview by saying that he had brought with him a present, which he hoped his majesty would do him the honor to accept. He then commanded Charlie to display the uniform, at the sight of which Lobossi broke into child-like exclamations of delight. He insisted upon arraying himself in it at once, in spite of Gambella's objections, and, when he had gratified his desire, walked several times around the hut with a martial stride; then, seating himself on the stool once more, he began to talk of business. He told the professor that it had been a long time since any of the Benguela traders had visited his country, and that he was anxious to have more come. He also desired to open a trade with the English at the Cape, as he wished to obtain arms and powder from them. Just now, he said, he was almost out of powder, and in great need of it, as he was carrying on a war with some of his subjects, who had rebelled against him.

"If I let you go on to the white men at the sea, will you send me guns and powder when you get there?" he asked.

The professor replied that, as he was not a trader, he could make no positive promise, but that as soon as he reached the white men he would tell them of the profitable trade that might be built up with the king, and added that his majesty might feel sure that when the white traders felt that they could enter his dominions with safety and profit they would be very quick to come.

This appeared to please the king; but Gambella, who was really an able man, endeavored to entrap the professor into replies that might be used to his disadvantage. Professor Moreton at once detected the crafty minister's object, however, and baffled him so completely that he ceased his questions.

The professor then stated the plan of his party. He said they had originally intended to descend the Liambai, or Upper Zambezi, to the great falls, and from that point make their way along the river by boat and on foot to the Zumbo, from which they could descend the stream to its mouth. Now, however, a new plan had presented itself, which was to march across the country from Lialui to Caineo, situated on an island in the Loengue, which river runs into the Zambezi below the Cariba rapids. From that point they could descend the Zambezi in boats to the Zumbo. To do this, however, they would have to ask the king to furnish them with men. He assured the king that it would be of infinite advantage for him to thus show that the Zumbo route was free to white traders, because, as soon as the fact was known, the Portuguese traders

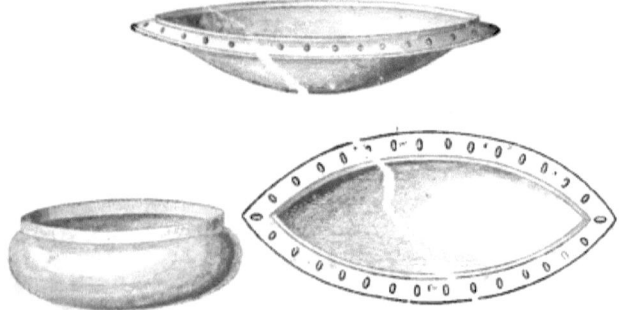

WOODEN PLATTERS OF THE LUINAS.

on the Lower Zambezi would eagerly embrace the opportunity to bring the articles he needed into his country. He himself would urge them to bring the arms and powder the king was so anxious to obtain.

Lobossi replied that he would think of the matter. In the mean time he was more than ever the friend of his white visitors, since they had given him such a magnificent present.

The professor then presented his request to be permitted to construct a camp near the town. Gambella at once urged the king to consent. He added that it would be the wisest course for all, as the whites would then be better able to control their men than in the town. The royal assent was given, and the interview came to an end.

When they returned to their own quarters Charlie told the professor that Caiumbuca had interpreted the interview correctly, but had omitted one of

Gambella's remarks to the king in support of their request to be allowed to build a camp. That astute statesman had advised the monarch that it would be much easier to deal with the whites when out of the town, as their ceasing to be his guests would relieve him of the obligations of hospitality, and leave him free in his dealings with them. These words sounded ominous to the party.

The next morning the professor arose quite ill, and it was evident that he was about to be taken with another attack of fever. He could not think of giving up, however. There was so much to do that required his personal attention, the future of the expedition was so uncertain, that he must keep on his feet as long as possible.

The day was the 6th of August, 1879, the anniversary of their landing at St. Paul de Loanda. One year before they had entered Africa full of hope and confidence. They had surmounted difficulties of the gravest nature, had carried their expedition almost to the centre of the continent, and now they were no longer masters of their own movements. They were really prisoners, dependent upon the caprice of a savage monarch and his unscrupulous minister. Nothing but courage and indomitable resolution could extricate them from their difficult position.

WOODEN SPOON OF THE LUINAS.

Early in the morning a large detachment of the carriers of the expedition was despatched under the command of Houston and Philip Lee to construct an encampment at a spot selected by the professor, about half a mile to the south of Lialui. They had orders to make it as strong as the means at their command would permit, and to hasten the work as much as possible.

Later in the day, in spite of the languor caused by his fever, the professor, with Ashton, Hubbard, and Charlie, went to call on the king, accompanied by Caiumbuca. They found him in one of the circular houses, surrounded by people, with six enormous pans of *capata* set before him, from which all were drinking. The king was very merry, and the whole court about half drunk. Caiumbuca was soon in the same condition, and as it had been agreed not to betray Charlie's knowledge of the language, the professor and his party, being thus left without an interpreter, withdrew.

On the morning of the 7th of August the professor was summoned by King Lobossi to appear before his great council to explain his plan to them. Though much worse from the fever, he set out at ten o'clock with his two companions and Charlie. Caiumbuca was charged to remain sober until the close of the interview.

They were received kindly by Lobossi, who, however, left the conduct of the proceedings to Gambella. The latter exerted all his arts to confuse the professor, but without success. Taking a stick, Professor Moreton traced upon the ground the course of the Zambezi, and to the east, running parallel to it, the course of the Loengue, which, under the name of the Cafueue, flows into the Zambezi below the Cariba rapids. He then marked the position of the village of Caineo on the Loengue, and showed that in fifteen days his party could reach that place, from which they could descend the Loengue to the Zambezi in boats, and pass down the latter river in the same way to the Zumbo. He declared that there were no cataracts in the Loengue, and that the Zambezi was perfectly navigable from Cariba to the Zumbo.

The king and the council were greatly astonished by the professor's knowledge of their country and Gambella, who knew the white man had spoken truly, was silenced. After much discussion it was resolved to allow the white travellers sufficient men to make the journey, and several of the members of the council declared they had long wished to see a trade opened with the whites on the Lower Zambezi. The council broke up amid great enthusiasm, and the king declared that the men who were to compose the expedition should be selected the next day.

The professor and his companions then returned to their quarters, and during the night the fever of the former increased to such an extent that he became delirious, causing grave anxiety to Ashton and Hubbard, who watched by him. The next morning he was better, but so weak that he had to keep his bed.

During the day Lobossi, who had heard of the professor's illness, came to see him, and brought with him his confidential doctor. The latter was a small, thin old man, with very white hair and beard, and a shrewd, cunning face. At the request of the king, Professor Moreton consented to allow the old man to determine what was the matter with him.

The doctor thereupon drew from his breast a string that was run through eight halves of the stones of some fruit, and solemnly pronouncing certain cabalistic words, threw the string upon the ground. Some of the stones fell with the inner side upward, and some the reverse. The doctor gravely examined the positions in which they had fallen, and then, turning to the professor, declared that he was possessed by the spirits of his deceased relatives, and that it was necessary for him to give the doctor something that he might charm them away. The professor pretended to believe all the doctor said, and dismissed him with a small present of gunpowder.

In the afternoon Houston and the carriers came in to say that the camp was in readiness. Preparations for a move were immediately begun, and by nightfall our travellers were comfortably established in the camp. All felt better satisfied and much freer than in the city of Lialui. Their quarters were cleaner and more to their taste, and they felt that if necessity should compel them to defend themselves they had here a better opportunity than in the crowded city.

The first act of Professor Moreton, after reaching the camp, was to turn over the command of the expedition to Ashton. He was himself too ill to undertake further negotiations with the king or Gambella, and the young man had so thoroughly proved his good sense and courage that he felt no hesitation in relinquishing the command to him until he himself should be fit to resume it.

LUINA HATCHET.

The next morning a considerable commotion was heard in the city, and Caiumbuca was sent to learn its meaning. There was an incessant beating of drums, accompanied by repeated musket-shots, sometimes singly and sometimes in volleys, and the greatest excitement seemed to be prevailing in Lialui. In a couple of hours Caiumbuca returned with an explanation of the extraordinary hubbub. News had just been received by the king of the defeat of his forces by the rebels in the Chuculumbe country. The latter had been aided by a band of white elephant-hunters from the eastern side of the continent,—Portuguese from the East Coast, Caiumbuca said,—and he added that these Portuguese were of a different race from those on the West Coast.

"It is fortunate for you," he said, "that you are not of the same race as these people; if you were, your lives would not be worth a day's purchase."

These words more than ever decided our travellers to adhere to the character of Englishmen with which the Luinas had invested them, and they also increased their anxiety for the future.

Caiumbuca reported the city in great excitement. The warriors had been called out by the war-drums, and messengers had been despatched to different parts of the kingdom to summon the royal forces.

The next morning our travellers were surprised to receive a visit from Gambella. He was entertained by Ashton, who informed him that during the sickness of the professor he would receive all communications from the king. Gambella then delivered a message from Lobossi, explaining the cause of the war, and the king's determination to prosecute it with vigor. He added that, as the scene of hostilities would be the Chuculumbe country, through which the party proposed to travel, the journey to Cainco would be impossible; therefore everything that had been agreed upon between the king and Professor Moreton must be considered as broken off. This was a sharp disappointment to the young man, but he concealed his feelings, and told Gambella that he hoped to make some other arrangement with the king that would be equally satisfactory. Gambella replied in a few polite phrases and then took his departure.

In the afternoon Ashton was informed that three of the Biheno pombeiros wished to speak with him. Upon making their appearance they told him that, not liking the condition of affairs in the country, they had concluded to return home, and were anxious to do so at once. In vain Ashton urged them to remain with the expedition awhile longer, and told them it would be cowardly to abandon it then. They were firm; they wished to depart at once,—that very afternoon, indeed.

Seeing that he could not move them, the young man sought the other pombeiros and asked their intentions. They replied that neither they nor their men were afraid, and would stand by the party. Caiumbuca and the five armed Benguela men also assured him of their fidelity to him, and soundly berated the Bihenos who wished to depart as cowards, and men who were acting in bad faith.

Thus reassured, Ashton caused the three pombeiros to surrender the arms and ammunition that had been issued to them and their men. This they did reluctantly, and only when Ashton had declared that without such a surrender he would not pay them the wages due them. The guns and powder were then delivered, and the pombeiros received the wages agreed upon for themselves and their men. Ashton then bade them leave the camp at once, and threatened them with severe punishment if any of them were found in it again. Yet it was not without a sad and foreboding heart that he watched the ninety-three men file out of the enclosure and take their way towards Lialui. This desertion left him with two pombeiros, sixty carriers, the five armed Benguela men, Charlie, Mombée, and Caiumbuca, making in all seventy blacks.

The next day, August 11, Lobossi paid a visit to the camp. Professor Moreton was too unwell to see him, and Ashton did the honors of the occasion. The king assured Ashton that the journey to the Chuculumbe was impossible, but told him that he would furnish the party with guides and a few people as far as the Zumbo, by way of the Zambezi. He then began to beg for various things, many of which were not in possession of the whites, and seemed like a spoiled child when told he could not have them. Ashton took occasion to question the king about a rumor he had heard that morning that Lo Benguela, the powerful monarch of the Matebelis, with whom Lobossi had been on bad terms for some time, was about to attack the Lui. This abrupt question seemed to disconcert the king, and he answered hastily that the rumor was false; that there was peace with the Matebelis, and he could easily crush the rebels with the forces he was raising.

The king then began to complain of the few presents his white visitors had given him, and ended by saying that as he was going to war they ought to let him have all their arms and gunpowder. He would guarantee their safety to the Zumbo, and as long as they were under his protection they would not need their weapons. Ashton told him that on the day of the departure of the expedition for the Zumbo he would give him a dozen guns and two kegs of gunpowder, but that under no circumstances would another gun or an ounce of powder belonging to the expedition be given to him. The king was displeased at this answer, and left the camp in a bad humor.

The next morning the party were surprised by a visit from one of the principal nobles of the kingdom, who brought an order from the king, commanding the whites and their followers to quit the country and go back to the Bihé. Ashton quietly told him to say to the king that he was committing a most unwise act, for if the white men were forced to return to the Bihé and Benguela they would prevent any more Bihé caravans from trading with the Lui. He also charged Caiumbuca to go with the messenger and repeat to the king what he had said. Later in the day Caiumbuca returned with a fresh order from the king to quit the country at once and take the road to the Bihé.

LUINA WOMAN.

On the morning of the 13th, Gambella himself made his appearance at the camp, fully armed, and, contrary to the custom of the country, did not lay aside his weapons upon entering the hut where Ashton received him. The only notice the young man took of this discourtesy was to remove his revolver from its case and place it in the front of his belt, where he could lay his hands on it at a moment's warning.

"I bring you the king's orders," said Gambella, shortly, "to quit the country at once. You will not go there, nor there, nor there," he added, sternly, pointing successively to the north, east, and south, "but will go back to the Bihé and Benguela. Refuse, and we will drive you away."

"Friend Gambella," said Ashton, coolly, looking the savage firmly in the eye, "go and tell Lobossi, or accept the message for yourself, that we will not move a step from here in the direction of the Bihé. It is true you have a numerous army, but you have no powder. My men are well armed. If we are attacked, we shall know how to defend ourselves. If we fall, the white king will call Lobossi to account for our death, for he loves us too well to allow us to die unavenged. You already have a civil war on your hands, and you are threatened by the Matebelis. Now let Lobossi provoke a war with the white king, and he is lost. You have my answer. We leave here only for the Lower Zambezi."

Gambella made no reply to this speech, which was uttered with an assurance Ashton was far from feeling, but, turning on his heel, left the camp in a towering rage.

The day was passed by our travellers in great anxiety, but nothing more was heard from the king. Professor Moreton, roused by the events occurring around him, was improving, but was still too weak to take an active part in them.

Towards nine o'clock at night Machauana came secretly to the camp, and told Ashton that Gambella, at a council held that day, had strongly advised Lobossi to have the white men put to death, but that the king had firmly refused to take such a step. He urged him to be on his guard, and promised to warn him if any unfriendly action were resolved upon. He added that he had great influence with the king, and would use it in behalf of his white friends.

The next day King Lobossi came to the camp unattended. He informed Ashton that he had changed his mind, and that all roads were open to the expedition. He would provide them with guides to the Quisseque, if the party decided to descend the Liambai, but, as he was going to war, could furnish no forces, and would not be responsible for anything that might happen. Ashton thanked him for his offer, and said the expedition would guarantee its own safety. The king then departed, and the young man subsequently learned that this new decision was due to the advice of Machauana, who had convinced him of the impropriety of compelling the whites to leave his dominions against their will. Machauana, they learned, was really more influential among the people than Gambella, though the latter was more in the confidence of the king. Between the two there was a bitter rivalry, and only the great popularity of Machauana saved him from the vengeance of the powerful minister.

On the 15th nothing further was heard from the city, and the day and night wore anxiously away. Late the next afternoon Ashton received a secret visit from Machauana, who told them that the question of putting them to death had again been raised in council by Gambella, but that Lobossi still refused to take such a step against those who had trusted to his hospitality. The old man said that he him-

LUINA WAR-CLUB.

self had warmly opposed the proposition, and had even threatened Gambella with the vengeance of the Luina race if he dared to violate the most sacred obligation of the nation,—that of hospitality. For the present his friends were safe, but they must be on their guard.

Soon after darkness had fallen, Ashton left the camp, and strolled slowly towards the city. He was anxious and oppressed, and was trying to see some way out of the troubles that surrounded him. Suddenly he was aroused from his reverie by a sharp whiz, as an assegai, hurled by some unseen hand, glanced by his left arm. Drawing his revolver and looking around him he saw, in the uncertain light, a tall negro preparing for a second throw. Quick as thought he raised his revolver and fired. A howl of pain from the black answered him, and the negro fell to the ground. Approaching him with caution, Ashton saw that he had thrown away his weapons. Placing his revolver at the negro's head, he compelled him to rise, and keeping him well covered with the pistol, drove him before him into camp. A hasty examination showed that the fellow had received a severe flesh wound in the right arm, but one not necessarily dangerous.

The man's wound was dressed, and then Ashton, summoning Caiumbuca, bade him accompany him to the king, taking with him also Houston and Charlie. Upon reaching the city they found Lobossi conversing with Gambella in one of the inner houses.

Ashton and his companions entered abruptly into the king's presence, pushing the would-be assassin before them. Leading the fellow before the king, Ashton demanded to know who and what he was. At the same moment the young man detected a hurried exchange of glances between the man and Gambella, which at once revealed to him the true author of the crime. Lobossi was horror-stricken at the sight of the blood on Ashton's hands, which the latter, in his haste to see the king, had forgotten to remove, and declared that he was in total ignorance of the attempt. The man he said was not one of his people. Clapping his hands to summon assistance, he ordered the negro to be removed, and requested Ashton to give him a minute account of what had occurred. Lobossi's indignation at the attempt on the young man's life was unfeigned, and he declared the wretch should suffer a terrible punishment. He said he should get but little sleep that night for thinking of the horrible affair, and begged Ashton to keep the matter quiet, assuring him that nothing of the kind should happen again while his white friends remained in his dominions.

Gambella was loud in his denunciations of the attempted assassination, and warmly applauded what Ashton had done. He said he only regretted that the negro had not been killed outright, and declared that he should pay dearly for his crime. Ashton, though firmly convinced that Gambella was the instigator of the attempt upon his life, thought it best to accept his protestations of friendship. A few more words passed, in which Lobossi repeated his promises of protection, and then Ashton and his companions returned to camp.

Ashton had scarcely risen the next morning when Charlie presented himself before him, and drawing him aside, said to him in a low voice,—

"Master Ashton, me right 'bout Caiumbuca. He bad nigger, and want to sell us all to Gambella. Last night when you see Lobossi and Gambella, me hear Gambella tell Caiumbuca to meet him near the city. When Caiumbuca come back to camp with us, he slip away and go see Gambella. Me follow, and hear what they say. Gambella say none of us understand the Lui language, and we not know what Caiumbuca say to Lobossi for you. When you talk one thing to the king Gambella tell Caiumbuca to say another that make Lobossi mad. Then he have you killed. Got to be cautious now, Master Ashton; got to watch every word and trust nobody."

"Well, Charlie," said Ashton, "it seems that we can trust no one but ourselves. You will continue to go with me when I see Lobossi; and as you understand the Lui tongue, you can warn me if Caiumbuca attempts to play us false. Then you must speak out plainly, and tell Lobossi the truth."

"Me do that," said Charlie. "Time to talk Lui then."

"To tell you the truth, Charlie," said Ashton, "I am more afraid of an

LUINA ASSEGAIS.

attack on our camp than anything else. If they attack us they will certainly try to set fire to the camp. Do you think we can trust the men?"

"Oh, yes," replied Charlie; "they will fight if attacked, because it will be for their lives."

"Yet if the camp is burned all our goods will go with it," said Ashton, speaking despondently for the first time.

"Look here, Master Ashton," said Charlie, "you got big camp; heap open ground in middle. You build house right in the middle, and cover it with green boughs, and throw earth over it, to keep fire away. You do it to-day, Master Ashton, and then you put guns and powder and stores in there, and when fire comes they in safest place."

"Your advice is good, Charlie," said Ashton; "I wonder we never thought of it before. The house shall be built to-day."

Early in the morning Gambella came over to the camp. He was in the friendliest mood, and said he had come to assure himself of his friends' safety, as he had not been able to sleep on the previous night for thinking of the dastardly attack on Ashton. Though his manner was friendly and his words pleasant, the young man could not help regarding his visit as a new evidence of danger.

"He has come," said Houston to Ashton, "to spy out our camp and detect its weak points. Suppose we seize him and hold him as a hostage for our safety?"

"No," replied Ashton; "we must not be the aggressors in anything. So far Lobossi is not hostile to us, though at heart he may not be our friend. To seize Gambella would convert the king into an open enemy and increase our difficulties."

"You are right, I suppose," said the young Californian, with a sigh; "but it seems too good a chance to be missed."

Gambella soon took his departure, and after he had gone Ashton commenced the construction of the store-house. It was finished by sunset, and the goods, powder, and spare arms of the party were placed in it. It was resolved that one of the young men or Charlie should stand guard over it every night. Lots were drawn, and the first night's watch fell to Charlie.

The night passed away peacefully, and the morning of the 18th of August dawned. Professor Moreton was now sufficiently recovered to leave his hut, and passed the day in making scientific observations. No word was received from the king; but during the afternoon Gambella sent in a present of ten loads of maize and massambala, with a friendly message. Just before sunset Ashton sent Caiumbuca to the king to say that they were now ready to depart as soon as he would furnish them with guides. Caiumbuca hurried off, but, as the hours passed on, failed to return, nor did our travellers see him again for several days.

It was Ashton's turn to guard the storehouse that night. All day he had been oppressed by a feeling that danger was close at hand. He tried to resist it, but could not shake it off. The silence of the king, and even the unexpected present from Gambella, served to deepen his forebodings. The absence of Caiumbuca also appeared conclusive proof of treachery. He communicated his fears to his companions, but the professor declared his faith in Lobossi's good intentions, and only Houston shared Ashton's fears of immediate danger.

"You may be right and I wrong, sir," said Ashton to the professor; "but I cannot resist the feeling that we are threatened with great danger. I shall expect all of you to remain in this hut all night, armed and provided with ammunition, and ready to answer my slightest call. I shall prepare the blacks in the same way, and have Charlie keep watch over them."

These preparations were accordingly made, and by nightfall the camp was quiet, but in readiness for an attack.

The day had been warm and trying, but after dark a strong and pleasant easterly wind had sprung up. Ashton, seated on a bench by the storehouse, with his rifle resting against his knee, was enjoying the cool breeze, and talking with Charlie, who was preparing to make a new round among the blacks. It was ten o'clock, and the camp was entirely silent. Not a sound came from the neighboring city, and Ashton began for the first time to hope that his fears were groundless.

Suddenly his quick eye caught the gleam of a light moving stealthily about beyond the encampment. This was followed by another, and another yet, until at least forty or fifty were seen glimmering beyond the enclosure. The meaning of this singular spectacle was at once plain to the young commander. His worst fears were about to be confirmed; the Luinas were about to attack and burn the camp.

"Charlie," he said, quietly, "go at once and bring up the blacks to the storehouse. Try to keep them as quiet as you can. We can't save the camp, but we *must* defend the storehouse."

Charlie was off at a bound, and at the same moment a burning brand was thrown in from without upon one of the huts of the encampment. This was followed by several others, and as the only covering of the huts was a light thatch of dry grass, several were soon in a bright blaze. Rushing to the professor's hut, Ashton shouted to his companions that the camp was attacked, and ordered them to bring out the cases containing the instruments, and such property as could be saved, and deposit them at the storehouse. This was quickly done, and by the time the whites reached the storehouse the flames, carried by the strong wind, were spreading in every direction. The camp was doomed,—the fight would be one for life.

The blacks, under Charlie's orders, had assembled around the storehouse, and to the delight of their white comrades appeared cool and collected. By the light of the burning camp Ashton could see a vast crowd of Luina warriors assembled without the line of huts, and from these a shower of assegais began to fall into the camp. Forming his men around the storehouse, which was located in the centre of the encampment, and beyond the reach of the flames, Ashton ordered them to open fire on the dark masses of their assailants, and to fire deliberately. He could see that the attacking party outnumbered his own at least twenty to one, and though he was well pleased at the firmness displayed by his own blacks, he knew the struggle must be a hard one. Calling Charlie to him, he said to him hastily,—

"Charlie, now is the time for your knowledge of the Lui tongue to save us. We can defend ourselves here for a considerable time, but the fight is an unequal one. You must make your way out of the camp, where and how you can. Then hasten to Lialui; there see Lobossi, and tell him his people are attacking us. See Machauana also, and inform him of our danger."

Charlie made no reply, but at once darted off towards the burning huts, and disappeared among them. Ashton watched him until he was out of sight, and then turned to the fight which was raging around him.

By this time the unequal struggle was at its height. The Luinas, uttering hideous yells, hurled their iron assegais upon the defenders of the camp, who answered with volleys of rifle and musket balls, which did considerable execution among the assailants. Ashton and his companions used their breech-loading rifles with terrible effect, and were everywhere along the line, encour-

THE DEFENCE OF THE BURNING CAMP.

aging their men to fight bravely. By this time several of the negroes of the expedition were wounded, none of them very badly, however, but they held their ground manfully. The Luinas continued steadily to gain ground, and the destruction of the huts having removed all barriers to their progress, they advanced in heavy masses into the encampment, and renewed the fight at close quarters, uttering the most fearful yells, and seeming like so many enraged demons in the light of the dying fires.

At this moment Mombée, who had been fighting like a tiger, and whose shoulder had been severely grazed by an assegai, rushed up to where Houston and Ashton were standing, and with a look of anguish on his face held up his rifle, which had just burst.

"Here, my brave fellow," said Houston, "take mine."

Handing his rifle and cartridge-belt to Mombée, Houston hastened to the storehouse to obtain another weapon. There was no longer any danger of the fire reaching the stores, but the iron hail of assegais was falling so thickly about the place that the effort to reach the entrance to the hut was accompanied with no little danger. Houston succeeded, however, in entering the hut unharmed. Leaving the door open, the light of the dying fires enabled him to see dimly the contents of the interior. The first object that met his eye was the large elephant rifle of the expedition, and near it a box of explosive cartridges. The balls of these cartridges were charged with nitro-glycerine, and had the property of exploding upon striking an object, and tearing open the flesh of an elephant. A single shot was thus sufficient to cause death to one of these monsters of the forest. Only that very morning Houston had been examining the rifle, intending to overhaul it and see that it was in thorough order the next day. Now, as he listened to the deadly conflict waging around him, the young Californian felt that the piece was worth a dozen ordinary weapons. Hastily securing the rifle and the cartridges, he darted from the hut and rejoined his companions, now hard pressed by the Luinas, who were advancing steadily towards the storehouse. The distance between the combatants was so slight that Houston had but to discharge his weapon into the dark mass opposite him, sure of bringing down a warrior at every shot. The first discharge of the elephant rifle was followed by a howl of dismay from the Luinas, who for the first time appeared to hesitate. Loading and firing rapidly, Houston discharged six shots at the warriors, each one being greeted with a yell of terror. The other defenders of the camp at the same time poured in a rapid and accurate fire, and the assailants were brought to bay. Suddenly they set up a wild chorus of yells, very different from their former war-cries, and the next moment turned and fled, panic-stricken, from the field. Houston followed them with several more shots from his rifle, which but increased their terror and hastened their retreat. In a few minutes not one of the attacking party was to be seen.

The rapid tramp of a large body of men approaching from the city was now heard, and soon after Charlie arrived with a considerable force, commanded by Machauana, which had been sent by the king to the rescue of the whites. Their services were not needed to repel the attack, but our travellers were well pleased to have them at hand in the event of a renewal of the conflict. Machauana brought a message from the king that he was ignorant of the whole affair, and he could only suppose that his people, thinking the whites meant to attack them in conjunction with the Portuguese who were aiding the rebels in the east, had taken the initiative, and fallen upon the camp of their own accord; but that he would use his whole power to prevent their being further molested.

"Lobossi may speak the truth," said Ashton to the professor; "but if he did not order the attack I am sure it was the work of Gambella."

Requesting Machauana to remain on the ground with his men until morning, Professor Moreton, who seemed to have recovered nearly all his former vigor during the battle, ordered fires to be built, and by their light proceeded to look after the wounded of the party. None of the whites had been injured save Ashton, whose forehead had been grazed by an assegai. The wound was trifling, but for a few hours was very painful. Mombée and twelve of the negroes had been wounded by assegais, but none of the Benguela men had been struck. The wounds were quickly dressed, and the injured men made as comfortable as possible. A search was then made for the wounded or dead of the attacking party, but none were to be found, their comrades having carried all of them off in their flight.

During the night a council of war was held by our travellers, at which Machauana was also present. The veteran warrior advised his white friends not to think of remaining in their present position, but to abandon it the next day and retreat to the mountains, near a place called Catongo.

"There," said he, "you can build another camp, and can resist more successfully any further attack that may be made upon you. Should fresh danger threaten you, I will try to warn you, and in the mean time I will try to provide you with food."

The advice of Machauana was adopted by Ashton, with whom, as the commander of the expedition, the decision lay, and it was resolved to begin the retreat to the mountains as early as possible the next day. Although no lives had been lost, the party had suffered severe losses in property, all their possessions save the articles in the storehouse having been destroyed in the burning huts. The camp equipage, the mackintosh boats, much of their clothing, their bedding, and many other articles, had thus been lost. But for Charlie's happy forethought in advising the construction of the storehouse, the expedition would have been ruined, for the attack was so sudden, and the fire spread so quickly, that it was with difficulty they had been able to remove even the scientific instruments and the few articles they had managed to rescue at the commencement of the assault.

Our travellers were very much perplexed, however, to account for the sudden panic and flight of the blacks. This was explained to them about daybreak by Machauana. He told them he had sent one of his men into the city for news. The Luinas had suffered heavily in the fight, and their defeat had spread consternation throughout the city. The warriors had been confident of victory, and upon entering the camp had made a vigorous advance upon the defenders, when suddenly the whites had directed against them some terrible and powerful sorcery, which they were unable to resist. Two of their bravest warriors had been literally torn in pieces, and three others had been decapitated by a terrible fire which seemed to burst from their bodies. It was this appalling spectacle that had caused the sudden panic and flight.

"It is as I suspected," said Houston to Ashton. "The nitro-glycerine bullets of the elephant rifle did it. It was a lucky thought of mine to use that rifle."

"We must keep the secret, however," said Ashton, "and allow them to think it sorcery."

Immediately after sunrise, Ashton determined to seek the king, and denounce him for the attack of the previous night. Taking with him Houston and Philip Lee, with Charlie as their interpreter, he set out at once for the city. They found Lobossi seated in the great square of the town, surrounded by his court and large numbers of his people. Lobossi was very friendly in his reception of the young men, but Ashton at once began to speak to him bitterly of the attack upon the camp.

"Before all your people, O Lobossi," said the young man, sternly, "I charge you with the responsibility for the cowardly attack upon us. The most sacred obligation of the Luinas, the law of hospitality, has been broken, and all your people who have lost relatives or friends in the battle, must blame you for their sorrow. You are king here, but you could not protect us. You allowed us to be attacked, and we defended ourselves."

In reply Lobossi repeated that he had known nothing of the affair until the sound of the firing and the receipt of Ashton's message had warned him of their danger. Then he had sent a force of warriors to their assistance. The king then endeavored, with all his ingenuity, to extract from Ashton the secret of the sorcery which had caused the attacking party to beat such a hasty retreat, for to sorcery and that alone he and his people attributed the terrible effects of the explosive balls so happily employed by Houston.

"King Lobossi," said Ashton, sternly, "we bore the attack of your people for a long time before we called to our aid the terrible powers we possess. Know that the sorcery of the white man is more destructive than that of the black man. As long as you treat us well we will not harm you; but if we are attacked again, we will call down the terrible fire and tear all your men to pieces. Woe to the Luina who raises his hand against us after this."

These words, which were faithfully translated by Charlie, produced a profound impression upon both the king and the people. Lobossi assured Ashton that he and his friends were safe, and advised him to build another camp.

"We shall build another camp," said Ashton, coldly, "but not here. We are going to the mountains, and shall camp at Catongo to-day. There we will await the fulfilment of your promise. Beware how you trifle with us, King Lobossi. We have power to destroy all your people if you again provoke us to anger."

With these words he abruptly quitted the king's presence, followed by his companions, and returned to camp.

"You have cheek enough for anything, Ashton," said Houston, as they walked along. "I never could have talked so to Lobossi."

"We are in a serious scrape," said Ashton, "and it will take cheek as well as courage to get out of it. As for the sorcery business, we must keep the true character of it secret. Not even Charlie must be told of it until we are out of this country."

Upon reaching the camp, Ashton hurried forward the preparations for the retreat, and at nine o'clock on the morning of August 19 the march was begun. The distance to Catongo was not great, being less than half a day's march. The party moved slowly, to accommodate the wounded, but the place was reached early in the afternoon. All the men save the wounded carried double loads, even the two pombeiros taking part in this labor.

Arrived at the mountain spur on which Catongo is situated, Ashton at once selected a site for the camp. It was on a little eminence, which sloped on one side to a lake of considerable size. It was well adapted for defence, and by nightfall a camp had been constructed.

The next day Ashton made a close examination of the stores on hand, and found that by putting the entire party on short rations he had food enough for six days. In the afternoon Houston made the discovery that the lake was full of fish.

"We shall not starve yet, professor," he said, cheerfully, "even if Lobossi refuses to allow his people to sell us food."

CHAPTER X.

ON THE ZAMBEZI.

ON the morning of the 21st of August, Charlie came to Ashton, and said Caiumbuca was in the camp, and desired to speak with him. Ashton signified his willingness to see him, and in a few moments the man approached. He came forward with a bold, confident air, which changed to one of cringing servility, as he met the cold, stern gaze of the young man.

Caiumbuca began to excuse his absence by saying that he had been sick at Lialui, and had been unable to come to the assistance of his companions during the attack upon them. Ashton cut him short by telling him coldly that they no longer needed his assistance, and that as he had managed to make such good friends in Lialui he had better return to them. He warned him that if he attempted to injure them any further with Lobossi, he would have the white man's fire that had done such havoc among the Luinas descend upon him and tear him to pieces. He concluded by ordering Caiumbuca to leave the camp at once, and never return to it again. The traitor, who was as firm a believer in the sorcery of the whites as was Lobossi himself, trembled at Ashton's threat, and quickly left the camp. Neither Ashton nor his companions ever saw him again.

Professor Moreton rallied quickly in the purer air of the mountains, and in the course of a few days was fully himself again. As Ashton had done so well in command of the party, however, he determined to allow him to retain the control until something definite could be agreed upon with the king.

On the 22d of August messengers arrived from Lobossi, bringing food, and bearing an invitation to the professor and his party to return to Lialui and be his guests until the question of their journey could be decided, which would be in a few days. Our travellers, however, were resolved not to quit their camp in the forest, and Professor Moreton bade the messengers inform the king that his wounded men were not yet well enough to bear the journey.

The next morning Ashton despatched Charlie at daybreak for Lialui, to learn something definite respecting Lobossi's intentions towards them. Charlie returned at nightfall, and reported that when he reached Lobossi's house the great council was in session, and a heated debate was going on. Carimuque, the chief of Quisseque, had sent several messengers to Lobossi with a request from an English missionary, who was at Patamatenga, to be permitted to enter the country, as he was very anxious to visit the Lui. Matagja, the minister of foreign affairs for the South, energetically opposed the request of the missionary. There were Englishmen enough in the land at present, he said, and it would not be wise to allow more to come. They were all sorcerers, and there was no telling what mischief they might bring upon the country. The debate, which Charlie stayed to hear, ended in a resolution not to allow the English missionary to enter King Lobossi's dominions.

As for their own affairs, all Lobossi would say was that he desired to see the professor and Ashton as soon as possible.

"No go to Zumbo now, Master 'Fessor," said Charlie. "How do to go see missionary?"

Charlie's question but expressed a thought that had sprung up in the minds of both the professor and Ashton. The journey to the Zumbo was clearly an

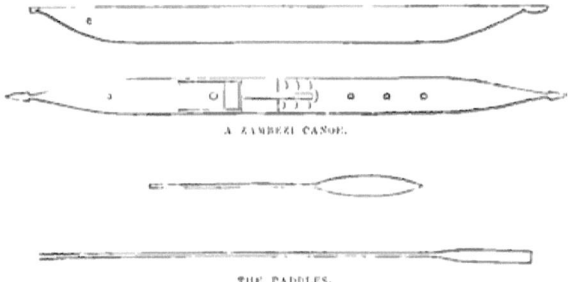

A ZAMBEZI CANOE.

THE PADDLES.

impossibility now, and the descent of the river was the only plan left open to them. The map was consulted, and they found that if Lobossi would give them boats they could reach Embarira, near the confluence of the Cuando or Linianti with the Zambezi, from which place they could march across the country to Patamatenga and join the missionary. Such a journey would require a month, if made in boats. From that point they could endeavor to reach the Transvaal and the English settlements in Natal. During the next two days the plan was earnestly discussed, and was adopted as the only resource left them.

On the morning of the 26th Professor Moreton and Ashton, accompanied by Charlie, set out from the camp at daybreak for Lialui. They were well received by King Lobossi, who was surrounded by his court and a number of his people. The king told his white friends that he hoped they were now convinced that he was not their enemy, and assured them that he had in no way connived at Caimmbuca's treachery.

Without replying to this, Professor Moreton said they had come to ask the

THE SONGUE.

SLOT OF THE SONGUE.

king to assist them in a journey to go and join an English missionary who they knew was at Patamatenga.

"How do you expect to get there without carriers?" asked the king. "You know you have none."

This question was loudly applauded by the bystanders.

"I have no carriers, it is true," replied the professor; "but there is the Liambai. You have boats, and if you will let me have what I want, and men to manage them, I can do without carriers."

"The Liambai is indeed there," said the king, "but it has cataracts. How will you get over them?"

Fresh applause greeted this question.

The professor replied that he was aware of the fact, but that where the rapids occurred the boats and their contents might be drawn ashore, carried around them, and relaunched in the stream below, and the journey be thus continued.

Lobossi retorted, with a broad grin, that his people had very little strength, and could not drag the boats ashore. This attempt at wit was greeted with a roar of laughter from the bystanders. The king instantly changed his manner, and demanded of the professor why he and his companions had not come to live at Lialui, as he had ordered them.

"We have not done so," replied the professor, rising to his feet, and speaking quietly but sternly, while at the same time he looked the king full in the eye,—" we have not done so for many reasons, the principal of which, King Lobossi, is that you are a crafty knave, who since our arrival has done nothing but deceive us, in order to try to rob us of all we have. I tell you, in presence of your people, that you are a robber and an assassin."

Then turning on his heel, the professor left the king's house, followed by his companions, amid a dead silence.

From the king's house the professor and his companions went to visit Machauana. The old man smiled as he listened to the professor's account of the interview with the king, and said it was the right way to talk to Lobossi. It would bring him to his senses. He said the king was really indignant at the attack that had been made upon them, and had censured Gambella severely for it. He had also refused to sanction any plan against their lives. He advised the professor, when he came back to Lialui, to claim the hospitality of Gambella. Once lodged in his house, the minister would not dare to plot against them. In the end he did not doubt that the king would send them on their way to join the missionary.

As they were leaving Machauana's house they were met by a messenger from Lobossi, who said the king earnestly desired to see them before they set out for their camp. They returned at once to the king's house, and this time found him alone.

Lobossi assured the professor that he and his companions had really no reason to doubt that he was their friend, that he intended to have some boats gotten ready for them, and that the Liambai was open to them.

"Lobossi," said the professor, "you have been badly advised by your councillors. We came here your friends, and we are your friends still. What gave the Macololo kings their great power was their generous and noble treatment of the great white traveller, with whom Machauana went to Benguela and Loanda.* The Luinas are pursuing a course that will drive away all

---

* Dr. Livingstone.

trade between your people and the white men. You already have a civil war on your hands, and you will need such articles as only the white traders can supply you with. Quarrel with my people, and you will inflict such misfortunes upon your country that your own people will rise against you and drive you from your throne."

Lobossi seemed much impressed by this speech, and renewed his protestations of friendship. He declared that he would give orders that very day for the boats to be gotten ready.

"When you come to me and tell me on your word as a king that the boats are ready, I will believe you, and we will all come back to Lialui," said the professor.

"Do not judge me hastily," said Lobossi, earnestly. "I am a king, and I am your good friend. Wait patiently for a day or two, and you will see that I will keep my word."

Thus the interview ended, and the professor and his companions went back to the camp, feeling more faith in Lobossi than at any previous time. They reached the camp sorely fatigued.

The next afternoon Machauana arrived with a message from the king, announcing that the canoes were in readiness, and inviting the party to return to Lialui the next day. Lobossi, the old man said, was acting in good faith now; the canoes were actually in readiness, and he advised them to lose no time in returning the next day. The professor promised to act upon his advice, and requested him to convey a message to Gambella for him, to prepare quarters for his party, as they intended to be his guests during their stay in the city, in order to show their confidence in his good faith. This Machauana promised to do, and added, laughingly, that after this Gambella would certainly do all he could to get them away on their journey, as the presence of so many guests would be expensive to him.

Early on the morning of the 28th of August the camp at Catongo was broken up, and the party set out on their return to Lialui. The march was slow, as the men were burdened with double loads. The wounded were nearly well, and were able to carry something, so that nothing was left behind at the camp. Lialui was reached at half-past two in the afternoon, and the party proceeded at once to Gambella's house. Gambella received his white guests with stately and even friendly courtesy, assigned them quarters in his own house, and provided shelter for the negroes of the expedition in some of the outhouses attached to his dwelling.

Late in the afternoon the professor and his young companions went to visit the king. Lobossi received them kindly, and remarked, with a peculiar smile, that they had done well to make Gambella their host, and that they would have nothing to fear as long as they had a claim upon his hospitality. He told them that all their troubles were due to the treachery of Caiumbuca, who had endeavored to have them killed in the hope of obtaining a part of their property. He added that he was now convinced that Caiumbuca had deceived both himself and Gambella, and that if he could lay hands on him he would punish him severely. The fellow had disappeared, however, and was nowhere to be found. The boats were in readiness, and the professor and his party could depart on the next day but one. He wished to make some final arrangements the next day, and in the mean time they would be safe and comfortable under the protection of Gambella.

The 29th of August was passed by our travellers in making preparations for the journey. The two Biheno pombeiros and their men, who had remained faithful to the party through all their misfortunes, were paid their wages by Professor Moreton, and were allowed to retain their guns and given a liberal supply of ammunition, as a reward for their gallant conduct on the night of the attack on the camp. They were well pleased with their rewards, and agreed to carry the baggage of the party to the boats the next morning, when they were to set out on their return to the Bihé. Professor Moreton spent a good part of the day in writing to Silva Porto. He related the adventures of the party in full, and did not fail to make known to the old trader the treachery of Caiumbuca. This letter he entrusted to one of the pombeiros, with orders to deliver it to Silva Porto's agent at Belmonte, who would forward it to his master.

While the professor was thus employed, Ashton was busy purchasing supplies for the party. With Gambella's aid he succeeded in procuring provisions for ten days. Gambella assured him he would have no difficulty in obtaining food along the river, and that the country along its course abounded in game of all kinds. The minister was now as anxious to hasten the journey of his guests as they were to depart. Having failed to get them out of the way in any other manner, he was only too glad for them to leave the country.

The expedition was now reduced to Professor Moreton, the four young men, Charlie, Mombée, and the five Benguela negroes, who remained faithful to their resolve to go on to the great sea, making in all twelve persons. With the assistance of the seven negroes our travellers were to make their way across fully half of the African continent, and through regions and dangers of which they had no knowledge. All recognized that they were now entering upon the most perilous part of their journey; yet all were eager to depart.

At daybreak on the morning of the 30th the entire party were in readiness to start. Soon after Lobossi came to say farewell. He brought with him a dozen negroes, who, he said, would go with the party and man the canoes. He would gladly send a larger force, he added, but the great council was opposed to sending any men away, with the necessity for raising troops on their hands. These men were his own slaves, however, and he could do as he liked with them. Then turning to the negroes, he commanded them to obey the orders of the whites as if they came from himself, and told them they would answer with their heads for their obedience. He informed the professor that these slaves would conduct him to the village of Itufa, on the Liambai, to the chief of which they bore positive orders to provide the travellers with fresh boats and men to man them for the voyage to Embarira. He gave the professor a small tusk of ivory as a present to the chief of the village, and said he had caused an ox to be slaughtered, and the flesh sent to the boats as provision for a part of the voyage.

"You see now," said Lobossi, "that I am not a bad man, and that I have kept faith with you."

He spoke with a simple dignity that touched the professor and his companions; and the former replied that he and his friends would forget the troubles they had passed through, and would remember only his last acts of kindness. He then presented the king with the twelve guns and two kegs of powder he had promised him when the boats should be ready, and to this added an excellent rifle and a supply of cartridges, which he asked his majesty to accept for his own use. Lobossi was delighted with the presents, and begged the professor to use his influence to induce the English traders to supply him with arms and ammunition. The king then bade the travellers a hearty farewell, and took his departure. Gambella's parting with them was less cordial, but was still friendly, and Ashton noticed that he heaved a long sigh of relief as he saw the party leave his house.

Our travellers set out from Lialui in a southwesterly direction. An hour's walking brought them to an arm of the river, which is called the Little Liambai. Here they found six good-sized canoes in readiness for departure, and in charge of two of Lobossi's servants, who delivered to the professor the flesh of the ox sent by the king.

No time was lost in loading the canoes with the baggage of the party, a portion being placed in each. The Bihenos, who had fulfilled their bargain to the letter, took leave of the whites, and as the canoes pushed off from the shore fired a salute from their guns, and shouted a cordial farewell.

Each of the canoes contained a portion of the baggage, and was provided with two of the king's slaves to paddle it. In the first canoe went Ashton and Charlie, in the second Houston and Mombée, in the third Professor Moreton and one of the Benguela men, in the fourth Hubbard and a Benguela man, in the fifth Philip Lee and another Benguela man, and in the sixth the other two Benguela men. Thus each canoe contained two members of the party, besides the two oarsmen; and as the former were armed, the safety of each boat and the property in it was insured. This order was preserved as far as possible during the entire descent of the river.

After leaving the shore the canoes pursued a southerly course for a quarter of a mile, and then, leaving the Little Liambai, entered a canal and steered southwest into a chain of lakes, through which the western branch pours a stream of water into the eastern or true Liambai. The spaces between these lakes were often nothing but muddy shallows, and at such places it was necessary to unload the boats and drag them from lake to lake. This was severe work, but all hands joined willingly in it. At six o'clock the party bivouacked in an open plain on the bank of a lake. The plain had been recently burned over, and there were no materials for constructing a shelter. Enough wood was procured on the opposite side of the lake to make a fire, and portions of the ox presented by Lobossi were roasted, and furnished a comfortable supper for both whites and blacks.

At daybreak the next morning, August 31, our travellers were astir. Breakfast was soon despatched, and the journey was resumed. Half an hour's paddling brought the canoes out of the lake into the main branch of the Liambai, which at that point was about two hundred and twenty yards wide and very deep. Noticing an abundance of game on the banks, Ashton caused the boats to land, and the four young Americans went ashore, and in half an hour succeeded in shooting six antelopes, which were placed in the boats. These, it was calculated, would furnish the party with meat for at least two days. The skins were carefully spread out to dry, as they would be useful for trading purposes along the river.

All day the canoes floated down the river, the swift current of which greatly assisted the exertions of the boatmen. Numerous hippopotami appeared, coming sometimes dangerously near the canoes; and as the boatmen were in mortal terror of the huge animals, they kept the canoes in the shallow water near the shore, where the hippopotami could not trouble them. Occasionally a crocodile would be seen swimming by, or basking upon the shore. The young Americans were sorely tempted to fire at the huge monsters, but Ashton's orders were positive. As the future was uncertain, no ammunition was to be wasted.

Nearly four days were passed on the river paddling down the stream, and camping upon its shores at night, and about noon on the 3d of September the village of Itufa was reached. The river here was fully a mile in width, and a strong east wind was blowing, which made the canoes rock so violently that there was danger of their being upset. The idea of being thrown out into a deep stream abounding in crocodiles was by no means pleasant to any of the occupants of the boats, and they were heartily glad when they were safely ashore at Itufa.

The chief of Itufa met the party at the landing place, and greeted them cordially. He gave them quarters in the village, and told them that their coming had not been unexpected by him, as Lobossi, not content with the instructions he had sent by the boatmen, had despatched a swift messenger overland with repeated orders to the chief to treat the white men and their companions with kindness, and furnish them with boats without delay. The boats, he said, would be ready as soon as possible; it would take a day to collect them, and in the mean time he was willing to sell the travellers what food they needed.

The chief was as good as his word, and spent the next day in getting together the necessary canoes. By nightfall six canoes of larger size than those by which our travellers had come from Lialui were collected at Itufa,

ITUFA HOUSE.

and the men who were to man them had been selected. Professor Moreton spent the day in purchasing food, and succeeded in obtaining a week's supply, which, with the provisions already on hand, and such game as they might be able to secure, would last the party to Quisseque. Lobossi's slaves were rewarded with presents, and the new boatmen were promised liberal wages, to be paid upon the safe arrival of the party at Embarira.

On the 5th of September the boats were loaded and in readiness to depart a little after sunrise. The chief of Itufa accompanied the party to the place of embarkation, and, when the moment of departure had arrived, said to the professor that he hoped he was satisfied, as he had fulfilled the orders of his king (Lobossi) to the letter. Professor Moreton replied that the chief had shown himself a faithful subject of his king, and that, as he had done so well, he would now give him the tusk of ivory which the king had intrusted to his white friend to be given to the chief in the event of his carrying out the orders sent him. The chief was greatly pleased with the present, which he said he prized more as a mark of his sovereign's good will than for its intrinsic value.

The party then set off, the order of the boats being the same as before, Ashton's leading. Though the canoes were larger than those of the Lui, our travellers soon found that they were quite as liable to upset, and as the broad river was considerably ruffled by a still east wind they left the shore with some misgivings. The boatmen kept in the shallow water, however, and no accident occurred. After a voyage of four hours, the boatmen declared they could go no farther that day, as the spirits that guarded that part of the river would visit their wrath upon them unless they halted there over night. They were firm in their decision, and the travellers were compelled to yield, and spend half a day in idleness.

The spot selected for their encampment was very different from anything they had seen since leaving the Bihé. It was at the extreme south of the vast Lui plain, where two mountain ridges converged, leaving only space for the bed of the Zambezi, there a mile and a quarter wide. A broken and rugged country succeeded the plain, and was covered with a luxuriant vegetation. Volcanic rocks were scattered thickly about, and rose abruptly from the stream, forming its banks. The change from the bare, flat plain to this bold and well-wooded region was so sudden and so decided as to be almost startling. It was very agreeable to our travellers, who were heartily sick of the tame and uninteresting country through which they had been journeying so long.

As the hour for the evening meal drew near, Mombée lit his fire to cook supper. Suddenly a spark from the flames flew into the lofty dry grass which covered the ground, and in an instant the whole place was ablaze. So rapidly did the fire spread that the entire party were obliged to make a rush for the canoes, and push out into the river to avoid it. This accident necessitated a removal to a camping place about a mile lower down the stream.

The next day was passed in paddling along the basaltic region, through which the great river breaks its way. Numerous small islands, rich in vegetation, were met, and on one of these the party encamped for the night.

The voyage was resumed early on the morning of the 7th, and for two hours the canoes glided by lovely islets and past bold masses of basaltic rock. Suddenly Ashton's boat paused and waited for the others to come up. When his companions had joined him, he pointed silently to two large lions on the right bank. They were drinking from the river, and had not noticed the boats.

"I think," said Ashton, in a low tone, "that notwithstanding the necessity for saving our ammunition, we might try a shot or two at them."

So saying, he ordered the boats to make for the bank of the river just above the animals. The four young men sprang ashore with their rifles, and set out cautiously towards the lions. At the same moment the animals caught sight of them, and, turning, walked slowly up to the top of a small hill, where they paused and surveyed their pursuers calmly. They allowed the young men to approach within a hundred yards of them, and then set off again up the stream, moving leisurely, and manifesting neither fear nor haste. After they had gone a short distance they stopped again, and allowed the young men to approach within fifty yards of them; then they resumed their retreat at a quicker pace, and disappeared in a low thicket close by. The hunters paused

HOUSTON AND THE LION.

at the same moment, uncertain what course to pursue. As he was about to turn to speak to his companions, Ashton, who was somewhat in advance of them, noticed the head of one of the majestic beasts peering through the bushes within twenty paces of him. Raising his rifle, he took deliberate aim and fired, and the head disappeared. Uncertain as to the effect of his shot, the young man was about to enter the thicket, when he was startled by a loud, wrathful roar, and the next moment the other animal, a huge lioness, bounded out of the undergrowth and dashed towards Houston.

The young men had been so intent upon watching Ashton's shot that the assault of the lioness took them by surprise. Houston's coolness did not desert him, however, and he calmly raised his rifle and fired at the beast, which was within less than five yards of him. At the same time Philip Lee and Hubbard discharged their rifles at the lioness. All the shots were well directed, and the huge animal, after staggering for a moment, and uttering a wild roar which seemed to shake the very ground, fell dead at Houston's feet.

"That was well done, boys," said Ashton, "and done not a moment too quick! She's a magnificent creature, and we must save her skin and paws. Now let us see what has become of the other."

Entering the thicket, they found the lion Ashton had shot lying stiff and motionless. The ball had penetrated the brain, and death had been instanta-

THE CAMP AT MOMA.

neous. Hubbard was sent back to the boats to bring up some of the negroes, who quickly stripped off the skin and claws of the lions. These were conveyed to the boats, and the voyage was resumed. The young men were very proud of their success, as each had had a share in the death of the noble beasts; but to Ashton all accorded the chief triumph, as his single ball had slain the proud king of the African forest.

In about an hour after, starting again, our travellers heard a distant and indistinct sound, like the breaking of the surf on the shore of the ocean. The sound grew louder as they proceeded down the stream, and finally changed to a dull heavy roar. Ashton, using Charlie as interpreter, asked the boatmen the meaning of it, and was told that they were nearing the great cataract of Gonha, the roar of which, they said, was like the thunder, and could be heard for many miles. Ashton caused his canoe to lie to for a few moments, and as his companions drew nearer shouted the news to them. Soon after the effect of the cataract began to make itself apparent in the stream, the current of which became so rapid as to render the most cautious navigation on the part of the boatmen necessary. Late in the afternoon the party paddled ashore near the hamlets of Sioma, and the camp was pitched close by the river side beneath the shade of an enormous sycamore. It was simply a bivouac in the open air.

THE CATARACT OF GONHA.

The next morning the party received a visit from the chief of the Sioma hamlets, who brought them a present of several measures of groundnuts. At the professor's request, he readily gave them a guide to the cataract. Leaving Charlie, Mombée, and the Benguela men to watch over the safety of their boats and baggage, the professor and the four young men set off early in the morning to visit the cataract of Gonha. They proceeded along the left bank of an arm of the Liambai or Zambezi, " which runs first to the southeast, then bends towards the west, and finally runs east and west, and in that position receives two other branches of the river, which form three islands covered with splendid vegetation. At the site where the river begins to bend westward, there is a fall in the ground of three yards in one hundred and twenty, forming the Situmba rapids. After the junction of the three branches of the Zambezi, it assumes a width of not more than six hundred and fifty-six yards, where it throws out a small arm to the southwest of trifling depth and volume. The rest of the waters, as they speed onward, meet with a transverse cutting of basalt, with a rapid drop in the level of forty-nine feet, over which they precipitate themselves with a frightful roar. The cutting creates three grand falls, a centre and two side ones. Between and over the rocks which separate the three great masses of water tumble innumerable cascades, producing a marvellous effect. On the north a third branch of the river continues running on the same upper level as the cataract, and then empties into the main stream in five exquisitely beautiful cascades, the last of which is four hundred and forty yards below the great fall."

Our travellers were deeply impressed with the richness and beauty of the scene, which, though lacking the grandeur of the great falls of the Zambezi, has a loveliness peculiarly its own. They spent the better part of the day viewing it from different points, and returned to the camp at nightfall, not a little saddened by the thought that they would see the beautiful scene no more.

From the Sioma hamlets to a point below the cataract of Gonha, called the Mamungo, the Zambezi was utterly unnavigable for canoes, and it now became necessary to transport the boats around the rapids and cataracts by land. The distance overland was three miles, and the route lay through a thick forest. The 9th of September was devoted to the task of carrying the boats from Sioma to the Mamungo. As only three boats could be conveyed at a time, the entire day was consumed in the undertaking. The task was performed by the natives of the Sioma hamlets, people of Calacas, or slaves, governed by a Luina chief. They are stationed there by the Lui government for the especial purpose of performing this work, which they are bound to do without the right to demand any recompense whatever. They executed their task so well and so patiently, however, that the professor bestowed a liberal reward upon them when the canoes were safely launched in the river at the Mamungo.

The night was passed on the river shore at the Mamungo, and on the 10th the party set out once more down the Zambezi. In an hour and a half after starting our travellers reached the mouth of the river Lambe, which flows into the Zambezi from the north, and is about twenty-one yards wide at its mouth. An hour was spent in examining the Lambe, which falls into the Liambai from an elevation of nearly one hundred feet by a series of beautiful cascades. Soon after camping, early in the afternoon, Houston, Philip Lee, and Hubbard succeeded in killing three antelopes, which were brought into camp.

In about an hour and a half after starting, on the 11th, the party reached the cataract of Calle. There the river, which was nearly a thousand yards in width, was divided by three islands into four branches. The river made a fall of about ten feet, and the swift waters rushed over the rocks which obstructed

CARRYING THE BOATS OVERLAND AT THE CATARACT OF GONHA.

all four branches, with a hoarse, sullen roar. To pass the cataract it was necessary to unload the canoes, and tow them along a little channel of comparatively smooth water, which skirted the right bank, and gave access to the river below the rapids. The goods were then brought forward by the negroes, the canoes were reloaded, and the voyage was resumed. Half an hour later some rapids of lesser importance were reached, and over these the boatmen steered the canoes with great skill, as they did also over a second series of rapids which were encountered somewhat later. The rest of the day was spent in paddling between jagged cliffs, which showed clearly the marks of the violent current which swept by them, and at night they bivouacked in the open air.

Soon after starting, on the morning of the 12th, the great rapids of the

Bombue were reached. The fall of the river here was only about six feet, and the stream was divided into four channels by islands. The force of the waters was so great, however, and the channels were so full of rocks, that the rapids were impassable. It was again necessary, therefore, to unload the canoes, and float them down the stream, close in to the banks. This was a most fatiguing operation, as the rapids were nearly a third of a mile in length, and consumed considerable time. It was safely accomplished, however, and the travellers reëmbarked in the quieter waters below the falls. In a little while another rapid was encountered, over which the canoes were carried safely by the boatmen; and after four hours more of paddling by lovely islets, green with foliage, the party went into camp near the mouth of the river Joco.

The professor now began to experience a slight return of his fever, and the whole party were more or less affected by the fatigue of sitting so long in the cramped position they were compelled to assume in the canoes, and also by sleeping so constantly in the open air. They therefore decided to spend the 13th of September in resting.

Breakfast was somewhat later that morning, as they were to remain at their camping-place during the day. The meal was scarcely finished when some of the negroes reported that they had seen elephants in the immediate neighborhood. The young men were on their feet in a minute, eager for an encounter with the animals; and even the professor, who was really sick, insisted on having a share in the sport. Houston, as the huntsman of the expedition, carried the elephant rifle, which he had handled so effectively on the night of the attack on the camp in the Lui, and which was now for the first time to be put to its legitimate use, and the others were armed with their breech-loaders. Leaving Charlie and Mombée in charge of the boats, they set out at once in the direction indicated by the negroes. They soon found the trail of the animals, and, following it, came up with them on the bank of the Joco.

Moving through the thick jungle which concealed them from the animals, the hunters saw seven large elephants wallowing in a marshy pool on the river's brink. They were of unusual size, and were rolling in the mud in happy ignorance of the near approach of danger. For a moment the entire party paused, and gazed at the huge monsters in silent admiration. Then moving cautiously through the jungle, which grew close up to the pool, they managed to approach within a very short distance of the elephants without being observed by them.

"I intend to fire at that large fellow in front," said Houston; "so aim at the others."

"We can't well fire at them while they are lying in the pool," said Ashton. "I'll give a shout, and that will bring them to their feet. Then we must do our best. Are you all ready?"

THE AFRICAN ELEPHANT.

Being answered in the affirmative, Ashton uttered a loud, ringing shout, which caused the animals to cease their sport, rise to their feet, and gaze around in alarm. At the same moment the reports of the five rifles rang out on the air. The elephant at which Houston had aimed fell instantly, and one of the others tottered for a moment, then sank to his knees, and, after a feeble effort to rise again, fell over on his side. The fall of the two monsters seemed to shake the very earth. The five remaining elephants now broke into a shrill trumpeting, and started off for the river at a full trot. Though the hunters sent another volley of balls after them, they succeeded in crossing the river, and disappeared in the forest on the opposite side.

Our travellers were much excited over their success, and hastened forward to examine the elephants they had slain. The ball from Houston's elephant rifle was charged with nitro-glycerine. It had struck the animal in one of the eyes, and had literally torn the head to pieces, causing instant death. The other animal had three rifle-balls in him, but there was no sign of a fourth. The professor laughingly said that he supposed his sickness had unsteadied his hand, and that his was the shot that had missed. As he was too weak to continue on foot much longer, he returned to the camp, and sent back several of the negroes to get out the tusks of the elephants. The extraction of these was a work of some difficulty, but they were at length safely removed, and were found to measure three feet in length, with a proportionate thickness. Charlie declared they were among the most valuable pieces of ivory he had ever seen, and were of great purity.

"They bring heap money, Master Hoosey," he said to Houston. "Maybe you have to use 'em 'fore you get out nigger's country."

The morning of the 14th saw the travellers on the river again, and they soon reached the rapids of Lusso, where they were obliged once more to unload the canoes, and tow them close to the shore to the quieter water below. Starting again, two hours more of paddling brought them to the cataract of Mambue. This cataract is divided into four distinct sections. "The first gives a fall of about a foot and a half; the second, which is nearly five hundred feet below the first, presents a fall of six feet, quite perpendicular; the third, one hundred and ninety feet still lower down, has a drop of about three feet; and the last, which has a similar fall of three feet, is three hundred and thirty feet distant from the previous one. The falls, therefore, cover an extent of ten hundred and fifty feet."

These falls presented the most serious obstacle our travellers had yet encountered. There was no means of getting the canoes over them, and the only way of passing them was by dragging the canoes overland. This Ashton was determined to accomplish that day. The negroes were at first unwilling to make the attempt, although the day's voyage had been but a short one; yet by promising them a liberal reward, Ashton succeeded in inducing them to undertake the task. It was a difficult one, and the young Americans turned to and assisted the blacks with a heartiness that put the latter on their mettle. It required four hours to get the boats into the smooth water below, but the task

THE CANOES IN THE RAPIDS.

was accomplished at last, and then the party went into camp for the night below the falls.

They were off again by half-past six o'clock on the morning of the 15th, and soon after floated over some small rapids, which were immediately succeeded by others that were highly dangerous. As the boats entered the rapids, several hippopotami appeared in the water below, right in their track. The boatmen, however, with great dexterity, managed to avoid both the rocks and the formidable animals, and the rapids were soon cleared. Within the next hour two more rapids, one of them of considerable extent, were passed, and then there rose on the air a loud rumbling sound like distant thunder. This caused Ashton to apprehend the presence of some great cataract, and he looked about for a convenient place at which to reach the shore; but a glance showed him that a landing would be impossible. On both sides rose up perpendicular masses of black basalt, with not room for even a goat to pass between them and the water. There was nothing to do but to go on with the swift current. In less than an hour six rapids of trifling inequality were passed, and at a little after nine Ashton saw at some distance before him a fall of fully three feet. The waters were rushing over it in masses of foam, and a loud roar rose from the gulf below. The shore was now more depressed, and admitted of a landing on the right bank; and Ashton, seeing the danger ahead, ordered his boatmen to make for the river bank, and at the same time shouted to Houston, who was in the next canoe,—

"Pass the word to make for the right bank! There's a large fall ahead!"

Houston obeyed the order, and the other canoes which were closer in shore than the first two at once turned towards the bank, which they succeeded in reaching. Not so with the boats of Ashton and Houston, however. The furious current baffled all their efforts to reach the shore, and swept them along with frightful rapidity towards the fall. The efforts of the oarsmen to resist the current caused both canoes to lose their steerage, and to swing around broadside to the stream, and in this position they sped onward towards the cataract. The boatmen, with a gesture of despair, shipped their oars and seated themselves in the canoes to await what seemed certain destruction. Ashton and Houston were silent, and both were convinced that the boats would never clear the fall in safety. The seconds seemed like hours to them, and in dumb despair they watched their canoes sweep downward to the abyss. A cry of horror was heard from their companions who had gained the shore, and the next moment the two canoes dashed over the fall, one after the other. They fell into the foaming waters below without upsetting, and were whirled on down the river by the raging current. Nothing but their loss of steerage, which caused them to swing around broadside to the stream, in which position they were carried over the fall, saved the canoes. Had they gone over headforemost, they would have been swamped, and their occupants drowned. The escape of the two boats and their crews was thus providential, and was in no way due to the skill of the oarsmen.

As soon as they found they were safe, Ashton and Houston directed their men to get the boats under steerage again, and make for the right bank. As the canoes were half full of water, it took them some time to do this, but at length they succeeded in reaching the shore. They were drenched through, but were overjoyed at their fortunate escape. Ashton at once despatched Charlie along the shore to his companions above the fall to inform them of the safety of the two boats and their crews, and to request them to join him as soon as possible. This they did in about an hour, towing the canoes by a small channel along the shore. The young men were heartily congratulated by their companions on their escape, for the latter had given them up as lost when they saw them swept over the falls.

After a rest of an hour the voyage was resumed, and during the remainder of the day seven more rapids, of greater or less extent, were passed, some not without great danger. By two o'clock in the afternoon they reached the rapids above the cataract of Catima-Moriro, or "The Fire Extinguisher," where they went into camp. The adventures of the day had been so exciting, and the men were so thoroughly worn out, that Ashton decided not to attempt to pass the cataract until the next day.

On the 16th the boats were carried around the falls, which are the last of the cataracts of the Upper Zambezi. From that point to the rapids which precede the great falls of Mozi-oa-Tunia, the navigation of the river is unobstructed. Below Catima-Moriro, the character of the country along the river changed, and to the high walls of black rock, succeeded extensive plains of sand on either hand. Many islands were passed, but these were mere cane-brakes. Late in the afternoon the party landed on the left bank, and passed the night there. They started again the next morning, halting for the night near the village of Catengo, and continuing their journey on the 18th camped in the afternoon near the village of Quisseque, or Chicheque.

Starting again on the 19th, an hour's paddling brought the boats to Quisseque. Ashton decided not to ask quarters in the village, but ordered the boats to a small island in the neighborhood, where the party went into camp. Sufficient cane and foliage was found on the island to enable the negroes to construct four huts; and thus, for the first time in many days, our travellers had a shelter over them.

The camp completed, Ashton despatched Charlie in one of the canoes to inform the native chief of Quisseque of their arrival, and to request him to sell them food. Charlie soon returned with the announcement that the chief would visit the white strangers that day, and as they had come direct from his king, would sell them provisions.

Charlie brought with him a strange negro, who was at once recognized by the professor as a native of the Orange country. The man spoke Sesuto, and

by the aid of Charlie, to whose knowledge of that language we have before
referred, our travellers were enabled to carry on a conversation with him. To
their great delight he informed them that he was the servant of the missionary
they were seeking, and that he was waiting at Quisseque for the answer of
King Lobossi to his master's application for permission to enter his territories.
He was delighted to hear that the "Englishmen," as he called the professor

THE CAMP NEAR QUISSEQUE.

and his companions, were going to seek his master, and declared they would
find him one of the best men in the world. The missionary was not an Englishman, he said, but a Frenchman. His own name, he stated, in reply to a
question from Ashton, was Eliazar.

While our travellers were conversing with Eliazar, the chief of Quisseque
arrived at the camp. His name was Carionoque, and he was known as one of
the bravest warriors in the service of King Lobossi. Professor Moreton informed him that he and his companions were anxious to continue their journey
without delay, and urged him to send them what food he could that very day.
This he promised to do, and during the afternoon kept his word, sending in
what amounted to about two days' scanty supply of provisions for the men.
He soon returned to his village, taking the negro Eliazar back with him.

Later in the day he came to the camp again, and, asking for the professor,
told him that the envoys he had sent to King Lobossi with the request of the
missionary to enter the Lui country, had just arrived with the king's answer,
which, our readers will remember, had been decided upon before the departure
of our travellers from the Luina capital. The royal answer, as repeated by

the chief to the professor, was a remarkable piece of diplomacy. It had been dictated by Gambella, and neither absolutely granted nor refused the desired permission. It expressed great pleasure at learning that the missionary had arrived in the country, but stated that, owing to the existence of war in the kingdom and the want of accommodations which the city of Lialui afforded, owing to its being a city so recently constructed, it was not advisable for him to proceed any farther. The king, therefore, requested him to delay his intention until another year, when he might return and renew his application. Carimuque added to the professor that he had received positive orders from the king not to furnish the missionary with the means of pursuing his journey northwards.

"You may tell the missionary this," he said; "but he must come to Quisseque to receive the king's answer in due form."

On the morning of the 20th our travellers were on the river again, and before noon they reached the mouth of the Machilla. This stream flowed through a vast plain, in which the occupants of the canoes could see many buffaloes, zebras, and antelopes grazing. Never in their lives had the professor and his companions seen so much game at one time; but as they were anxious to push on, they made no effort to secure any. Towards five o'clock they camped upon the bank of the Zambezi. A search was at once made for wood with which to kindle a fire, but none was to be found. The prospect of having to go supperless was rapidly becoming a certainty, when Charlie spied an old tree floating down the river. The boats were sent out for it, and it was towed ashore, where it furnished material for a fire, which was soon sending its ruddy light through the camp.

The next day, the 21st of September, was their last on the river. They started at an early hour, and, after paddling for five hours, reached the head of a rapid of considerable size, the first of a chain which terminates in the cataract of Mozi-oa-Tunia, the Great Falls of the Zambezi. A landing was at once made on the right bank of the river, and the canoes were unloaded, and concealed by the boatmen in the thick grass. The loads were then assigned to the negroes, even Charlie and Mombée being compelled to carry their share, and the party set off across the country for the village of Embarira, which was reached after a march of six miles.

The party were well received by the chief of Embarira, a village of the Macalacas, situated on the Cuando River, near its mouth, the sources of which river our travellers had visited and examined in June. Two houses in the village were assigned the party, one for the whites, and the other for the blacks. The chief informed the professor that a white man, who was neither a missionary nor a trader, was encamped opposite the village, on the other side of the Cuando. This news greatly astonished our travellers, and many were their conjectures as to the character and nationality of the white stranger. The chief also told them that the camp of the French missionary was at Lechuma, about fourteen miles to the southeast of Embarira.

The house assigned our travellers proved anything but a comfortable habitation. It was overrun with vermin, and the mosquitoes were so troublesome that they were forced to quit the hut and pass the night in the open air.

The next morning the professor despatched a messenger to Lechuma with a note to the missionary, telling him of their arrival and requesting him to

THE LAST BOAT OVER THE CUANDO.

visit them as soon as possible. Immediately after breakfast, the work of paying the negro boatmen their wages began. They were given in full all that had been promised them, and to the pay of each the professor added a slight present as a reward for their good conduct. The men were at first well satisfied with their pay, but, in about an hour later, came to Ashton and declared that they wanted more, as they had a long journey back home. After a little questioning, the young man found that they had been prompted to make this demand by the chief of the village, who had already become covetous of the goods of the strangers. Ashton firmly refused to submit to the claim of the blacks, and sent them away with the threat that if they sought his presence again he would have his own men seize and flog them. He also told them if they did not start on their homeward journey that very day, he would cause King Lobossi to be informed of their conduct. This last threat had the desired effect, and the boatmen promised to set out at once, begging Ashton not to report them to the king, as it was all the fault of the chief.

Ashton soon after sought an interview with the chief, and, thinking it better not to mention his knowledge of the latter's bad faith, simply requested him to furnish him with a boat, in order that he might go over and see the white man on the other side of the Cuando. The chief replied sulkily that he had no boat, but, upon Ashton offering him a few charges of gunpowder, agreed to send one of the negroes over the river with a message to the white man. He would not consent, however, to send Ashton or any of his companions across. As this was the best that could be done, the young man wrote a note to the stranger, and entrusted it to Charlie, who was allowed by the chief to use a miserable little cockle-shell of a canoe, which seemed hardly fit to carry him over the river.

In a couple of hours Charlie returned, bringing with him an Englishman of about twenty-eight or thirty years, short, thick set, and powerfully built. He wore a coarse linen shirt, the unbuttoned collar of which showed a strong, massive throat, and his sleeves, which were rolled up, displayed a pair of muscular arms, burned brown by the African sun. He wore a straw hat, and trousers of ordinary material, which were secured about the waist by a belt, into which were thrust a revolver and a bowie knife. He advanced toward our travellers, who moved quickly to meet him, and held out both hands.

"Who are you?" he asked, laughing as he spoke, "and where do you come from? Your man would tell me nothing, except that you wanted to see me."

In a few words the professor explained to him who they were, and gave him a general idea of their journey across the continent.

"It is wonderful!" exclaimed the stranger. "Who would have thought of a party of youngsters making such a journey! However, you Americans seem equal to anything!"

He then told them that his name was Harris, and that he and a companion, Dr. Edward Humphreys, were engaged in a zoological expedition. The doctor, he said, was a distinguished scientist in England, and he had accompanied him as his companion and prepared his specimens.

"How many are in your party?" he asked.

"Twelve, white and black," replied the professor.

"Are your negroes trustworthy?"

"Entirely so."

"Then you had better cross the river and camp beside us," said Mr. Harris. "The people of this village are a bad lot, and the chief is the greatest rogue of all. They will certainly give you trouble if you remain here."

"We have no means of crossing the river," said Ashton. "The chief tells me they have no boats."

"They have plenty of them," replied Mr. Harris. "We have two of our own, fortunately, which are at your service. Let one of your men go back with me, and he and I will bring the boats over, and in two or three trips you can cross your whole party with your traps."

Our travellers at once gratefully accepted the kind offer of the Englishman, and Mombée was selected to return with him and bring over one of the boats, it being necessary to retain Charlie, as he was their only interpreter. Mr. Morris and Mombée then set off, and the men were ordered to get their loads, which had been considerably lightened by the consumption of provisions and the payment to the boatmen, in readiness to be transported to the river shore.

The chief of the village, who had watched the interview between the white men from a distance, now came forward and demanded to know what the "Englishman" wanted. Ashton explained to him, through Charlie, that they had found friends in the Englishman and his companion on the other side of the Cuando, and that they were about to cross the river and encamp with them. The chief declared that this was impossible, as no boats were to be had; but Ashton assured him they would find the boats they needed. The chief then said that he felt hurt at the withdrawal of his white visitors from his village. Ashton thanked him for his hospitality, but said they preferred to be with their own people on the other side of the river. The chief then changed his tone, and insolently declared that if the party attempted to cross the river he would prevent it.

"Listen to me, Mocumba," said Ashton, addressing the chief by his name. "We owe you nothing, and do not even ask you for boats to cross the river. We are free to go where we like, and you will not dare to molest us. We are the friends of King Lobossi, and are travelling under his protection. Attempt to harm us, and he will punish you for it."

"Lobossi is far away," said the chief, with an insolent laugh. "He will never hear of what is done here."

"But Carimuque will hear of it," said Ashton. "He has the king's orders. If I send to him, he will come here and burn your village."

"I am not afraid of him," said Mocumba, boastingly.

"Very good," exclaimed Ashton, looking at him fixedly, and speaking sternly. "We do not depend upon either Lobossi or Carimuque for our protection. We are twelve resolute and well-armed men, and more than a match for your whole village. Attempt to interfere with our crossing the river, and we will destroy you."

Then turning to the men, he told them to carry the loads to the river shore. At the same time he drew his revolver, and pointing it at the chief's head, ordered him to accompany the party, on pain of instant death.

"You must not hurt him, Ashton," said the professor, earnestly.

"I have no intention of doing so," replied the young man. "I shall only hold him as a hostage for our safety until the last boat has left this side."

The entire party now moved down to the river shore, taking with them the trembling chief. As they reached the water they saw the canoes, manned by Mr. Harris and Mombée, leave the opposite shore. They were soon on the Embarira side, and then the work of passing the river began. It required several trips and a couple of hours to accomplish this. Ashton, Houston, and Charlie remained on-guard over the chief until the rest of the party and all the goods were safe on the opposite shore. They then set off in the last boat. Before doing so, however, Ashton told the chief that he and his party desired to be on good terms with him, but were ready at any moment to meet and repel an attack. He told him, if he would come over to their camp the next day, he would make him a present in return for his hospitality to them.

Upon arriving on the opposite shore of the Cuando, our travellers were warmly welcomed by Dr. Humphreys, a' tall, fine-looking man, with a long beard and white hair, and a face prematurely old from suffering and labor. Setting the negroes to work to construct a camp, the professor and his companions joined the English gentlemen, and were soon engaged in conversation with them. Dr. Humphreys stated that the objects of their journey to the Cuando having been accomplished, he and his companion were making their preparations to leave for another part of the country, when they heard of the arrival of the Americans at Embarira. They listened with wonder to the professor's account of the march of his party across the continent, Dr. Humphreys declaring, repeatedly, that without the evidence before his eyes he would not have believed it possible for the young men to accomplish such an undertaking. He complimented them highly upon their courage and endurance, and assured the professor that his skill in preserving the health of his party through so trying a journey was beyond all praise.

Upon repairing to their own quarters for the night the professor and his companions began to discuss the prospect before them. Their stores were now so greatly reduced that it would not be possible for them to carry out their original plan, which was to march overland to the Zumbo, and thence descend the Zambezi to the Portuguese settlements at its mouth. All agreed that the only thing left them now was to endeavor to reach the Dutch and English settlements in the Transvaal, from which they could proceed to Port Natal, from which there was regular steamer communication with Europe.

The morning of the 23d brought the chief of Embarira to the camp to receive the present promised him by Ashton. He expressed great regret for his conduct on the previous day, and said a bad spirit had made him do so. Ashton accepted his apology, and gave him the promised present. Mocumba then begged that he would not let either King Lobossi or Carimuque know what had happened, as he did not want to get into trouble with them. Ashton told him that on leaving the Cuando he and his party would pass by Embarira, and that if they were not molested they would forget all that had happened, but that if trouble arose they would defend themselves, and would also send word to Lobossi and the chief of Quisseque of the matter. With this promise Mocumba was well satisfied, and soon took his departure.

About noon the French missionary reached the camp, having been sent over the river by Mocumba, with whom he had succeeded in establishing friendly relations upon his arrival in the country. He was the Reverend Pierre Gaillard, who had been sent out to Africa by a missionary society of France, to take charge of the Leribe mission in the Basuto land. He had labored there successfully for several years, and, being anxious to carry his work farther, had sent to Lialui to ask the permission of King Lobossi to enter the Lui country, with what result the reader already knows. He was a little over forty, and was well browned by the African sun, under which he had lived so long. He spoke English fluently, and was also acquainted with the language of the country. He was very cordial in his greetings of the travellers, and was soon made acquainted with their adventures. He was much interested in their account of their adventures in the Barôze, and was greatly disappointed when Professor Moreton told him of the result of his application to King Lobossi. He said, however, that he hoped to persuade Carimuque to allow him to pass above Quisseque, and would leave for that place the next day, to receive the king's answer. He then asked the plans of the professor and his companions for the future, and upon being told of their intention to try to reach the Transvaal, he advised them to go first to Lechuma, where his own camp was located, and where he had left his wife and her sister, under the protection of his faithful blacks. At Lechuma, he said, they would find the agency of an English trading firm, with which they might be able to make arrangements that would help them on the rest of their journey. He would give them a letter of introduction to Madame Gaillard, and could assure them of a hospitable reception at his own camp. As for himself, he should start for Quisseque early the next morning, and, whatever the result of his efforts, would return to Lechuma in about ten days. During the conversation which followed, Mr. Gaillard gave our travellers much valuable information concerning the country through which their journey to the coast would lie.

It was determined by the professor and his companions to recross the

MR. AND MRS. GAILLARD.

Cuando at an early hour the next morning, and set out at once for Lechuma. Mr. Gaillard would cross the river with them, and then proceed to Quisseque.

Accordingly, at a little after sunrise on the 24th of September, our travellers took leave of their good friends, Dr. Humphreys and Mr. Harris, who placed their boats at their disposal, and crossed over to Embarira, accompanied by Mr. Gaillard. In parting with him they agreed to await his return at Lechuma, when they would determine upon their future movements. Mocumba, who met the party on landing, supplied Ashton with several carriers, which greatly lightened the loads of Charlie, Mombée, and the five Benguela men, who were now the only means of transporting the goods remaining to the party.

Embarira was left about eight o'clock. The day was intensely hot, the road very sandy, and the progress of the party was painful and slow. The ground began to rise as it receded from the river, and the progress of the travellers was up hill all the way. They suffered intensely from thirst, but after about four hours' steady marching reached a clear spring of cool water, in the shade of a little grove, where they slaked their burning thirst. Two hours more brought them to Lechuma.

The place was situated in a narrow valley, running due north and south, and shut in by richly wooded mountains of low elevation. On the east side of the valley our travellers saw a collection of huts, which, they subsequently learned, formed the establishment of Mr. Phillips, an English trader. Nearly opposite were two abandoned hamlets, which were occupied as a trading-post by Mr. George Westbeech. A little to the north of Mr. Westbeech's factory stood a strong stockade, enclosing a circular space about one hundred feet in diameter. Within this were a thatched cottage, a hut built after the manner of the country, and two travelling wagons. This was the camp of Mr. Gaillard, the missionary.

Immediately upon arriving, Ashton set the Benguela men and Charlie and Mombée to work to collect material for a camp, and by nightfall a strong stockade and four huts had been erected for the accommodation of the party within a few hundred yards of Mr. Gaillard's camp.

While the work was in progress, Professor Moreton and his young companions went to the missionary's camp to call upon Madame Gaillard and her sister. Entering the stockade, they found the two ladies sitting at the door of the cottage, engaged in sewing. The sensations of the travellers at finding themselves once more in ladies' society were curious and hard to describe. Their travel-worn and rough appearance contrasted strangely with the neatness of the ladies and their surroundings, and for a moment they hesitated to approach. Madame Gaillard, however, had been expecting them, and the cordial reception given them by herself and her sister soon put them at their ease. She said she had been looking for them all the afternoon, as her husband had told her he would endeavor to persuade them to go on to Lechuma that day. She and her sister had, therefore, deferred their evening meal until the arrival of the travellers, whom she now invited to share it with them. The invitation was accepted, and for the first time since leaving St. Paul de

Loanda our travellers sat down to a table graced by the presence of ladies. A pleasant evening was spent with them, and then the professor and the young men went back to their own camp.

The next morning Professor Moreton and Ashton made a visit to Mr. Westbeech, who told them he was greatly surprised by their arrival, as he had heard nothing of their being in the country. He was much interested in their story, and declared it the most remarkable narrative he had heard during the many years he had spent in Africa. He was a man of good education and

ENCAMPMENT OF THE GAILLARD FAMILY IN LECHUMA.

generous impulses, though he was a thorough trader when it came to a question of bargain. He readily purchased the four elephant tusks and the few extra guns they had still with them, paying them in provisions, but buying them at his own price.

Ashton now astonished his companions by producing a twenty-pound note of the Bank of England, and asking Mr. Westbeech to give him change for it. The trader laughingly assured him that he had no money.

"Money would be of no use to me here," he said, "as all my transactions are merely matters of barter. Since you are responsible, however, I will let you have what you want, as far as I can furnish it, taking your notes for the same. These notes I will send to my correspondent at Shoshong, where English money is used, and you can pay them to him."

This arrangement was satisfactory to all parties, and our travellers felt that Ashton's foresight had smoothed away one of the greatest difficulties in the remainder of their journey. The young man told the professor, that, knowing they would want money should they succeed in reaching the East Coast, he had placed some Bank of England notes in a water-proof belt which he had worn under his clothing through the whole journey, not caring to mention the matter until there was occasion to use the money.

Mr. Westbeech expressed his willingness to aid the party to continue their journey. He told them that one of the wagons of his firm was expected to arrive from Shoshong in about ten days with a supply of goods. He intended to send it back immediately to bring up more, but as he had very little to send by it, it would go back nearly empty. It was large enough to hold their entire party, and such goods as they had left, and he would place it at their disposal for a nominal sum. The offer was gladly accepted, and an agreement was drawn up by Mr. Westbeech, and signed by himself and Professor Moreton.

"Fortune seems to favor us at last, professor," said Ashton.

"You deserve her favors for the pluck you have all shown in your journey across this abominable continent," said Mr. Westbeech. "Your arrival here is timely, to say the least. Had you come ten or twelve days later, it would not have been in my power to serve you. You must then have made the journey to Shoshong on foot, and you would have found it more trying than any of your past experiences. You will have to traverse a terrible country, and even with the wagon it will take you nearly a month to reach Shoshong."

The time passed by our travellers at Leehuma was the pleasantest rest they had yet enjoyed in Africa. Their minds were free from the anxiety which had hitherto kept them constantly on the strain; they were well supplied with provisions; their quarters were comfortable; and the society of the ladies of the neighboring camp afforded them a pleasure to which they had long been strangers. Each day some of the party went out in search of game, and they generally succeeded in obtaining enough not only to supply their own wants, but also to furnish the table of their kind friends,—the French ladies. Twelve days were spent in this pleasant manner, and on the 6th of October the wagon from Shoshong arrived at Mr. Westbeech's establishment. On the same day Mr. Gaillard returned from Quisseque. He was alone, however, his faithful servant, Eliazar, having fallen a victim to the fever at that place.

Mr. Gaillard was much pleased to learn of the arrangement made between our travellers and Mr. Westbeech respecting the wagon. He told the former that, since his efforts to enter the dominions of King Lobossi had failed, he had determined to return to Shoshong to replenish his supplies before starting for another field of labor. They could travel together as far as that place, and the journey would thus be pleasanter to all parties.

One thing, however, stood in the way of this arrangement. Professor Moreton and his companions were anxious to visit the Great Falls of the

INTERIOR OF MR. GAILLARD'S CAMP IN LECHUMA.

Zambezi. They were too near to them to pass them by, and the visit would consume at least ten or twelve days. Mr. Gaillard was anxious to move on to Patamatenga as soon as possible, as his oxen were suffering from the attacks of the tsee-tsee fly.

Upon consulting with Mr. Westbeech, that gentleman informed Professor Moreton that his wagon would not be ready to start for Shoshong for a week. He advised the Americans to accompany the missionary as far as Guejuma's kraal, about three days' march to the southeast, and begin their journey to the falls from that point. Mr. Gaillard could then move on to Patamatenga, at which place the travellers could rejoin him on their return. The trader's wagon could start at the appointed time, proceed to Patamatenga, and there await the arrival of the party from the falls.

This arrangement being satisfactory to all parties, Ashton instructed Mr. Westbeech to provide the wagon with provisions for a month, and to furnish them with supplies sufficient for the journey to the falls and back to Patamatenga. The travellers decided to take with them only their arms, such clothing as had been left to them, the scientific instruments, and the provisions for the journey. Mr. Gaillard offered to transport the latter in his wagons, and thus save the blacks the fatigue of carrying them.

There was nothing now to detain the party, and it was decided that they should start with the missionary the next morning. Accordingly, on the 7th of October, the two camps were broken up. Mr. Westbeech bade a hearty farewell to the occupants of both camps, and assured Professor Moreton and Ashton that they could depend upon his carrying out his part of the arrangement to the letter. About ten o'clock the journey was begun, and Lechuma was soon left behind. The route for the better part of the entire way lay through the forest, and often the road was found to be obstructed by fallen trees or loose rocks. These had to be removed before the wagons could pass, and the work was difficult and fatiguing. Charlie and the Benguela men, assisted by the blacks in Mr. Gaillard's service, worked manfully at the task of removing the obstacles. The road was also very sandy, and the wheels of the vehicles sank so deep in the sand that progress was very slow. The ladies, of course, rode in one of the wagons; but as the professor and his companions had to make the journey on foot, Mr. Gaillard refused to avail himself of the comfort of the vehicles, and marched by the side of his friends. Very little water was met with, and the oxen which drew the heavy vehicles suffered greatly from thirst. A good supply of water having been laid in at Lechuma, the members of the party were not subjected to this inconvenience.

At last, on the 10th of October, the travellers reached Guejuma's kraal, a wretched place, established by the English traders as a depository for their herds, which they cannot keep in Lechuma, owing to the presence of the terrible tsee-tsee fly. Water was obtained there for the oxen, and a halt was made for the night.

As time was now a matter of importance, the professor and his companions decided to set out the next morning for the great cataract of Mozi-oa-Tunia. They were up betimes on the 11th, and the loads, which consisted of the instruments and provisions, were assigned to Charlie, Mombée, and the Benguela men. After a hearty breakfast, and a cordial farewell to the missionary and his family, our travellers set off in a northeasterly direction. They had no guide but a map, but with this and their compass they did not doubt their ability to reach their point of destination. Their only fear was that they might suffer from a scarcity of water.

The first days of the march passed without anything of interest occurring, and on the morning of the 12th our travellers heard, for the first time, a distant booming sound, like the reverberation of thunder from the mountain sides. All paused and listened intently.

"It is the roar of the great cataract," said the professor. "The wind is

THE BURIAL OF ELIAZAR.

from the north, and everything is so still that we can hear the sound, although we are fully two days' march from the falls."

During the day the party shot a number of partridges, which were very abundant in this region, and these furnished an excellent supper.

The country through which our travellers journeyed for the first two days was rugged and stony, but was well wooded. On the 13th they entered a deep valley, entirely destitute of trees. Huge fragments of rock, terminating in

18

pinnacles, rose on either side and at different points in the valley. A wilder, gloomier scene could not be imagined. Towards noon the wind suddenly shifted to the north-northeast, and a furious storm, which had been gathering all morning, burst over the valley. The thick black clouds seemed to swoop down to the ground, and poured forth torrents of water, accompanied by the most terrific display of lightning the party had ever witnessed. The sharp rocky pinnacles attracted the lightning, which darted upon them and dashed down their sides. One not far from the party was struck by a fiery bolt, and riven in two from top to bottom. A singular feature of the tempest was the manner in which the lightning divided itself. A ball of fire would dart from the clouds, and when near the ground would separate into several, which glanced horizontally from their centre and struck in as many different points. This was repeated several times. All the while zigzag flashes of fire played about the atmosphere in every direction, until the whole upper air seemed ablaze. Never before had the Americans witnessed so sublime and awful a spectacle.

As for the negroes, they were panic stricken. They dropped their loads and threw themselves flat on the ground, where they lay moaning in terror, unable to seek shelter from the water which was running over them. But for the fact that their loads were securely encased in water-proof coverings, they would have been hopelessly ruined. Professor Moreton and his companions endeavored to calm the poor fellows, by putting on an appearance of ease which they were far from feeling, for they could not conceal from themselves that the danger to the whole party was actual and imminent. The storm raged for over an hour, and then suddenly ceased, and the travellers, drenched through, started on their way once more. They were forced to stop again in the afternoon to allow another, but a less severe, rain-storm to pass over. Towards five o'clock they arrived at some deserted huts about three miles distant from the falls. The huts were rendered habitable, and a halt was made for the night. Bright fires were soon blazing, and by these the travellers dried themselves.

During the night a fresh storm broke over the huts, deluging them with water, putting out the fires, and again drenching the party through and through. The roar of the thunder was mingled with the hoarse tones of the great cataract, and the lightning was violent and continuous. About four in the morning the storm passed away as suddenly as it had come.

The morning of the 14th of October broke clear and beautiful; the clouds had vanished, and the sun was out in all his power. The roar of the falls was louder, and filled the whole party with a more eager desire than ever to gaze upon them. Breakfast was late, owing to the difficulty of making a fire with the wet wood, and the day's march was not begun until nine o'clock.

Guided by the roar of the waters, which grew louder as they advanced, the travellers, about noon, reached the western extremity of the great cataract.

The cataract of Mozi-oa-Tunia (a Sesuto term, meaning "the smoke is rising") was first seen by Dr. Livingstone in 1855, and again in 1860, since which time it has been visited by many Europeans. Livingstone named it the "Victoria Falls," in honor of the Queen of England. It is the sublimest cataract in Africa, and perhaps the most remarkable in the world. It is more than twice as high as the Falls of Niagara, and possesses many features peculiar to itself. Major Serpa Pinto, who visited it, and took accurate measurements of it, thus describes the cataract:

"Mozi-oa-Tunia is neither more nor less than a long trough, a gigantic crevasse, an abyss profound and monstrous into which the Zambezi precipitates

MOZI-OA-TUNIA.

itself bodily to an extent of nineteen hundred and seventy-eight yards. The cleft in the basaltic rocks which form the northern wall of the abyss is perfectly traceable, running east and west. Parallel thereto, another enormous wall of basalt, standing upon the same level, and one hundred and ten yards distant from it, forms the opposite side of the crevasse. The feet of these huge moles of black basalt form a channel through which the river rushes after its fall, a channel which is certainly much narrower than the upper aperture, but whose width it is impossible to measure.

"In the southern wall, and about three-fifth parts along it, the rock has been riven asunder, and forms another gigantic chasm, perpendicular to the first; which chasm, first taking a westerly curve and subsequently bending southwards and then eastwards, receives the river, and conveys it in a capricious zigzag through a perfect maze of rocks.

"The great northern wall of the cataract over which the water flows is in places perfectly vertical, with few or none of those breaks or irregularities that one is accustomed to see under such circumstances.

"The Zambezi, encountering upon its way the crevasse to which we have alluded, rushes into it in three grand cataracts, because a couple of islands which occupy two great spaces in the northern wall divide the stream into three separate branches.

"The first cataract is formed by a branch which passes to the south of the first island, an island which occupies, in the right angle assumed by the upper part of the cleft, the extreme west. This branch or arm consequently precipitates itself in the confined space open on the western side of the rectangle. It is one hundred and ninety-six feet wide and has a perpendicular fall of two hundred and sixty-two feet, tumbling into a basin whence the water overflows to the bottom of the abyss, there to unite itself to the rest in rapids and cascades that are almost invisible, owing to the thick cloud of vapor which envelopes the entire foot of the falls. The island which separates that branch of the river is covered with the richest vegetation, the leafy shrubs extending to the very edge along which the water rushes, and presenting a most marvellous prospect. This is the smallest of the falls, but it is the most beautiful, or, more correctly speaking, the only one that is really beautiful, for all else at Mozi-oa-tunia is sublimely horrible. That enormous gulf, black as is the basalt which forms it, dark and dense as is the cloud which enwraps it, would have been chosen, if known in biblical times, as an image of the infernal regions, a hell of water and darkness, more terrible, perhaps, than the hell of fire and light.

"As if to increase the sensation of horror which is experienced in presence of this prodigy of nature, one must risk one's life in order to survey it. To survey it thoroughly is impossible; Mozi-oa-tunia forbids such an operation.

"At times, when peering into the depths through that eternal mist, one may perceive a mass of confused shapes, like unto vast and frightful ruins. These are peaks of rocks of enormous height, on which the water dashes and becomes at once converted into a cloud of spray, which rolls and tumbles about the peaks where it was formed, and will continue to do so as long as the water falls and the rocks are there to receive it.

"Opposite Garden Island, through the medium of a rainbow, concentric to another and a fainter one, I could perceive from time to time, as the mist slightly shifted, confusedly appear a series of pinnacles, similar to the mina-

MOSI-OA-TUNYA. THE WEST FALLS.

rets and spires of some fantastic cathedral, which shot up, as it were, from out the mass of seething waters.

"Continuing our examination of the cataract, we find that the beginning of the northern wall, which starts from the western cascade, is occupied to an extent of some two hundred and eighteen yards by the island I have before alluded to, and which confines that branch of the river that constitutes the first fall. It is the only point whence the entire wall is visible, simply because along that space of two hundred and eighteen yards the vapor does not completely conceal the depths.

"After the first island comes the chief part of the cataract, being the portion comprised between the above island and Garden Island. In that spot the main body of the water rushes into the abyss in a compact mass, thirteen hundred and twelve feet in length; and there, as is natural, we find the greatest depth. Then follows Garden Island, with a frontage of one hundred and thirty-two feet to the rift, and afterwards the third fall, composed of dozens of falls which occupy the entire space between Garden Island and the eastern extremity of the wall. This third fall must be the most important in the rainy season, when the masses of rock which at other times divide the stream are concealed, and but one unbroken and enormous cataract meets the eye.

"As the water which runs from the two first falls and from part of the third near Garden Island rushes eastward, it meets the remainder of the third fall coursing west, and the result is a frightful seething whirlpool, whence the creamy waters rush, after the mad conflict, into the narrow rocky channel before alluded to, and go hissing away through the capricious zigzag chasm.

"The islands of the cataracts and the rocks which lie about it are all covered with the densest vegetation; but the green is dark, sad-colored, and monotonous, although a clump or two of palms, as they shoot their elegant heads above the thickets of evergreens which surround them, do their best to break the melancholy aspect of the picture.

"Never-ending showers of spray descend upon all objects in the proximity of the falls, and a ceaseless thunder growls within the abyss.

"Mozi-oa-tunia cannot be properly either depicted or described. The pencil and the pen are alike at fault; and in fact, saving at its western extremity, the whole is enveloped in a cloud of vapor, which, perhaps fortunately, hides half the awfulness of the scene."

High above the falls, which were nearly four hundred feet in height, rose a dense mass of snow-white vapor, which, after reaching an altitude of about eight hundred feet, floated away in a sort of fine rain.

Our travellers were deeply impressed by the sublime scene before them, and for a long time regarded it in silence. The first to speak was Charlie, who gravely declared that it must be a "very big devil" that lived there, and that he hoped they would not fall into his power. The rest of the day was spent in examining the falls and viewing them from different points. Late in the afternoon the party withdrew about a couple of miles back from the cataract and went into camp. When they sank to sleep that night the last sound they heard was the ceaseless roar of the mighty waters.

The next two days were passed by our travellers at Mozi-oa-tunia, the professor devoting the time to a survey of the falls. The task was not altogether an easy one, and was accompanied with no little danger. In order to measure the height of the principal fall it was necessary to see the foot of the wall in the depths of the abyss. There was but one way to accomplish this, and that was for the professor to allow himself to be lowered over the side of the precipice on which they stood. In spite of the protests of his companions, Professor Moreton made Charlie and Mombée strip off their garments, which were of striped cotton cloth. These he tied together, and so improvised a rope, which he wound about his body under the arm-pits. Giving the ends to Charlie and Mombée, he told them to hold on tight, and then, taking his sextant in his hand, walked out coolly to the very edge of the cliff. Bracing his feet upon the rock, he leaned far over the side, until he could see the foot of the opposite wall, and quietly proceeded to determine the angle with the base he had already established. The young men looked on with terror, not daring to speak, scarcely to breathe, while the two faithful blacks trembled violently. The professor seemed suspended in mid-air. The slightest loosening of their hold by the negroes, the parting of the cloth that held him, or even the slip of a foot, would send the adventurous explorer headlong to certain death. The observation occupied but a few minutes, but these seemed like hours to the spectators; and when the professor called to the blacks to pull him back, and was once more safe on solid ground, a sigh of relief went up from the whole party.

On the 16th the travellers spent the morning in taking a last look at the falls, and at mid-day set out to rejoin the missionary and his family at Patamatenga. This was a much more difficult undertaking than the journey to the falls. The latter it had been easy to find, as their roar made their locality known afar; but the task before our travellers now was to find a small kraal or settlement not laid down on the map, and which they might easily pass by without knowing it. Still the professor was convinced that Patamatenga kraal lay due south of the falls, and in that direction he resolved to direct the course of the party, without deviating from it in the least; therefore the march was directed to the place where the party had found the abandoned huts on the 13th, and in these the night was passed.

The next morning the journey was resumed, the course being due south. The route lay over a broken and stony country and through a narrow and desolate valley, with not a tree nor a shrub in sight. The sky was overcast, and the gathering clouds betokened the coming of bad weather. Several lions were seen during the day; but as their pursuit would have involved too much

PROFESSOR MORETON MEASURING THE FALLS.

delay, no effort was made to molest them. At the point where the halt for the night was made no wood was to be had; but the negroes, after a long search, succeeded in finding some dry branches, which they brought into the camp. These, upon being split, were found to be full of enormous scorpions, which scampered away in fright as the blows of the hatchet laid open their dwellings. During the night a severe rain-storm broke over the camp, and lasted till near morning, wetting the travellers through and damaging the provisions, which had been imprudently left exposed. Upon examination, the next morning, Professor Moreton found that they had but two days' scanty supply left. They might be three days yet on the road; and should game prove as scarce as it had been throughout the march, there was a certainty of having to travel one day at least on empty stomachs.

The march on the 18th was through a rugged and stony district, and progress was necessarily slow. After five hours' steady walking a little pool of water was reached, by the side of which the party went into camp. On the 19th they had a seven hours' tramp across a sandy plain covered with shrubs and tall grass. Not a vestige of water had been seen during the day; and when the party came to a halt, late in the afternoon, it was with the belief that the thirst from which all were suffering greatly would continue to torment them during the night. As the men laid down their loads there was suddenly heard from the branches of a tree close by the soft cooing of a flock of African doves. Charlie's face brightened at once.

"Hear that, Master 'Fessor!" he exclaimed. "Water close by. Doves come at sundown to drink. Stay there till morning. Me go look for water."

With this he started off in the direction of the sound. He returned in half an hour, and reported that he had found a small spring of good water about half a mile farther on. The loads were lifted with a will; and the party, setting out at a rapid pace, were soon at the spring, beside which they encamped. There was an abundance of water for their wants; but when supper was served, it was necessary to put the whole party on half rations, in order that there might be food enough left for a scanty breakfast the next morning.

They were on the road again very early on the 20th, and almost immediately plunged into a jungle, through which they were half an hour in making their way. Upon clearing it they came upon a large brook running swiftly over its stony bed; and beside it stood a well-built kraal, surrounded by a strong stockade, above which rose the roofs of several houses built after the European plan. This was Patamatenga, close to which they had camped on the previous night in ignorance of its whereabouts.

An Englishman came down to the brook to meet them as they were crossing, and welcomed them cordially. He informed the travellers that the missionary and his family had gone on to Daca, five hours distant, and that Mr. Westbeech's wagon had passed by Patamatenga only an hour before. He would not hear of the professor and his companions going on to Daca that day, and persuaded them to spend it with him, and rest after their long tramp. He then led them into the kraal, and, giving orders to his servants to provide for the blacks, invited the Americans into his house, where they were soon seated at a well-spread table.

The day was passed pleasantly with the hospitable owner of the kraal, and on the morning of the 21st of October the party set out for Daca, where they found Mr. Gaillard and his family, and the wagon sent by Mr. Westbeech awaiting them.

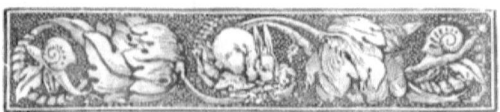

CHAPTER XI.

TO THE INDIAN OCEAN.

AS there was nothing to detain them at Daca, our travellers readily consented to Mr. Gaillard's proposal to start on their journey to Shoshong the next morning. Upon examining the wagon sent by Mr. Westbeech, Ashton found that the trader had not only filled his order for provisions to the letter, but had generously added a number of articles which he begged the young man, in a note sent by the driver of the wagon, to accept, with his compliments.

The wagon to be used by our travellers and their men was much larger than those of the missionary's party, and was drawn by twelve stout oxen. It afforded ample room for the goods of Mr. Westbeech, the property of the professor and his companions, and for the members of the expedition, who found places on the skins and blankets laid over the "freight," which was securely packed in the bottom of the vehicle.

Ten o'clock on the morning of the 22d of October saw the travellers on their way. The first eight days of the journey were spent in traversing a monotonous, uninteresting country, in which water was found only at long intervals. The oxen suffered greatly from thirst, and it was necessary to make frequent halts in order to rest them. The weather was warm and enervating, and our travellers experienced more discomfort from the heat than during any previous portion of their sojourn in Africa. The soil was sandy, and the oxen found it hard to pull the heavy wagons along the deep road. On the 29th a forest of gigantic trees was crossed, and it was often necessary to clear the road of fallen timber and the thick undergrowth which obstructed it. On the 30th the travellers entered the dry, sandy plain of the Kalahari, the terrible Sahara of Southern Africa. This desert, which stretched away far to the southward, was crossed first by Dr. Livingstone, with whose description of it the professor and Ashton were familiar. They agreed that the great explorer had in no wise exaggerated its terrors. It was covered with a thick growth of stunted thorn-trees, through which it was often necessary for the negroes to cut a way for the wagons, foot by foot, with their hatchets; and frequently, for as much as ten miles at a time, the sand was twenty inches deep, rendering it impossible to travel much more than a mile an hour. Water was not to be found, and both the oxen and the travellers suffered severely from thirst. On the 1st of November the dry bed of a river was crossed. The banks were so steep that it was with the greatest difficulty the oxen could drag the wagons up the opposite side. When they had succeeded in doing so, the camp was formed, and a search for water resulted in finding several pools of it still remaining in the bed of the river. All hastened to them eagerly, but only to meet with a terrible disappointment,—the water in the pools, so clear and tempting to the eye, was as salt as if it had been drawn from the sea. A further search was

CROSSING THE "GREAT SALT PAN."

rewarded by finding seven wells of considerable depth, not far from the camp, containing a plentiful supply of clear, sweet water. As soon as the travellers had slaked their thirst, the negroes were set to drawing water for the cattle, which were so sadly in need of it.

The dry river bed was that of the Nata, which along the lower part of its course is called the Chua. In the rainy season it is quite a good-sized stream. The southern portion of the Desert of Kalahari is better watered than the northern, and is frequented by a nomadic population, called the Massaruas, to whom the English settlers in Southern Africa apply the general term " Bushmen." They are exceedingly black, with projecting teeth, very bright eyes, and but little hair. They are savages, and are almost as low down in the scale of humanity as the Mucassequeres, with whom our travellers, it will be remembered, met near the upper Cuando. Some of them came into the camp soon after it was pitched, and Ashton gave them a little powder and tobacco, with which they were highly delighted. They gave very discouraging accounts of the scarcity of water along the route the party intended to pursue. During the next three days, the travellers were greatly annoyed by parties of Massaruas, who followed them, begging for various articles. They ceased their importunities at once when spoken to sternly, and at the least gesture indicating resentment would take to their heels.

On the 7th of November a portion of the route lay across the extreme southeastern edge of the remarkable basin known as the Great Macaricari, or "Great Salt Pan," the most singular feature of the Kalahari Desert. It is an "enormous basin, where the ground has sunk from nine to sixteen feet, and which at its longer axis must be from one hundred and twenty to one hundred and fifty miles, and at the shorter, from eighty to one hundred miles in extent." It is elliptical in shape, and has its greater axis due east and west. In the Massarua language the term Macaricari "signifies a basin covered with salt, or salt pans, where the rain-water is held for a certain time, disappearing in the summer season through the evaporation, and once again leaving behind it the salts which it had dissolved. The lining of the pans is of coarse sand, covered with a crystalline layer of salt, which attains to a thickness varying from an inch to an inch and a half. The great lake receives during the rainy season an immense volume of water through its tributaries the Nata, Simoane, Cualiba, and others; in fact, the whole of the rains which fall in those latitudes between the lake and the frontier of the Matabeli country drain into it. These waters, which form enormous torrents, must fill the Great Macaricari very speedily. This vast basin communicates with Lake Ngami by the Botletle or Zonga, and its level is the same as that of the latter lake, a circumstance which gives rise to a remarkable phenomenon. As the two lakes are some degrees distant from each other, the great rains will frequently fall in the east and cause the Macaricari to overflow, whilst the springs which feed the Ngami have not increased in volume. The Botletle then runs westward from the Macaricari to the Ngami. At other times the

THE OUCO.

reverse of this takes place, and the Ngami uses the same conduit to drain its surplus waters into the Macaricari."

At the time our travellers crossed it the great basin was quite dry, and its white layer of salt was painful to the eyes, and the dust ground from it by the wheels of the wagons caused no little smarting to the throats of the party.

On the 18th a mountainous country—through which ran the dry bed of the Letlotze—was crossed, and during the next day the route lay along the defile by which that stream breaks through the mountains. On the morning of the 20th of November the party were on the road at an early hour, cheered by the knowledge that this was to be the last day of their wearisome journey. They pushed on as fast as the oxen could travel, and about noon arrived at Shoshong, the great capital of the Manguato. They were met at the entrance to the town by messengers from King Khama, the sovereign of the country, and were assigned quarters in a half-ruined house, which had been at one time occupied by some English missionaries. Dilapidated as the house was, it was still a shelter, and, with some little exertion on the part of the travellers, was soon made habitable. It was situated near the river, and close to a convenient supply of good water.

The Manguato, or country of the Bamanguatos, occupies a large part of Southern Africa, immediately north of the western part of the Transvaal. Its capital is Shoshong, a city which contained at the time of our travellers' visit fifteen thousand people. The city is situated in the valley of the Letlotze, which is here about three miles in width, and shut in by high mountains. It stands on the north side of the valley, close to the mountains, and is traversed by a torrent which divides it into two sections. The city consists of three quarters or wards, one of which is occupied by the natives, the second by the English residents, and the third by the missionaries, their church and school. The greatest drawback to the prosperity of the place is the scarcity of water, which is painfully felt during the dry season.

The houses of the native quarter are built of reeds and covered with thatch; they are cylindrical in shape, and have conical roofs. The missionary's quarter contains a church, a comfortable dwelling, and school-houses, built of brick, and covered with roofs of galvanized iron. On the opposite side of the city, in the open plain, is the English quarter, the houses of which are of brick, and are well built.

The greater portion of the native population is Christian, having been converted by the labors of the English missionaries. All dressed in the European style, and our travellers were told that there was not an inhabitant of the city that did not possess a gun. The natives are prosperous, being devoted to agriculture and cattle-raising. Women as well as men take part in the field work, their ploughs and other implements being of English manufacture. Many of the residents of the city possess large herds of cattle, which graze in other parts of the country. Mr. Gaillard assured his American friends that they would find the Manguato, on the whole, the best governed and most prosperous of the native African monarchies.

Soon after the arrival of the travellers at their quarters, King Khama, the sovereign of this prosperous country, sent word to Mr. Gaillard that he would make him a visit in the afternoon. He arrived on horseback a little before sunset, accompanied by two mounted attendants. He was a striking-looking man, tall and robust, and with a countenance which showed him to be far above the average African ruler in both intellect and natural kindness. He was dressed simply in the English style, and with great taste. His manners

THE ENGLISH QUARTER AT SHOSHONG.

were dignified but friendly, and our travellers declared that he was "every inch a king."

He welcomed the missionary and his family warmly, smilingly remarking that he had felt sure that Lobossi would not permit him to enter the Lui country, and had been expecting his return for some time. Mr. Gaillard then presented Professor Moreton and the young Americans, who were cordially received by the king. He expressed great interest in their movements, and told them that as he was coming to breakfast with his friend, Mr. Gaillard, the next morning, he hoped to hear an account of their adventures. Then, congratulating them heartily upon having carried the journey so far with success, he exchanged a few more words with the missionary and took his leave. He spoke English fluently, and it was in that language that he conversed on this occasion.

"Well," exclaimed Houston, after Khama had departed, "I must say he is something like a king!"

"Khama," said Mr. Gaillard, "is the most remarkable man in Africa. His father was a barbarous old heathen, and treated his people very cruelly. Khama was the eldest son of this monarch, and the heir to the crown. At an early age he conceived a great liking for the English missionaries who were laboring here, and was converted to Christianity, and educated by them. You would be surprised to find how well-read he is. He is a man of fine intellect and great nobility of character. His education, his conversion to Christianity, and his friendship for the missionaries drew upon him the hatred of his father, who persecuted him in various ways, with the avowed intention of getting him out of the way, and securing the succession for his second son, Camanhane. This conduct at length induced Khama, who was now thirty-one years old, to withdraw from Shoshong to the country along the Botletle. On the road his cattle were dispersed for want of water. They were caught by the Massaruas and taken back to his father. Khama sent at once to the king to reclaim them, but his messengers were told to inform him that if he wanted them he must come to Shoshong for them, and that his presence in that city would be the signal for his death. Khama coolly sent word that he would return to Shoshong in the spring and demand them, and then set to work to collect an army from the people on the borders of the Botletle and Ngami. In the spring he marched upon the capital, defeating the forces sent against him in several battles, and finally entered Shoshong in triumph. The people received him with joy, deposed his father, and proclaimed him king. Khama then ascended the throne, and having restored to his father all his wealth and herds, and having also made a liberal provision for his brother, he sent them away to the south, on the borders of the Corumane. The condition of his people began to improve from the commencement of his reign, and they were delighted with their new sovereign. After a year had elapsed, he committed a great indiscretion, prompted thereto by his natural kindness of heart. He recalled his father and brother to Shoshong, and loaded them with favors. They repaid his kindness by renewing their plots against him; and Khama, disgusted at finding himself the object of new intrigues, resigned the crown to his father, and withdrew to the north. The Bamanguatos, however, who were warmly attached to Khama, were dissatisfied with this arrangement, and soon rose against the old king, deposed him, and recalled Khama, who, after once more loading his father and brother with riches, again banished them to the south. This was seven years ago, and since then Khama has reigned wisely and happily. He has carried on several successful wars with the neighboring kings, and has thus established his reputation as a great captain. It is to him that the people owe their present prosperity, and they are devotedly attached to him. He has no guards, and visits the people in their homes and fields, treating both rich and poor with equal kindness. He encourages them to work, and takes great interest in all their pursuits. He is very wealthy, but spends his money freely for the good of his people. You will see much of him while here, and the more you see the better you will like him."

King Khama kept his promise, and breakfasted with the Gaillards and our travellers the next morning. At his request, Ashton related the adventures of his party in their march across Africa. The king was especially interested in the account of their sojourn in the Lui country, and was much amused at the way in which they had baffled the schemes of Gambella, whom he knew well by reputation.

"Gambella is a man of ability and energy," said the king. "If he were civilized and a Christian, his power for doing good to his country would be immense. What you tell me of Lobossi gives me a better opinion of him than I have ever had before."

When the king had taken his departure Ashton and his companions went over to the English quarter, and seeking out Mr. Westbeech's correspondent, discharged his indebtedness to that gentleman. This was easily done, as the English had succeeded in introducing into Shoshong the currency of their own country. This had been a difficult matter at first; but at the time of our travellers' visit all transactions, even with the natives, were carried on with English money, and the system of barter was among the things of the past.

Ashton had carried with him Bank of England notes to the amount of three hundred pounds; so that, now that they had reached a country in which money could be used, he had no difficulty in procuring such articles as he and his companions were in need of. Among these was a new suit of clothes for each member of the party, including the blacks.

Our travellers remained in Shoshong for a week, and greatly enjoyed their return to civilization. They made the acquaintance of the English missionary residing in the town, who was a friend of Mr. Gaillard, and of a number of the English merchants and their families, whose hospitality was cordially extended to them. King Khama conceived a warm liking for the young men, especially for Ashton, and during the latter part of their stay invited them to accompany him on a hunting expedition. This was made on horseback, the king furnishing the mounts. Ashton's horse was a small but wiry, fleet-footed black, which pleased him so much that on the return from the hunt he was loud in his praises of it. The king smiled at the young man's enthusiasm, and replied that it was a very good horse indeed. He also complimented Ashton upon his riding.

Immediately upon their arrival at Shoshong our travellers began to look about them for a wagon for the journey to Pretoria, the capital of the Transvaal. While engaged in their search one of the English merchants, with whom he had become acquainted, met Ashton on the street, and told him that he was about to despatch a wagon to Pretoria to bring up some goods that were awaiting him there.

"The wagon will go empty," he said, "and it is large enough to hold your whole party and the two negroes I shall send with it. I don't think you can do better than to make use of it as far as Pretoria, where you can easily find a conveyance for the rest of your journey."

Ashton readily accepted the offer, which was a most generous one. The Englishman refused to receive any pay for the use of the vehicle, which he

THE OPUMDELUME.

said he intended to send to Pretoria anyhow, and only asked that Ashton should pay for the food of the negroes who were to accompany it.

"I am the gainer by the arrangement," he said. "You and your party will be a protection to my wagon and oxen, and I shall feel easier in my mind than if I sent them on alone. The country is comparatively safe, but still one never knows what may happen in Africa."

"When will your wagon be ready to start?" asked Ashton.

"Promptly on the 28th," was the reply. "Can you get ready by that time?"

"We can start at any moment," answered Ashton.

"Then we can consider the arrangement settled," said the English merchant.

The next thing was to lay in stores sufficient for the journey, which would occupy nearly a month, and these Ashton purchased from the owner of the wagon that had been placed at his disposal.

The evening of the 27th of November was spent by our travellers with the Gaillard family, whose many kindnesses had been gratefully appreciated by them. Everything was in readiness for the start the next morning, and Madame Gaillard now brought from her own slender stores some delicacies which she bestowed upon them as a parting gift. The regret at separating was mutual, for the missionary and his family had conceived a warm liking for their American friends.

All the members of the household were astir at an early hour on the morning of the 28th. King Khama came to breakfast with the party, and to

KHAMA.

take leave of the departing Americans. He announced his determination to ride with them a few miles on their way, and invited Mr. Gaillard to join him, telling him that he had provided a horse for him. Breakfast over, the professor and his young companions bade farewell to Madame Gaillard and her sister, and walked over to the wagon which was awaiting them a short distance from the ruined dwelling. Upon reaching it they found the horse that Ashton had ridden at the king's hunt standing near by, held by one of the royal servants. In a few minutes King Khama and Mr. Gaillard came up on horseback, and the king, pointing towards the horse, said to Ashton that he had brought him as his parting gift to his young friend.

"Accept him, with my good wishes," said Khama, kindly. "He will enable you or any of your friends to vary the monotony of the journey by changing from the wagon to the saddle, and you will find him useful in many ways."

Ashton warmly thanked the king for the handsome gift, and joyfully sprang into the saddle. The rest of the party took their places in the wagon, and the journey to Pretoria was begun, the three horsemen riding beside the vehicle. About four miles from Shoshong the king and the missionary bade adieu to the travellers, wishing them a safe and pleasant journey, and returned to the city. The latter watched them until they were out of sight, and then the wagon, drawn by its twelve oxen, set off again. About five o'clock a halt was made for the night at a spot where there was no water. The 29th and 30th were passed in journeying through a dull, uninteresting country, the road lying for a great part through a thick forest.

Soon after starting, on the morning of the 30th, the wagon, in descending a hill, met with a decided mishap. The wheels on one side got into a deep rut, and the ponderous vehicle tilted over, and would have capsized had it not been caught by two trees which grew close by the roadside, and which prevented it from going over entirely. The driver, a good-natured negro, who spoke English with tolerable ease, sprang out, looked at the wagon for a moment, and then quietly seated himself on the side of a bank, the picture of despair.

"Get up there, you black rascal," cried Houston, angrily, "and help us to get this wagon straight!"

"It will tax our ingenuity to right it," said Professor Moreton. "Still, we must try."

The professor then ordered the men to unyoke the oxen from the wagon, and to cut down three long, stout poles, which he made them lash to the fallen side of the vehicle. To the tops of these poles he attached ropes, which he fastened to trees on the opposite side of the road. Then, hitching a yoke of oxen to the ropes, he drew them tight, and so raised the wagon into its natural position. The negroes were set to work to fill up the rut with earth, pieces of wood, and the boughs of trees, so that the wheels might be on a level with those on the opposite side. The ropes which held the wagon in position were then removed, the oxen hitched to it again, and by considerable effort the vehicle was drawn out into the road once more. The undertaking was fatiguing in the extreme, and consumed four hours. During the last hour a heavy rain fell, and soaked the party through and through. They were off again at half-past three in the afternoon, but the storm increased so in violence, and the road became so deep in mud, that they were obliged to halt two hours later. The storm raged with great fury until ten o'clock that night, and the lightning played about wildly in every direction, striking large forest-trees frequently, and bringing them to the ground with a heavy crash. The violence of the tempest rendered it impossible for any of the party to leave the wagon, the interior of which fortunately kept dry, and the night was passed without supper.

The next morning an early start was made, and in an hour an open plain was reached. The rain had rendered the ground so boggy that the wheels sank into it almost up to the hubs, and scarcely a mile an hour was made. After struggling for several hours across this plain, a slight eminence was reached where the ground was drier. When the top of the hill was gained the travellers found themselves on the left bank of the Limpopo, at that point called the Crocodile River. As the ground was firm and comparatively dry, the summit of the hill was chosen as the camping-place for the night.

KHAMA CHASING THE ONGIRIS.

Ashton rode down to the river to try to ascertain its depth. Khama, for so he had named the horse, in honor of its giver, moved along leisurely until near the water, when he suddenly pricked up his ears, bounding into the grass, and darted off with the utmost rapidity. Ashton endeavored to rein him in; but finding this in vain, seated himself firmly in the saddle, and allowed the animal to take his own course. In a few minutes the heads of several ongiris appearing above the grass explained the cause of Khama's rapid movements. He had scented the animals, and being a trained hunter, had set off in pursuit of them. For fully half an hour the race continued, the horse gradually gaining upon the antelopes. At last they were near enough for Ashton, who was anxious to bring the pursuit to a close, to try the effect of his rifle; and raising the weapon to his shoulder, he fired at the group of flying animals. One fell to the ground, but the others bounded off and were soon lost to sight. As he reached the dead antelope Khama stopped still, and Ashton dismounted, threw the game over his saddle-bow, and started to return to his companions. He endeavored to ride to the eastward, thinking the halting-place was in that direction, but Khama persistently moved northward, and Ashton at last let him have his own way. The instinct of the horse proved correct, and in about an hour he reached the wagon, where he found his companions alarmed at his long absence.

The river was still too high to be forded on the 2d of December, and the party were forced to remain on its bank during the day. Houston and Philip Lee went out in the afternoon with their rifles, and succeeded in killing two fine leopards, which the negroes skinned for them. On the 3d, by the advice of the driver of the wagon, the party gave up the idea of fording the river, and moved off again, this time in the direction of the Ntuani, which they reached a short distance above its confluence with the Limpopo. The road was so deep in mud that their progress was very slow. They found the river too deep to be forded, and went into camp on its bank. The 4th and 5th were spent in waiting for the water to fall, and on the 6th it was found to have receded far enough to admit of a possibility of its being forded. Charlie volunteered to try its depth; and stripping off his clothes, waded into the stream, and succeeded in crossing it and returning, the water coming up a little above his waist. As there was a probability that a fresh rain-storm might again swell the stream, it was determined to try to pass it without waiting for a further fall. The professor ordered the negroes to unload the wagon and carry the goods on their heads over to the opposite bank. This was accomplished in the course of an hour, and then began the real difficulty of the passage. Three of the six yoke of oxen were sent over the river in charge of the negroes, and Khama swam the stream in good style, with Ashton on his back. The other young men followed the example of the negroes, and forded the river with their clothes on their heads. When all were over, Professor Moreton entered the wagon, and taking the lines from the driver, ordered him to urge the six oxen, which were still attached to it, forward at full speed. The animals ran rapidly down the hill, dragging the heavy vehicle after them, and, dashing into the stream, succeeded, after a brave struggle, in reaching the opposite bank. The river was safely passed, but the men were so tired that the party encamped on the bank of the stream for the rest of the day. The river thus crossed marks the northern boundary of the Transvaal, and our travellers were now in English territory. On the 8th the journey was continued along the left bank of the Limpopo, on which the camp was fixed at a late hour in the afternoon.

While at Shoshong Professor Moreton had been presented with a magnesium lamp, which had been left there by a previous traveller, and shortly after nightfall he determined to make use of this lamp, in some observations he wished to take in order to determine the exact position of their camp. Mombée was given the light to hold, and the professor busied himself with his instruments. He had scarcely begun his observations, however, when a loud, angry roar startled the whole party. Houston and Ashton at once caught up their rifles, which were lying by them, and Mombée silently turned the brilliant light in the direction from which the sound had proceeded. The bright glare at once revealed two large lions, crouching and ready to spring, a few yards

ANT-HILLS NEAR THE LIMPOPO.

distant from the spot where the professor was standing. The blinding rays of the lamp, shining full in the faces of the lions, caused them to pause for a few moments, and thus gave the young men time to take deliberate aim, and fire. Both beasts fell to the ground, shot through the head.

The danger was over, but the oxen and Khama, who had been seized with terror at the roar of the lions, struggled violently to break from their fastenings, and it took the combined efforts of the whole party to pacify them. The negroes were then set to work to strip the skins from the dead lions, and the professor resumed his observations.

During the next few days the journey was continued to the southward; the Marico River was crossed on the 13th, and on the afternoon of the 17th the party arrived at Soul's Port, the mission of the Piland's Berg or Mountain.

They took up their quarters in some ruins not far from the dwelling of the missionary, who, noticing their arrival, came at once to welcome them.

Piland's Berg is one of the principal missions in the Transvaal, and takes its name from the lofty mountain on which it is situated, and which rises abruptly from the plain. The surrounding country is well cultivated, and the white houses of the Boer settlers could be seen dotting the mountain side. The next two days were spent at the mission, the travellers being hospitably entertained by the missionary, who proved to be a friend of Mr. Gaillard. He was greatly pleased to hear news of his fellow-worker, and paid a high tribute to his unselfishness and energy.

On the 20th the professor and his companions set off again, and crossing the plain beyond Piland's Berg, entered a rugged country, and on the afternoon of the 23d reached the mission of Betania, a Boer settlement. Soon after starting, the next day, they passed through a Boer village, the inhabitants of which received them with the most demonstrative hospitality, pressing upon them presents of potatoes, fruits, fresh vegetables, and even fowls. The cause of this unusual demonstration was explained by one of the old men of the village, who spoke English imperfectly, and who told the professor that it was "Christmas eve." The announcement and the hearty kindness of the settlers profoundly affected the professor and his companions, who had been so long used to savage life that they had not once thought of the approach of the great festival of the Christian world. After a brief halt, and many wishes for a "Merry Christmas," the wagon was off again. The Limpopo was reached and forded, though still quite high, and the camp was pitched on its right bank.

Christmas morning, 1879, dawned bright and fair, and after a hearty breakfast the travellers set out again, stimulated by the knowledge that two days more would bring them to Pretoria. During the day they crossed the huge chain of mountains known as the Magalies Berg, which divides the Transvaal by a barrier running nearly due east and west. The pass by which they crossed the range was a very difficult one, and it was a hard task for the oxen to draw the heavy wagon up the northern ascent. The descent of the southern side was exciting and difficult. The wagon, unprovided with a brake, plunged heavily down the steep road, frequently running on to the oxen, and threatening to send the whole team to destruction. The danger was so great that the professor made the whole party dismount from the vehicle and descend the pass on foot. No accident happened, however, and the camp was pitched late in the afternoon, at the foot of the pass. On the night of the 27th the party encamped in an open country destitute of wood; and on the afternoon of the 28th arrived at Pretoria, the capital of the Transvaal.

The country known as the Transvaal, or the "territory beyond the Vaal,"

A NIGHT VISIT FROM THE LIONS.

in the heart of which our travellers now found themselves, lies between the Limpopo River, on the north, and the Orange Free State, Natal, and Zulu Land, on the south. The Vaal River separates it from the Orange Free State. It is divided into two unequal parts by the lofty range known as the Magalies Berg, or Kashan Mountains, which run across the entire country from east to west. The northern portion, as we have seen, consists of large plains broken by ranges of mountains, and is deficient in water. The southern portion comprises vast undulating plains, from four thousand to seven thousand feet above the level of the sea, well watered and rich in game. The whole country is fertile, yields good crops, and affords fine pasturage for the extensive herds of cattle and sheep that graze over it. Tobacco, cotton, and sugar are grown in the

STORE IN PRETORIA.

northern section. The native population are principally Bechuanas. The whites consist chiefly of Boers, a people of Franco-Dutch origin, the descendants of the original settlers of the Cape Colony. The English population is small.

The Transvaal owes its origin to the hostility of the Boers to the sovereignty of England. When the Cape Colony was transferred to Great Britain in 1814, the measure met with a silent but steadfast opposition on the part of the Boers. This was intensified by the emancipation of the slaves in 1833, a measure which threatened to overturn the entire domestic system of the Boers, and in 1836 they emigrated in large numbers to the Orange River country, and founded the Orange Free State. The next year a large band of them moved into Natal, and founded the town of Pietermaritzburg. In 1840 Great Britain took possession of Natal, and the majority of the Boers crossed the

NATIVES OF THE TRANSVAAL.

mountains, and settled in the Vaal country. In 1848 Great Britain, under the pretext of protecting the savage Griquas from encroachments upon their territory, took possession of the Orange Free State. This measure led to a war with the Boers, under Pretorius, the president of the Orange republic.

The Boers were successful at first, and drove the English garrison from Bloemfontein on the 17th of June, 1848. They were defeated, however, by the English at Boomplaats, on the 29th of August of the same year, with great loss. Unwilling to submit to English sovereignty, Pretorius and the majority of his followers emigrated to the Vaal region, and founded the town of Pretoria, which became the capital of the Transvaal republic. The country soon became prosperous, but it was not to escape the hand of the old enemy of the Boers. In 1877, Great Britain, under the pretext of putting an end to disorder in the country and preventing a general rising of the natives, took possession of the Transvaal. The British occupation was quietly effected, but was bitterly resented in secret by the Boers. This was the state of affairs at the time of our travellers' arrival at Pretoria.*

The Boers, as has been stated, are of Franco-Dutch descent, and sprang from a union of the original Dutch settlers of the Cape Colony and the French refugees, who, escaping to Holland after the revocation of the edict of Nantes, were sent out to the Cape of Good Hope by the Dutch East India Company in the latter part of the seventeenth century. The term "Boer" means simply "farmer," or "cultivator of the soil." Our travellers found these people a hardy, active race. All could read and write, but beyond these rudiments they were ignorant. They were frugal, industrious, temperate, and moral. They were brave and determined, as their resistance to the savage natives and the English had abundantly proved. Absolute equality prevailed among them. Their lives were regulated upon a system almost patriarchal, and their Bible, with which all were familiar, was the only book they read. The sole distinction that could be observed between them was that of age, the younger naturally yielding to the persuasion of the elder. The women were as industrious as the men, and devoted themselves indefatigably to the labors of the household.

Pretoria our travellers found to be a small town, with about one thousand inhabitants, and an English garrison. The streets were wide and spacious, and were lined with well-built and often elegant houses, for the most part but one story in height, and frequently placed in the midst of handsome gardens. The town, constructed upon an inclined plane, was abundantly supplied with water from springs in the upper portion. A few churches, a court-house, and the barracks of the garrison, the last placed on a commanding point above the town, constituted the public buildings. The town was growing rapidly, and

---

* The hostility of the Boers culminated in open war against the English towards the end of 1880. Peace was concluded in 1881, after a gallant resistance by the so-called rebels. The Boers were granted the right of self-government under the suzerainty of the British crown, which retains the control of the external relations of the state, and a veto on all future enactments affecting the natives.

it was evident that in a few years it would become a place of considerable importance. The shops were numerous, and were well supplied with all the necessaries, and many of the luxuries, of civilized life.

Halting their wagon, and leaving it in charge of Charlie and the other blacks at the outskirts of the town, Professor Moreton and the young men went into Pretoria to see if quarters for their party could be obtained. They sought out a Mr. John Taylor, a prominent merchant of the place, to whom they had been given letters of introduction by their friends in Shoshong, and were fortunate enough to find him at his place of business.

A TRANSVAAL FARM.

Mr. Taylor received them with cordiality, but told them they would find it difficult to obtain such accommodations as they desired. His own house, he said, was too small to ask them there, or he would gladly invite them to be his guests. He had, however, a large piece of vacant ground near his residence, and a number of tents in his warehouse. These he offered to place at their disposal, and with them they could form a camp. They would then be his near neighbors, he laughingly added, and he would be happy to see them at his house at any time. He advised the professor to send one of the young men to bring up their wagon and people at once, and he would have the tents in readiness for them by the time the wagon reached the store.

Houston volunteered to attend to bringing up the wagon, and at once took his departure.

Upon learning the plans of the party, Mr. Taylor advised them to lose no time in pushing on to Durban, the seaport of Natal. They could easily reach it in eight days, by taking a wagon to Pietermaritzburg, from near which place there was a railway to Durban. The next steamer would sail on the 11th of January, and there would be no other for a month. He told them there would be no difficulty in procuring such a wagon as they desired, and that he would assist them in securing a comfortable vehicle.

PROFESSOR MORETON AT PRETORIA.

From Mr. Taylor our travellers heard for the first time of the Zulu war, and its successful close a few months previous to their arrival. The roads, he said, were now safe, and they might travel without fear of danger. There were numerous towns along the route where they could purchase such provisions as they might need, and it would not be necessary to encumber themselves with a stock of stores.

Houston now came up with the wagons and the negroes, and Mr. Taylor caused the tents to be brought out and placed in the vehicle. He then conducted the party to their camping-ground, where the tents were soon erected. Mr. Taylor then left them, saying he should expect the professor and his companions to dine with him. The wagon was unloaded, the two negroes who were in charge of it were liberally rewarded, and Ashton mounted his horse and accompanied them to the establishment of the merchant to whom the vehicle was consigned, and delivered it to him.

Three days were spent by our travellers at Pretoria. From the first the camp became an object of great interest to the people of the place, and when the latter learned the character of its occupants, their curiosity to see the bold adventurers who had so daringly crossed the continent knew no bounds. All day the camp was thronged with visitors, and invitations to dinners, balls, and receptions were showered upon the professor and his companions from all quarters. Some of these were accepted, others declined from lack of time, and wherever they went the travellers found themselves the lions of the hour. They found the English society at Pretoria, though small, both cultivated and pleasant, and were in their turn amazed at the amount of luxury to be seen in this far-off quarter of Africa. After being so long cut off from the pleasures of civilization, their intercourse with their new acquaintances was very delightful.

Ashton succeeded, with Mr. Taylor's assistance, in securing a couple of light covered wagons, drawn by four horses each, and driven by negroes who spoke English well. With these Mr. Taylor assured him they could reach Durban in full time for the steamer, and have even a day or two to spare at that place.

At last all was in readiness, and early on New Year's Day, 1880, the wagons were at the camp, in readiness to start. Mr. Taylor gave them a parting breakfast at his house, to which a number of the prominent citizens and officers of the garrison were invited. The health of the travellers was drunk amid great applause, and all present wished them a speedy and pleasant journey to the coast, and a safe return to their own country.

The breakfast detained the party longer than they had expected, and it was not until ten o'clock that they were able to set out. Then, with a hearty good-by to the friends that had assembled to see them off, they started on the last stage of their memorable journey, Ashton mounted on Khama, and the other members of the party seated in the wagons. Pretoria was left at a rattling gallop; and after a day's ride through a rugged country, the town of Heidelberg was reached about nine o'clock at night. The party found quarters at a hotel, the first house of European construction they had slept in since their departure from Benguela; and they enjoyed greatly the rest in bed, hard and stiff as their couches were.

After an early breakfast they set off again, and about two o'clock in the afternoon reached the Waterfalls River, which they forded with considerable difficulty, the stream being very high. The day's ride was across an enormous plain, utterly devoid of trees, and covered with grass, without a single object to break the view in any direction. At eight o'clock at night they reached the village of Standerton, where they crossed the Vaal River, and passed the night in a wretched inn. Still, after their hard experiences, the place seemed comfortable enough to them. Standerton was left at seven the next morning, and early in the afternoon the party entered the defiles of the Drakensberg. The pass was steep and difficult, and they toiled slowly along it. Scarcely had they entered it when a terrific thunder-storm, accompanied with violent wind and rain, broke upon them, drenching them through in spite of the coverings of the wagons. Ashton, who was mounted on Khama, received the full force of the storm; but the horse, accustomed to such tempests, showed neither alarm nor uneasiness, but trotted along as peacefully as though it had been clear sunshine. Night overtook the party in the defile, and compelled them to move cautiously. The storm ceased as they left the pass, and towards nine o'clock Ashton, who was riding ahead of the wagons, saw a bright and steady light some distance ahead. He halted until his companions came up, and pointed it out to them. They moved forward slowly until within a quarter of a mile

THE DRAKENSBERG.

of the light, and then stopped, hesitating whether to approach it or not. Ashton volunteered to go forward and reconnoitre, and leaving his horse with the wagons, set out towards the light on foot. Approaching it cautiously, he saw that it came from a couple of fires, around which a number of men in European dress were gathered. Venturing still farther, he soon came within the line of light, and the next moment was halted by the stern challenge, "Who goes there?" Answering, "A friend," he was told to halt, while the sentry summoned the guard. Upon the arrival of the sergeant he was led to one of the fires, by which three English officers were standing. They accosted him politely, and upon learning who he was, told him that he was in the bivouac of a small detachment of English troops on their way to join the garrison at Pretoria. The commander of the detachment cordially invited him to share their fire, and sent one of his men back to the rest of the party to bring them up. The wagons soon arrived, and the same cordial greeting was extended to the professor and his companions.

"Your wagons will furnish better quarters for the night than we can offer you," said Captain Layne, the commander of the detachment; "but you are welcome to a share of the fire, and we can offer you some hot coffee, which I have no doubt will be acceptable, after the drenching the storm has given you."

The offer was gladly accepted, and the travellers and their military hosts were soon seated around the fire, engaged in friendly conversation. The coffee was served in tin cups, but it seemed delicious to the wet and tired Americans. None of the party thought of sleep, save the negroes, who curled themselves up in one of the wagons; and the night was passed by the fire, the English officers listening with deep interest to the story of the journey across the continent.

Professor Moreton and his companions parted from their new acquaintances at daybreak on the 4th, and travelling all day reached a Boer farm-house at sunset, having eaten nothing since the previous day. Their request for supper was readily granted by the hospitable farmer, who set before them a hearty meal, to which they did full justice. They had to pass the night in their wagons, as the farmer had no room for them in his house. He promised them a good breakfast the next morning, however, and kept his word. He refused to take any pay for his hospitality, saying that it was one of the precepts of his religion to show kindness to strangers.

With many thanks to their kind host, our travellers started again, and about sunset reached Newcastle River, on the opposite bank of which stood the town of Newcastle. The river was rising rapidly, and it was with the greatest difficulty that they forded it. They spent the night in the only hotel in the place, and keenly enjoyed the wretched supper and breakfast of which they partook there. On the 6th they started at seven in the morning, and travelled through a rugged but interesting country. Early in the afternoon Sunday River was reached, and here an excellent dinner was procured for half a crown each. Thus refreshed, they resumed their journey, and arrived at Ladysmith about eight o'clock in the evening. The little inn at this place was sadly lacking in accommodations, and they spent the night on the parlor floor, on which the landlord spread mattresses for them without coverings. They slept soundly, however, and woke with wonderful appetites for breakfast, which was served for them soon after sunrise. Starting immediately after breakfast, the party reached Colenso in three hours. Here they were conveyed, with their wagons, across the Tugela River in a good-sized ferry-boat. About three in the afternoon the charming little village of Howick was reached, and here our travellers spent a pleasant hour in visiting the beautiful cataract which has made the place famous. Pietermaritzburg, the capital of the colony of Natal, was reached at ten o'clock that night, and the party found excellent quarters at the Royal Hotel, the principal public-house.

NEAR PIETERMARITZBURG.

Pietermaritzburg, a city founded by the Boers in their unsuccessful attempt to colonize Natal, is fifty miles from Durban, and contains over ten thousand inhabitants. It is well built, and possesses some handsome edifices, among which are several fine churches. It is noted for its handsome gardens and beautiful flowers, and boasts a fine park.

Our travellers did not see much of the town, for they were anxious to push on to Durban without delay. The landlord of the hotel informed them that they would have to drive twenty-three miles the next day to reach the railway, which was not yet finished to the capital, and advised them to start about ten o'clock the next morning. They were off at that hour, and at three o'clock arrived at the terminus of the railway. As the wagons had been paid for at Pretoria, Ashton had only to bestow some gratuities upon the drivers, and transfer their property to the luggage van of the train which was to take them to Durban.

As they beheld the train of cars standing in the station, the locomotive with steam up, ready to start, Houston, who had been silent for some time, exclaimed, in a voice trembling with emotion,—

"It may be all foolishness, but I tell you, boys, to get back to civilization, and a real railway train once more, makes the salt water come into my eyes!"

Charlie and the other blacks were taken to see the locomotive, and were lost in astonishment at the sight of it. They were afraid to venture near it; and Charlie, after looking at it from what he considered a safe distance, turned to Houston, and said, timidly,—

"Him one very big devil, Master Hoosie! Me 'fraid of him!"

The party crowded into a second-class carriage, as the professor and his companions were curious to witness the effect of this mode of travelling upon their followers, who had never experienced the like before. The train started at four o'clock, and as the locomotive gave a long, shrill whistle before moving off, the Benguela men sank back in their seats with a howl of terror. Mombée's face was a study, and even the brave Charlie showed unmistakable signs of fright.

"Him no hurt us, Master Hoosie?" asked the poor fellow, in a low tone.

"Oh, no, Charlie," replied Houston, laughing. "This is the way we travel in my country and in Europe. It is a very good devil that is pulling us along."

The negroes were soon reassured by seeing that their white companions were not afraid, and when the train increased its speed gave utterance to many expressions of wonder and delight at the rapid and easy motion of the carriage.

Durban was reached at six o'clock, and the party proceeded to the principal hotel of the place, where they secured comfortable quarters. The windows of the rooms assigned to the professor and his companions commanded a fine view of the harbor and the sea, and all crowded around the one at which Professor Moreton stood, and gazed with feelings that it would be hard to describe upon the vast expanse of blue water which stretched away to the horizon.

"Well, boys," said the professor, after a long silence, "the 'Young American Expedition to South Central Africa' is a success. We have, with God's help, triumphed over every difficulty; we have crossed the continent, and this is the Indian Ocean. I think we have something to be proud of for the rest of our lives."

It was the 9th of January, 1880, eighteen months and three days since they had landed at St. Paul de Loanda to begin their journey across Africa. All their difficulties and dangers had been safely passed; and the thought uppermost in each heart, as they stood gazing upon the sea, was one of devout thankfulness that they were all together, and that none of the party had been left sleeping in the "dark continent."

"If any of you had died," said Ashton, speaking as if to himself, "I should never have forgiven myself for urging this expedition."

"Well, old fellow," said Houston, "we have pulled through all right, and, the Lord be thanked, we are all here, safe and well!"

The steamer was to sail on the 11th; and Ashton, on the morning after their arrival, set about finding some means of sending Mombée and the five Benguela men back to their home. He proceeded at once to the office of the American consul, where he was warmly welcomed, and there had the good fortune to meet with the captain of an American clipper ship, which had put into the harbor the day before. When the skipper heard the young man's story, as he related it to the consul, he told Ashton that his vessel was bound for St. Paul de Loanda, and that he would very cheerfully receive the six negroes on board, and would land them at Benguela. This he offered to do at a very moderate cost.

"I'd go a couple of hundred miles out of my way to do this for you, young man," he said, heartily. "The pluck you youngsters and your professor have shown in your travels and troubles gives you a claim upon the assistance of any fellow-American. Now it seems providential," he added, "that my ship should come into this port just in time to help you out of your scrape about these niggers. You might have had to wait here for a pretty long time before you could have found such another chance."

"Your arrival is certainly most fortunate for us, captain," said Ashton; "but we should have sailed to-morrow, even if this lucky chance had not occurred, and have carried them to Europe, and sent them from there to Benguela by the Portuguese steamer."

"I sail with the tide to-morrow morning," said Captain Gray. "Now I'll tell you what to do, Mr. Ashton. Bring your whole party on board of my ship this afternoon, and dine with me. We'll have the consul there, and I'll give you a real Yankee dinner. I dare say it will do you good, after your long absence from home. Bring your negroes along with you, and they can remain on board."

Ashton accepted the invitation, and the captain soon left the office. With the assistance of the consul, the young man succeeded in getting a bill, which he drew upon his London bankers, cashed. He then proceeded to the agency of the steamship on which they were to sail the next day, and secured passage for himself and his companions to Zanzibar, where they were to change to a

| Professor Moreton. | Mombée. | Charlie. |
Benguela negro. | | Benguela negroes.

PROFESSOR MORETON AND THE NEGROES OF THE EXPEDITION.

steamer for Aden. Having thus accomplished all his business, he rejoined his companions at their hotel, and delivered Captain Gray's invitation to dinner.

Mombée and the Benguela men were then paid the wages due them, were allowed to retain their guns as a reward for their fidelity, and were each furnished with a new suit of clothes. They were loud in their thanks, and declared that they would be great men when they returned to Benguela, and would always be treated with respect by their countrymen, since they had "discovered so many countries."

At four o'clock the entire party proceeded to the harbor, where the boats of the "Columbia" were waiting to convey them to the ship. They found the vessel gayly decked out in bunting in honor of their visit. High above all floated the national ensign of the Great Republic of the West; and as the professor and his companions stepped on board, and came once more under the stars and stripes, they gave three ringing cheers for the "old flag," which were answered with a will by the crew.

A pleasant afternoon and evening were spent on board the "Columbia," and about nine o'clock our travellers and Charlie prepared to go ashore. Professor Moreton delivered to Mombée a long letter to Silva Porto, which he had written during the morning, informing the old trader of the success of their expedition, and renewing the thanks of himself and his companions for the many kindnesses the old man had shown them. This letter he charged Mombée to present in person. A hearty farewell was then said to the negroes who were to return to Benguela, and the faithful blacks cried like children at parting from their kind employers.

"You can depend upon it, gentlemen," said Captain Gray, as the party were leaving the ship, "these fellows shall be well treated on my ship. The way they stood by you in all your troubles gives them a claim to every kindness I can show them."

During the night the "Danubio," the steamer in which our travellers were to sail to Zanzibar, arrived and anchored in the roads, the harbor of Durban being too small to admit a vessel of her tonnage. She was to sail promptly at four o'clock on the afternoon of the 11th of January, and at noon the party embarked, with their baggage, on the little tender which was to convey them to the steamer. They were soon on board, and were cordially welcomed by the captain, who had been made acquainted with their story by the agent of the line at Durban.

The "Danubio" was a fine steamer, and our travellers were given excellent accommodations on board of her. Charlie, who had never been on a steamer before, was delighted with the vessel, and spent hours during the voyage in watching the working of her machinery, which seemed to him even more wonderful than the locomotive.

The steamer sailed at four o'clock in the afternoon, and was soon at sea. The weather was fine, and the voyage proved very delightful. Calls were made at Lourenço Marques, and Mozambique, and in due time Zanzibar itself was reached. Here it was found that the steamer for Aden would not sail for two days, and the captain of the "Danubio," who had been very attentive to the professor and his companions during the voyage, insisted that the party should remain on board of his ship, as he declared they could not get decent accommodations in the town. He placed a boat at their disposal, and thus enabled them to go ashore whenever they wished.

At Zanzibar our travellers parted from Charlie, who, besides being paid the wages promised him, was given a handsome present in money. The faithful fellow wept bitterly at parting from his friends, especially from Houston, to whom he was greatly attached, and they, on their part, were deeply grieved to separate from one who had been so devoted to them, and to whose intelligence and courage they owed so much. Houston offered to take him to America with him, but Charlie declined to go. He said he had an old father, whom he had not seen for many years, and he must now stay with him until his death.

"He very old, Master Hoosie," said Charlie. "He not live long. When he die me go to 'Merikee. Me find you out, and never leave you again."

Houston, thinking it by no means unlikely that Charlie would carry out his intention some day, gave him his address, and desired him to preserve it carefully.

Two days after their arrival at Zanzibar, our travellers, now left to themselves, went on board the steamer "British India," and sailed for Aden, which was reached in due time. They were fortunate enough to find one of the Austrian Lloyd steamers about to sail for Suez, and immediately transferred themselves and their property to that vessel. The voyage up the Red Sea was uneventful, and at last Suez was reached. Here our travellers left the ship, and took the train for Cairo.

It does not form a part of our purpose to describe the adventures of the party in Egypt. Our task was finished with their arrival at Durban, and we can only glance rapidly at their homeward journey. Being anxious to catch the first steamer for Europe, they gave a day to seeing the sights of the Egyptian capital, another to a visit to the Pyramids, and on the third day took the train for Alexandria, where they embarked on one of the Peninsular and Oriental steamers for London. The British metropolis was reached on the 1st of March, six weeks having been passed in the voyage from Durban. These were very delightful weeks to Professor Moreton and his companions, and enabled them to recover thoroughly from the fatigues of their trying journey. They arrived in England in excellent health and spirits, and eager to return to their own country. They made but a brief stay in London, and hurried on to Liverpool, where they took passage for Philadelphia on one of the steamers of the "American Line." A pleasant voyage of ten days brought them to the Capes of the Delaware, and the next day saw them safely landed in Philadelphia.

The comrades in so many memorable adventures were reluctant to separate, and two more days were spent together, the other members of the party being the guests of Ashton, who, it will be remembered, was a Philadelphian. The third day brought the inevitable breaking-up of the party, and they separated with many promises of future meetings.

"Well, old fellow," said Houston, as he wrung Ashton's hand at parting, "when you get ready for another exploring expedition, don't fail to let me know; only choose some other country than Africa."

"I am done with explorations for some time to come," said Ashton, laughing. "I, for one, am satisfied with the adventures of the 'Young American Expedition to South Central Africa.'"

THE END.

www.ingramcontent.com/pod-product-compliance
Lightning Source LLC
Chambersburg PA
CBHW022053230426
43672CB00008B/1158